CAMBRIDGE TEXTS AND STUDIES IN
THE HISTORY OF EDUCATION

General Editors

A. C. F. BEALES, A. V. JUDGES, J. P. C. ROACH

MATTHEW ARNOLD
AND THE EDUCATION OF THE
NEW ORDER

IN THIS SERIES

Texts

Fénelon on Education, edited by H. C. Barnard

Friedrich Froebel, translated and edited by Irene Lilley

Matthew Arnold and the Education of the New Order, edited by Peter Smith and Geoffrey Summerfield

Robert Owen on Education, edited by Harold Silver (in preparation)

James Mill on Education, edited by W. H. Burston (in preparation)

Studies

Education and the French Revolution, by H. C. Barnard

OTHER VOLUMES IN PREPARATION

MATTHEW ARNOLD
AND THE EDUCATION
OF THE NEW ORDER

A SELECTION OF ARNOLD'S WRITINGS
ON EDUCATION, WITH AN
INTRODUCTION AND NOTES BY

PETER SMITH

*Lecturer in English, St John's College
of Education, York*

AND

GEOFFREY SUMMERFIELD

*Lecturer in Education,
University of York*

CAMBRIDGE

AT THE UNIVERSITY PRESS

1969

Published by the Syndics of the Cambridge University Press
Bentley House, 200 Euston Road, London N.W.1
American Branch: 32 East 57th Street, New York, N.Y. 10022

This Selection, Introduction and Notes © Cambridge
University Press 1969

Library of Congress Catalogue Card Number: 69–10433
Standard Book Number: 521 07341 3

Printed in Great Britain
at the University Printing House, Cambridge
(Brooke Crutchley, University Printer)

To

Bill Grant, Cabrillo College, California

AND

Richard Hamilton, Edinburgh University

CONTENTS

INTRODUCTION   *page* 1

DEMOCRACY   41

A FRENCH ETON   76

THE TWICE-REVISED CODE   157

EXTRACTS FROM ARNOLD'S REPORTS
  ON ELEMENTARY SCHOOLS, 1852–1882   198

EXTRACTS FROM ARNOLD'S SPEECH ON
  HIS RETIREMENT   241

NOTES   244

CHRONOLOGICAL TABLE   256

SELECT BIBLIOGRAPHY   257

INDEX   259

ACKNOWLEDGEMENTS

Anyone now working on Matthew Arnold must acknowledge his debt to R. H. Super, whose edition of *The Complete Prose Works of Matthew Arnold* is in the process of publication by the University of Michigan Press. Except in the case of Arnold's *Reports* and the Speech on his Retirement we have followed Super's text, which is 'in each case...the last one over which Arnold is known to have (or may be presumed to have) exercised any supervision; ordinarily this is the last version printed in his life-time'. We are grateful both to Mr Super and to the University of Michigan Press for their permission to use the text in this way, and for detailed textual comment we refer the reader to Super's edition.

It is a pleasure to express publicly our gratitude to, and our admiration of, the work of this editor of Matthew Arnold.

P. S.
G. S.

INTRODUCTION

Such is the distinction which, in our own day, Matthew Arnold has achieved as a literary critic and poet, and such was the notoriety he won in his own day as a controversialist writer on social and religious topics, that his professional concern with education tends to be obscured. His work as a school inspector, and his writings which resulted directly from such work, have been neglected, or seen perhaps as some necessary but unfortunate drudgery which sustained him and his family while he was engaged in other and more auspicious labours. Such neglect has been unfortunate, for this work is central to the thought and ambitions of this educator, and is of a piece with much of his other writings. His social and, indeed, his literary criticism, and his educational writings are interdependent, are mutually illuminating, and both form part of a body of thought the terms of which are not always capable of exact definition, but which nevertheless possesses a real coherence.

In this volume we publish some of Arnold's educational writings, all of which resulted directly from his work as a school inspector. They demonstrate the extent and variety of Arnold's interest in, and concern for, the provision of public education in his own day; they also show a mind dealing with both the principles and the practice of education. In 'Democracy', for instance, Arnold is outlining the political philosophy which resulted from his conception of the contemporary educational needs, whilst in his *Reports* he is discussing the issues involved in the day-to-day functioning of the schools which he visited. But all of the writings we include form part of and enrich a body of thinking which is further expounded in his other, less obviously educational writings. In our Introduction we seek to outline, by reference to some of his other work, the attitudes and social and political philosophy which stemmed from Arnold's concern with the 'bad civilisation' of his own day.

Throughout his life, Arnold was deeply interested in the public affairs of his own day—'these are damned times', he wrote to Arthur Hugh Clough as early as September 1849; and proceeded in his letter to show his interest and condemnation of them.[1] The extent of his later disquiet may be judged from a letter he wrote to his sister, Mrs Forster, in which he linked the death of his son, Basil, 'with so much other "suffering in the flesh,"—the departure of youth, cares of many kinds, and an almost painful anxiety about public matters.'[2] Earlier, in November 1865, Arnold wrote a longer and more detailed exposition of his anxiety:

Whatever Mary [his sister] may say, or the English may think, I have a conviction that there is a real, an almost imminent danger of England losing immeasurably in all ways, declining into a sort of greater Holland, for want of what I must still call ideas, for want of perceiving how the world is going and must go, and preparing herself accordingly. This conviction haunts me, and at times even overwhelms me with depression; I would rather not live to see the change come to pass, for we shall all deteriorate under it. While there is time I will do all I can, and in every way, to prevent its coming to pass. Sometimes, no doubt, turning oneself one way after another, one must make unsuccessful and unwise hits, and one may fail

[1] *The Letters of Matthew Arnold to Arthur Hugh Clough*, ed. H. F. Lowry (Oxford, 1932), p. 111.
[2] *Letters of Matthew Arnold*, ed. G. W. E. Russell (2 vols. 1895), I, 382.

after all; but try I must, and I know that it is only by facing in every direction that one can win the day.[1]

This letter reveals more than his interest in and concern with contemporary affairs, for it also demonstrates his determination to work for some reformation in the lives of his fellow-countrymen. In his first prose work, *England and the Italian Question*, published in 1859, he made clear what was to become his purpose as a prose writer:

In attempting to fulfil it, [the forming of a clear judgement on the question of Italian independence] I have enjoyed peculiar opportunities for correcting myself of certain misconceptions current in England. I venture to hope that in endeavouring to record the lessons which I have learned, I may possibly be of some use to others.[2]

Writing with a modesty[3] that disappeared as he warmed to his task, he stated what that purpose was to be: the correction of 'misconceptions current in England'. Had he needed to write his *Apologia*, Arnold might well have said with Newman, 'I begin to think I had a mission'. Certainly Fitzjames Stephen, a frequent opponent of Arnold's who complained of the moral enthusiasm of Rugby and its sons, was to say in his 'Mr Matthew Arnold and His Countrymen' that Arnold's 'self-imposed mission [was] to give good advice to the English as to their manifold faults'.[4]

---

[1] *Letters*, I, 309–10. For his feelings about the representative significance of Holland, see ibid. 90–2.

[2] *The Complete Prose Works of Matthew Arnold*, ed. R. H. Super (Ann Arbor, 1960–; 5 vols. published to date), I, 65.

[3] In a letter to his mother of 29 October 1863, he wrote: 'It is very animating to think that one at last has a chance of *getting at* the English public. Such a public as it is, and such work as one wants to do with it!' *Letters*, I, 201.

[4] *Saturday Review*, 3 December 1864, p. 683.

The seriousness of his concern and the consequent missionary zeal are essential parts of Arnold's thought and intrinsic to much of his prose writing; they also stem from an analysis and appraisal of contemporary society which, though they were never stated in their entirety in any one piece of work, may be gathered from his various writings. Writing in the early part of the second half of the nineteenth century when rioting and political disturbance were common, and when the 1867 Reform Act was to complete the enfranchisement of the middle class begun by the Reform Act of 1832, Arnold was constantly referring to his own age as an epoch of change, 'an epoch of dissolution and transformation'. (Cf. W. E. Houghton, *The Victorian Frame of Mind*, pp. 1–8.) In his essay on Heine, he explained what he felt was happening:

Modern times find themselves with an immense system of institutions, established facts, accredited dogmas, customs, rules, which have come to them from times not modern. In this system their life has to be carried forward; yet they have a sense that this system is not of their own creation, that it by no means corresponds exactly with the wants of their actual life, that, for them, it is customary, not rational...To remove this want of correspondence is beginning to be the settled endeavour of most persons of good sense. Dissolvents of the old European system of dominant ideas and facts we must all be, all of us who have any power of working; what we have to study is that we may not be acrid dissolvents of it.[1]

To recognise this change, that his was an era of dissolution and transformation, was to Arnold the prime need of the contemporary Englishman; indeed, he

[1] Super, III, 109–10.

maintained that such recognition and consequent adaptation was all that could be asked of him:

> Perfection will never be reached; but to recognise a period of transformation when it comes, and to adapt themselves honestly and rationally to its laws, is perhaps the nearest approach to perfection of which men and nations are capable.[1]

Compare the following extract from Dr Thomas Arnold's *Englishman's Register* (*Miscellaneous Works*, p. 116):

> England cannot remain what it has been; and the endeavour to detain a state of things which is passing away is, at the best, a waste of those efforts which might be better employed in preparing for the approaching and inevitable change, and in making the passage from the old system to the new as easy and imperceptible as possible.

Society was changing and one section that was becoming less important was the aristocracy. Although it continued to administer, Arnold considered it an anachronism, the days of which were numbered. As early as March 1848, after the riots in Trafalgar Square, he wrote to his mother:

> It will be *rioting* here, only; still the hour of the hereditary peerage and eldest sonship and immense properties, has, I am convinced, as Lamartine would say, struck.[2]

Many years later, Arnold gave, in his essay 'Equality', his explanation of the original function of the arisocracy:

> Their reason for existing was to serve as a number of centres in a world disintegrated after the ruin of the Roman Empire, and slowly re-constituting itself. Numerous centres of material force were needed, and these a feudal aristocracy supplied. Their large and hereditary estates served this public end.

[1] Ibid. II, 29.   [2] *Letters*, I, 4.

The owners had a positive function, for which their estates were essential.[1]

That time was an 'epoch of concentration', as was the period which followed the French Revolution, when the aristocracy fulfilled its function splendidly and led and unified the effort of the whole nation in combating the aggression of Napoleonic France. In *Friendship's Garland* one of Arnold's 'foreign friends' makes the following comments upon the English aristocracy in that era of concentration, comments which we can accept as Arnold's own views:

This aristocracy was high-spirited, reticent, firm, despising frothy declamation. It had all the qualities useful for its task and time; Lord Grenville's words, as early as 1793: 'England will never consent that France shall arrogate the power of annulling at her pleasure, and under the pretence of a pretended natural right, the political system of Europe,'—these few words, with their lofty strength, contain, as one may say, the prophecy of future success; you hear the very voice of an aristocracy standing on sure ground, and with the stars in its favour. Well, you succeeded, and in 1815, after Waterloo, you were the first power in Europe.[2]

By the middle of the nineteenth century, however, the aristocracy had outlived its purpose. Despite certain qualities it possessed, which Arnold was ready to acknowledge and respect, he considered not only that it was inadequate to deal with the contemporary situation, but also that it had a pernicious and stunting effect on society. Democracy, Arnold urged, was the living force, and, although in England it had been slow in developing itself, yet the English people, he maintained,

becomes more and more sensible to the irresistible seduction of democratic ideas, promising to each individual of the

[1] *Mixed Essays*, in *The Works of Matthew Arnold* (Edition de luxe, 15 vols. 1903–4), X, 84.
[2] Super, V, 14.

multitude increased self-respect and expansion with the increased importance and authority of the multitude to which he belongs, with the diminished preponderance of the aristocratic class above him.[1]

This spread of democratic ideas he saw as inevitable and irresistible. In 1861, in the introduction to *The Popular Education of France*, he wrote:

Life itself consists, say the philosophers, in the effort *to affirm one's own essence*...Democracy is trying *to affirm its own essence*; to live, to enjoy, to possess the world, as aristocracy has tried, and successfully tried, before it...So potent is the charm of life and expansion upon the living; the moment men are aware of them, they begin to desire them, and the more they have of them, the more they crave.[2]

Arnold recognised the spread of democracy, and conceived the modern spirit as 'the motion, as we say, of making human life more natural and rational,—or, as your philosophers say, of getting the greatest happiness for the greatest number'.[3] For the aristocracy, however, the increasing importance of such ideas was creating a situation with which it was completely incompetent to deal. It was incompetent—and this is a celebrated judgement of Arnold's—because of its incapacity for ideas:

It is the old story of the incapacity of the aristocracy for ideas,—the secret of their want of success in modern epochs ...Themselves a power reposing on all which is most solid, material, and visible, they are slow to attach any great importance to influences impalpable, spiritual, and viewless.[4]

Already Arnold saw this intellectual poverty of the aristocracy as resulting from the extent of its posses-

[1] Ibid. II, 13.
[2] Ibid. 7. This introduction was later published as the essay 'Democracy'.
[3] *Friendship's Garland*, Super, V, 17–18.
[4] 'Democracy', Super, II, 11.

sions, and when he wrote *Culture and Anarchy* he emphasised the fact:

> But the aristocratic class has actually, as we have seen, in its well-known politeness, a kind of image or shadow of sweetness; and as for light...it is not that it perversely cherishes some dismal and illiberal existence in preference to light, but it is lured off from following light by those mighty and eternal seducers of our race which weave for this class their most irresistible charms,—by worldly splendour, security, power, and pleasure.[1]

Thus the aristocracy, as a result of its inherent limitations, could neither appreciate the situation when new ideas were stirring among the masses nor, consequently, adapt itself to deal with the democratic challenge as a governing class. Arnold realised that the coincidence of the two facts was to weaken further the power of the aristocracy, and wrote: 'At the very moment when democracy becomes less and less disposed to follow and to admire, aristocracy becomes less and less qualified to command and to captivate.'[2] And, despite the closing paragraph of *England and the Italian Question*, where Arnold foresaw, a little doubtfully perhaps, the possibility of the aristocracy ruling the new world as it had done the old, by 1861 he was reiterating the opinions expressed in his letters in 1848 and 1856: 'The time has arrived, however, when it is becoming impossible for the aristocracy of England to conduct and wield the English nation any longer.'[3]

In contrast to the fine, albeit ineffective, style of the aristocracy, Arnold saw the working class—or, as he called it in his 'new...and convenient division of

[1] Super, v, 140.
[2] 'Democracy', ibid. II, 15.
[3] Ibid. II, 6. See also *Letters*, I, 4, and I, 50.

English society', the Populace—as a body of immature men, brutalised by the squalor in which they lived and depressed by the social inequalities which existed in England. In the urgent times of 1867 he wrote:

But that vast portion, lastly, of the working class which, raw and half-developed, has long lain half-hidden amidst its poverty and squalor, and is now issuing from its hiding-place to assert an Englishman's heaven-born privilege of doing as he likes, and is beginning to perplex us by marching where it likes, meeting where it likes, bawling what it likes, breaking what it likes,—to this vast residuum we may with great propriety give the name of *Populace*.[1]

Excluded from political power and brutalised though this class was, Arnold was yet perspicacious enough to realise that this 'vast residuum' was ultimately to possess great political power. Soon after he had become a school inspector he wrote to his wife:

I think I shall get interested in the schools after a little time; their effects on the children are so immense, and their future effects in civilising the next generation of the lower classes, who, as things are going, will have most of the political power of the country in their hands, may be so important.[2]

Despite the restless times in which he was living, Arnold retained, unlike Carlyle for instance,[3] his belief in democracy and in the possibility of transforming the 'lower Classes'. And the agent for the civilising, the transforming of this potentially great political power was to be the middle class.

The Reform Act of 1832 had enfranchised half the middle class and the Act of 1867 was to ensure that it was to govern. As a result of his estimate of the worth

[1] *Culture and Anarchy*, Super, v, 143.
[2] *Letters*, I, 17.
[3] For Carlyle's response to the problems of reform, see 'Shooting Niagara: and After?', *Macmillan's Magazine*, XVI (August 1867).

and effectiveness of the aristocracy and the working class, the middle class was, in Arnold's eyes, in a pivotal position. In 1864 he had great hopes of this class and to Cobden he wrote:

At the same time there is undoubtedly just now a ferment in the spirit of the middle class which I see nowhere else, and which seems to me the greatest power and *purchase* we have; and all that can be done to open their mind and to strengthen them by a better culture should I think be done; we shall then have a real force to employ against the aristocratic force and a moving force against an inert and unprogressive force, a force of ideas against the less spiritual forces of established power, antiquity, prestige, and social refinement.[1]

In the same month he wrote to his mother about his sending, and Cobden's receipt of, the articles which were to be published as *A French Eton:*

From Cobden I had an interesting letter, written on the receipt of the articles, before he read them, to say that he should certainly read them and was prepared to be interested, but that his main interest was in the condition of the lower class. But I am convinced that nothing can be done effectively to raise this class except through the agency of a transformed middle class; for, till the middle class is transformed, the aristocratic class, which will do nothing effectively, will rule.[2]

For Arnold, then, the middle class was doubly important—first because, at the time, it was the only possible effective political force since the aristocracy was incompetent, and the working class raw and under-developed; and secondly because it had to fulfil the function of civilising the masses, who were, he felt sure,

[1] W. H. G. Armytage, 'Matthew Arnold and Richard Cobden in 1864. Some recently discovered letters', *Review of English Studies*, xxv (1949), 252.

[2] *Letters*, I, 224. For a statement of similar views, see Arnold's 'Ecce, Convertimur ad Gentes', *Irish Essays and Others, Works*, XI.

soon to possess the greatest political power. And now it becomes apparent why Arnold devoted so much of his writings to the middle class, and why he waged his war against the Philistines. To govern England effectively, the middle class had to be transformed, and it was by his writings that he hoped to assist such a transformation. Later in life, in his 'The Future of Liberalism', Arnold wrote: 'The master-thought by which my politics are governed is rather this,—the thought of the bad civilisation of the English middle class.'[1]

As Leslie Stephen realised, it was also the master-thought which governed much of his prose writing, for he comments thus on Arnold's statement: 'This was, in fact, the really serious aim to which his whole literary activity in later life converged.'[2]

Before considering Arnold's views on the 'bad civilisation' of the middle class, and on the need for its transformation, it might be well to remember that, despite his condemnation of its deficiencies, he could recognise and respect its virtues. In October 1854 he wrote from Oxford to his wife, complaining of the apathy of the people he met there, and continued:

However, we must hope that the coming changes, and perhaps the infusion of Dissenters' sons of that muscular, hard-working, *unblasé* middle class—for it is this, in spite of its abominable disagreeableness—may brace the flaccid sinews of Oxford a little.[3]

Twenty years later, Arnold, showing that his opinion of the middle class remained unchanged, wrote:

The Puritan middle class, with all its faults, is still the best stuff in this nation. Some have hated and persecuted it, many

[1] *Irish Essays, Works*, XI, 135.
[2] *Studies of a Biographer* (4 vols. 1898–1902), II, 95.
[3] *Letters*, I, 39.

have flattered and derided it,—flattered it that while they deride it they may use it; I have believed in it. It is the best stuff in this nation, and in its success is our best hope for the future. But to succeed it must be transformed.[1]

His respect for the middle class, qualified though it is, tends to become obscured by Arnold's insistence on its deficiencies—an insistence that would help, he hoped, in its transformation.

In *Culture and Anarchy* he continued to use for the members of the middle class 'the designation of Philistines' that he had first used in his essay on Heine. In the same book Arnold also discusses the appropriateness of the name for them, and in so doing enumerates what he considers to be some of their shortcomings:

For *Philistine* gives the notion of something particularly stiff-necked and perverse in the resistance to light and its children; and therein it specially suits our middle class, who not only do not pursue sweetness and light, but who even prefer to them that sort of machinery of business, chapels, tea-meetings, and addresses from Mr Murphy, which makes up the dismal and illiberal life on which I have so often touched.[2]

One of the celebrated essays in which he considered that dismal and illiberal life was 'My Countrymen', later to become part of *Friendship's Garland*, a book which, though light-hearted and ironic in tone and technique, was a serious attack upon the middle class and their culture. In this essay, Arnold is answering the *Saturday Review*'s criticism that he had committed 'the indecency of talking of "British Philistines"', and, in his justification of the name, his summary of the life led by the middle class is essentially the same as that just quoted from *Culture and Anarchy*. 'Can any life',

[1] 'Irish Catholicism and British Liberalism', *Mixed Essays*, *Works*, x, 137–8.
[2] Super, v, 140.

one of his foreign friends wonders, 'be imagined more hideous, more dismal, more unenviable?'[1] In both *Culture and Anarchy* and *Friendship's Garland*, however, Arnold is not content merely to demonstrate how mean, dreary and restricting that life was; he seeks also to reveal the cause of such Philistinism.

The members of the middle class, he maintains—and here one must mention that he considered the middle class to be largely composed of Dissenters—denied the existence of certain of man's instincts and powers. In *Culture and Anarchy*, he divides these instincts and powers into two main groups—moral and intellectual:

This [the claim that in religion can be found a 'full law of conduct and a full law of thought'] might, no doubt, be so, if humanity were not the composite thing it is, if it had only, or in quite over-powering eminence, a moral side, and the group of instincts and powers which we call moral. But it has besides, and in notable eminence, an intellectual side, and the group of instincts and powers which we call intellectual.[2]

Using different terms, Arnold writes in 'My Countrymen' of the 'factors of modern life', and specifies them as:

the growth of a love of industry, trade, and wealth; the growth of a love of the things of the mind; and the growth of a love of beautiful things. They are body, intelligence, and soul all taken care of.[3]

And as late in his life as 1882, in an address delivered at the opening of the session of the University of Liverpool, he further detailed the needs of man that must be satisfied for his complete development:

Money-making is not enough by itself. Industry is not enough by itself. I speak now of the kinds of stimulus most in use

<hr>

[1] Ibid. 19.   [2] Ibid. 177.   [3] Ibid. 19.

with people of our race, and above all in communities such as Liverpool. Respectable these kinds of stimulus may be, useful they may be, but they are not by themselves sufficient. The need in man for intellect and knowledge, his desire for beauty, his instinct for society, and for pleasurable and graceful forms of society, require to have their stimulus felt also, felt and satisfied.[1]

Arnold believed, then, with William von Humboldt, that

the end of man, or that which is prescribed by the eternal or immutable dictates of reason and not suggested by vague and transient desires, is the highest and most harmonious development of his powers to a complete and consistent whole.[2]

For a man to reach his full stature, his various needs, insisted Arnold, must be met. It is culture, he wrote in *Culture and Anarchy*, which

leads us...to conceive of true human perfection as a *harmonious* perfection, developing all sides of our humanity; and as a *general* perfection, developing all parts of our society.[3]

And perfection, then, is only possible for the individual as a member of a society where

he is required, under pain of being stunted and enfeebled in his own development if he disobeys, to carry others along with him in his march towards perfection, to be continually doing all he can to enlarge and increase the volume of the human stream sweeping thitherward.[4]

Arnold saw the reason for the rawness and hideousness of middle-class life in the fact that its members had 'developed one side of their humanity at the expense

[1] *Five Uncollected Essays of Matthew Arnold*, ed. Kenneth Allott, (Liverpool, 1953), p. 88.
[2] *The Sphere and Duties of Government*, p. 11.
[3] Super, v, 235.   [4] Ibid. 94.

14

of all others, and have become incomplete and mutilated men in consequence'.[1] In *A French Eton* he denied that all which the best of the middle class cared for was '*Business and Bethels*', and all that the rest cared for was '*Business* without the *Bethels*', although in the same book Arnold insisted at length on the need for the middle class to transform itself before it could have 'the right or the power to assert itself absolutely'.[2] In *Culture and Anarchy*, however, written in more urgent times, he showed that he believed that its business and its religion were the central and all-important facts in the life of the middle class. This belief he states most emphatically in 'My Countrymen' when he quotes one of his 'foreign friends'—a fiction which allows Arnold to attack without reserve—who says: 'Drugged with business, your middle class seems to have its sense blunted for any stimulus besides, except religion; it has a religion, narrow, unintelligent, repulsive.'[3]

The middle class, then, had found the law of its life in its religion, and that 'a hole-and-corner' religion, too. Such exclusive concern with religion and business had made the life of the middle class narrow, one-sided, and incomplete so that 'in what we call *provinciality* they abound, but in what we may call *totality* they fall short'.[4] Its members concerned themselves mainly with conduct—intelligence or *Geist*, beauty, and pleasurable and graceful forms of society were of little importance to them. Theirs was the care, Arnold maintained, for 'strictness of conscience, Hebraism, rather than the care for sweetness and light, spontaneity of conscious-ness, Hellenism'.[5]

[1] Ibid. 236.
[2] Ibid. II, 317.
[3] Ibid. v, 19.
[4] Ibid. 237.
[5] Ibid. 179.

Such a class, whose life was so inadequate and restricted, was, although in a position of great political importance, quite unworthy, he insisted, to rule until it had transformed itself. What concerned Arnold as much as the 'bad civilisation' of the middle class was its smugness—its self-satisfaction and inability to recognise its own shortcomings. In 'The Function of Criticism at the Present Time', after quoting Mr Roebuck's words, 'I pray that our unrivalled happiness may last', Arnold continued: 'Now obviously there is peril for poor human nature in words and thoughts of such exuberant self-satisfaction, until we find ourselves safe in the streets of the Celestial City.'[1] And in *Culture and Anarchy* he pointed out the dangers of this complacency:

The Puritan's great danger is that he imagines himself in possession of a rule telling him the *unum necessarium*, or one thing needful, and that he then remains satisfied with a very crude conception of what this rule really is and what it tells him, thinks he has now knowledge and henceforth needs only to act, and, in this dangerous state of assurance and self-satisfaction, proceeds to give full swing to a number of the instincts of his ordinary self.[2]

It was this smugness and lack of ideals that Arnold strove to remedy. His was the task, he considered, to reiterate to the middle class that 'Jerusalem is not yet'.

One of Arnold's answers to this self-satisfaction of the middle class was to recommend 'culture as the great help out of our present difficulties'. In his essay on Wordsworth he had said that the world 'is forwarded by having its attention fixed on the best things', and throughout *Culture and Anarchy* he elaborates that idea. Culture he defined as a 'study of perfection' or more

[1] Super, III, 272.   [2] Ibid. v, 180.

dynamically as 'a pursuit of our total perfection'. The means by which such perfection might be approached was the

> getting to know, on all matters which most concern us, the best which has been thought and said in the world; and through this knowledge, turning a stream of fresh and free thought upon our stock notions and habits, which we now follow staunchly but mechanically, vainly imagining that there is a virtue in following them staunchly which makes up for the mischief of following them mechanically.[1]

Culture, then, must work by 'criticism' as Arnold had already defined it in 'The Function of Criticism at the Present Time'. In that essay he advocated that the critic, in the combined sense of literary and social critic, should be 'disinterested', and concern himself with ideas, and not with 'those ulterior, political, practical considerations about ideas'.

But it would be a mistake to assume, as did some of Arnold's contemporaries, that culture merely recommended 'this free play of the mind on all subjects which it touches'. For the 'inward condition of the mind and spirit' ultimately and inevitably heralds the 'moral and social passion for doing good'. This aspect of culture is, indeed, the more important:

> There is a view in which all the love of our neighbour, the impulses towards action, help, and beneficence, the desire for removing human error, clearing human confusion, and diminishing human misery, the noble aspiration to leave the world better and happer than we found it,—motives eminently such as are called social,—come in as part of the grounds of culture, and the main and pre-eminent part.[2]

[1] Ibid. 233–4.
[2] Ibid. 91. See also 'Equality', *Mixed Essays*, *Works*, x.

And yet Arnold insisted that the men of culture of his day should abstain from direct political action:

> Now for my part I do not wish to see men of culture asking to be entrusted with power; and, indeed, I have freely said, that in my opinion the speech most proper, at present, for a man of culture to make to a body of his fellow-countrymen who get him into a committee-room, is Socrates's: *Know thyself!* and this is not a speech to be made by men wanting to be entrusted with power.[1]

There is, of course, no illogicality in Arnold's position. He insisted that criticism must precede action—that, before trying to make 'reason and the will of God prevail', the aspirant to culture had to make sure that he had first determined what they were. Moreover, it was 'at present' and in England where the man of culture was to recommend the Socratic dictum, because already sufficient consideration was being given to the practical application of ideas.[2] And Arnold looked at the political actions of his liberal friends who were, as Arminius maintains in *Friendship's Garland*, 'for the spiritual development of your democracy by rioting in the parks, abolishing church-rates, and marrying a deceased wife's sister'[3] and insisted that they were not basing those actions on 'the best that is thought and known in the world'. Arnold's desire was that 'by learning to think more clearly, they may come at last to act less confusedly'.[4]

Although he urged the need for disinterestedness and abstention from action, Arnold was himself being practical, if only by the act of publication, and interested

---

[1] Super, v, 88.
[2] See 'The Function of Criticism at the Present Time', Super, III, 269-70.
[3] Ibid. v, 46.   [4] Ibid. 226.

in that he was emphasising only one aspect of truth as he saw it. To combat the complacency and lack of idealism he stressed the need for criticism, for lucidity and flexibility, for *Geist* which must precede the political action by which culture ultimately works also. This position Kenneth Allott has concisely described:

Ideally detachment and zeal are the two sides of a single responsibility: the critic (using the term in the convenient Arnoldian sense to cover social commentator as well as literary critic) is loyal to the whole truth, but his judgement of what the public needs at a particular moment causes him to floodlight one fragment of it rather than another.[1]

Arnold's insistence upon the need for criticism before action annoyed some at least of his contemporaries, as he himself pointed out in his introduction to *Culture and Anarchy*. Frederic Harrison, in his 'Culture: a Dialogue', amusingly protested:

death, sin, cruelty stalk among us, filling their maws with innocence and youth; humanity passes onward shuddering through the raging crowd of foul and hungry monsters, bearing the destiny of the race like a close-veiled babe in her arms, and over-all sits Culture high aloft with a pouncet-box to spare her senses aught unpleasant, holding no form of creed, but contemplating all with infinite serenity, sweetly chanting snatches from graceful sages and ecstatic monks, crying out the most pretty shame upon the vulgarity, the provinciality, the impropriety of it all.[2]

The leading articles in the *Daily Telegraph*, that constant enemy of Arnold's, besides complaining of the indifference to practical politics that Arnold was advocating, also fulminated about his fondness for

[1] *Matthew Arnold*, British Council pamphlet in series 'Writers and Their Work' : No. 60 (1955), p. 8.
[2] *The Choice of Books* (1886), p. 111.

quoting and recommending Continental habits and virtues to his fellow-countrymen:

Then, when we have learned to make no fuss either about the heaven above, the earth beneath, or the waters under the earth, we are to cross the Channel and take lessons from Germany and France...None the less are we to be humble pupils of a people which cannot govern itself, which cannot advance without revolutions, and which has borrowed more thoughts from us than it has ever repayed.[1]

Arnold was aware and concerned about the fact that his praise of certain aspects of Continental life was exciting such criticism. After he had published a reply to the criticism contained in two letters which had appeared in the *Pall Mall Gazette* under the pseudonym 'Horace', he wrote to his mother: 'I was glad to have an opportunity to disclaim that positive admiration of things foreign, and that indifference to English freedom, which have often been imputed to me...'[2]

He was, of course, a patriot and, as A. P. Kelso has said, 'his vehemently cordial admiration of the Continent, his apparent disparagement of ways English are but further proofs of how genuine an Englishman he was'.[3] The need of his own time was for criticism, and for that, he maintained, one must go abroad. Quoting himself, he began 'The Function of Criticism at the Present Time' by stating that for many years the main effort of European literature had been a critical one, and added: 'almost the last thing for which one would come to English literature is just that very thing which now Europe most desires...'[4] Just as Arnold

[1] 8 September 1866.
[2] Letter of 24 March 1866; *Letters*, I, 323.
[3] *Matthew Arnold on Continental Life and Literature* (Oxford, 1914), p. 2.
[4] Super, III, 258.

did not underestimate the merit of the middle class, although by emphasising its deficiencies he appeared to do so, in the same way he appeared to some of his contemporaries to value more highly the Continental life than the English. For Arnold, the 'real *unum necessarium* for us is to come to our best at all points',[1] and therefore one had to emphasise the short-comings rather than the achievements of one's fellow-countrymen, and, as he was to write in a preface to *Higher Schools and Universities in France*, 'a criticism of our way of acting, in any matter, is tacitly supplied by the practice of foreign nations, in a like matter, put side by side with our practice'.[2]

Arnold was not making a complete comparison between the social and political life of England and that of France, and finding England lacking, but he was selecting those matters which he felt were ordered 'better in France' and recommending them to his countrymen. Indeed, concerned as he was with the needs of the moment, he was prepared to recommend to the consideration of his countrymen institutions and practices which he certainly would not like to see them adopt:

If I were a Frenchman I should never be weary of admiring the independent, individual, local habits of action in England, of directing attention to the evils occasioned in France by the excessive action of the State; for I should be very sure that, say what I might, the part of the State would never be too small in France, nor that of the individual too large. Being an Englishman, I see nothing but good in freely recognising the coherence, rationality, and efficaciousness which characterises the strong State-action of France, of acknowledging the want of method, reason, and result which attend the feeble State-action in England; because I am very sure that,

<hr>

[1] Ibid. v, 180.　　　　[2] *Works*, xii, 89.

strengthen in England the action of the State as one may, it will always find itself sufficiently controlled.[1]

But besides his advocacy of the need for criticism, Arnold had another suggestion, and an obviously practical one, to make for the solution of the problems of his day. The provision of adequate secondary schooling for the middle class would, he was sure, assist greatly in the transformation of that class. In *A French Eton* he wrote:

In that great class, strong by its numbers, its energy, its industry, strong by its freedom from frivolity, not by any law of nature prone to immobility of mind, actually at this moment agitated by a spreading ferment of mind, in that class, liberalised by an ampler culture, admitted to a wider sphere of thought, living by larger ideas, with its provincialism dissipated, its intolerance cured, its pettiness purged away,—what a power there will be, what an element of new life for England! Then let the middle class rule, then let it affirm its own spirit, when it has thus perfected itself.

And I cannot see any means so direct and powerful for developing this great and beneficent power as the public establishment of schools for the middle class.[2]

Here Arnold had forsaken the disinterestedness of criticism and begun to advocate practical reforms. It is important, however, to realise that he saw the reforms which he urged as serving criticism which would—and thus culture works—at some later date influence practical politics. True, he had apparently abandoned his contention that 'our main business at the present moment is not so much to work away at certain crude reforms',[3] but, by choosing to reform the educational system, Arnold himself was still trying to create 'a frame of mind out of which the schemes of really fruitful reforms may with time grow'.[3]

---

[1] 'Democracy', Super, II, 16–17.
[2] Ibid. 322.   [3] Ibid. V, 221.

Matthew, the son of Dr Thomas Arnold of Rugby, examined both the Educational Homes daily advertised in *The Times* where education was provided for '£20 per annum, no extras', and the establishments he typified in *Friendship's Garland* as Lycurgus House Academy, the *alma mater* of Bottles Esq. Such schools, he knew, provided schooling that was totally inadequate for the politically powerful middle class, and in no way prepared it for meeting its responsibilities towards the 'Populace'. Thus, each of his books dealing with the educational administration on the Continent became an eloquent plea for the provision of proper secondary education for the middle class. Such provision, he insisted, would be the greatest help in the transformation of that class; with such an advantage, the middle class, at last beginning to 'see the object as it really is', would devote its virtues of 'energy and honesty' to making 'reason and the will of God prevail'. Throughout his life, Arnold remained convinced of both the need for and the benefits that would result from the establishment of such schools; many years after his educational reports were published he wrote:

To generate a spirit of lucidity in provincial towns, and among the middle-classes, bound to a life of much routine and plunged in business, is more difficult. Schools and universities ...are in this case the best agency we can use.[1]

and:

But good secondary schools...this, I repeat, is what American civilisation in my belief most requires, as is what our civilisation, too, at present most requires.[2]

And effective secondary schools, argued Arnold, must be provided by the State. The middle class, des-

[1] *Five Uncollected Essays*, ed. Allott, pp. 92–3.
[2] Ibid. pp. 21–2.

23

pite the assertions of the *Daily News* and the *Nonconformist* to the contrary,[1] was failing miserably to educate its sons to discharge their duties. By enlisting the aid of the State, better schools would be provided than those which then existed as the result of the private efforts of middle-class parents, and the commercial activites of many self-styled schoolmasters:

The State can bestow certain broad collective benefits, which are indeed not much if compared with the advantages already possessed by individual grandeur, but which are rich and valuable if compared with the makeshifts of mediocrity and poverty. A good thing meant for the many cannot well be so exquisite as the good things for the few; but it can easily, if it comes from a donor of great resources and wide power, be incomparably better than what the many could, unaided, provide for themselves.[2]

For secondary education to be thus provided by the State would confer another benefit—not only would schools be provided cheaply and be accessible to all, but there would also be a 'valid security' for the teaching:

By public establishment they [the schools] may give securities for the culture offered in them being really good and sound, and the best that our time knows. By public establishment they may communicate to those reared in them the sense of being brought in contact with their country, with the national life, with the life of the world; and they will expand and dignify their spirits by communicating this sense to them. I can see no other mode of institution which will offer the same advantages in the same degree.[3]

Such words, besides demonstrating Arnold's faith in the State provision of education, reveal his belief in the need for some central standard of thought and taste.[4]

[1] See 'My Countrymen', Super, V, 5.

[2] 'Democracy', Super, II, 21.

[3] *A French Eton*, Super, II, 322–3.

[4] See 'The Literary Influence of Academies', Super, III, 232–57.

The danger of democracy was, Arnold saw, the lack of ideals. At one time the aristocracy, with 'its lofty spirit, commanding character, exquisite culture', served to maintain standards and to prevent the country from becoming provincial and third rate. But, 'since in a time of expansion like the present, a time for ideas, one gets, perhaps, in regarding an aristocracy, even more than the idea of serenity, the idea of futility and sterility',[1] on what action, Arnold asked,

may we rely to replace, for some time at any rate, that action of the aristocracy upon the people of this country, which we have seen exercise an influence in many respects elevating and beneficial, but which is rapidly, and from inevitable causes, ceasing?...what influence may help us to prevent the English people from becoming, with the growth of democracy, *Americanised*?[2]

His questions were rhetorical, for immediately he replied: 'I confess I am disposed to answer: on the action of the State.'[2]

Self-governing democracy was only to be effective if, as Arminius says in *Friendship's Garland*, 'it is government by your better self'.[3] Such arguments, Arnold replies, in his character of the ironic champion of the middle classes, arise from the inability of Arminius to rise 'to an Englishman's conception of liberty'.[3] That Arminius speaks for the real Arnold becomes apparent when we read in his essay, 'Democracy':

Nations are not truly great solely because the individuals composing them are numerous, free, and active; but they are great when these numbers, this freedom, and this activity are employed in the service of an ideal higher than that of an ordinary man, taken by himself.[4]

[1] Super, v, 125.
[2] 'Democracy', Super, II, 15–16.
[3] Super, v, 49.   [4] Ibid. II, 18.

For the citizens, the State, that is '*themselves* in their collective and corporate character',[1] was to maintain high ideals and to become the 'organ of our collective best self, of our national right reason'.[2] As J. Dover Wilson has said, in his essay on Arnold in *The Social and Political Ideas of some Representative Thinkers of the Victorian Age*:

But, above all, Arnold looked to the State to become the centre of national life, transcending all *classes*. He is fond of quoting Burke's famous apostrophe to the State as a 'partnership in all science, a partnership in all art, a partnership in every virtue and in all perfection.'[3]

Such a conception of the State was one which culture suggested with its basis in our best self.[4] Arnold, however, was quite prepared to recommend the intervention of the State as he knew it—that is an executive power in the hands of an aristocracy but based on middle-class support—in areas hitherto regarded as reserved for personal choice. He would have it intervene in home affairs and curtail personal liberty both to safeguard the State as it was, and also to help to transform itself by providing secondary education for the middle class. In *Culture and Anarchy* he was prepared to emphasise the purely police functions of the State, but both in that book and in his educational writings he advocated the intervention of the State as he knew it to produce the State as he conceived it should be:

But we, beholding in the State no expression of our ordinary self, but even already, as it were, the appointed frame and prepared vessel of our best self, and, for the future, our best

[1] *A French Eton*, Super, II, 294.
[2] *Culture and Anarchy*, Super, V, 136.
[3] Ed. F. J. C. Hearnshaw (1933), p. 185.
[4] See *Culture and Anarchy*, Super, V, 134–5.

26

self's powerful, beneficent and sacred expression and organ—
we are willing and resolved, even now, to strengthen against
anarchy the trembling hands of our Barbarian Home Secre-
taries and the feeble knees of our Philistine Alderman-
Colonels; and to tell them, that it is not really in behalf of
their own ordinary self that they are called to protect the
Park railings, and to suppress the London roughs, but in
behalf of the best self both of themselves and of all of us in the
future.[1]

With order maintained, then, the provision of secondary schools for the middle class by the State would,
Arnold was sure, help to supply the urgent need for
lucidity, flexibility of mind, *Geist*—in a word, criticism
—and, with society thus transformed, the State would
become just such a partnership as Burke had described.
Such a statement is, admittedly, a foreshortening of
Arnold's argument but at least it does properly stress
his view of the importance of the middle class, and the
urgency of the need for their adequate education.

But the greatest difficulty in the way of such effective
state action in England was, in Arnold's view, the
excessive worship of personal liberty. Culture, it will be
remembered, requires the individual to strive not only
for his own perfection but also 'under pain of being
stunted and enfeebled in his own development if he
disobeys, to carry others along with him in his march
towards perfection'.[2] And such a conception of perfection, Arnold continues, 'is at variance with our
strong individualism, our hatred of all limits to the
unrestrained swing of the individual's personality, our
maxim of "every man for himself".'[3] It is concerning
this particular shortcoming of the English that Arnold
has much to say, not only in *Culture and Anarchy*, but

[1] Super, v, 224.
[2] *Culture and Anarchy*, Super, v, 94.   [3] Ibid. 95.

also in *Friendship's Garland*, in some senses a companion work although less well known. Arnold, in the dedicatory letter of that book, makes great play with the Englishman's 'fetish-worship of mere liberty', whilst in what was, as originally published, the last letter, one to 'Horace', he shows himself concerned 'to work out a deliverance from the horrid dilemma in which "Horace" and others try to fix us;—liberty and Philistinism, or else culture and slavery'.[1] As Arnold often maintained, there was a third alternative—liberty and culture, as much liberty as was compatible with the pursuit of perfection, 'a *harmonious* perfection, developing all sides of our humanity; and...a *general* perfection, developing all parts of our society'.[2]

We have already seen that Arnold was a writer with well-defined aims—to expose the shortcomings of the middle class and to try to remedy them. Consequently he wrote for them, but in fact he had another audience in mind whom he particularly wanted to reach. Despite his division of society into three estates, he knew that there were those who did not share the faults of their respective class. Among the Barbarians, even, there were, he said, those 'who are (as are some of us Philistines also, and some of the Populace) beyond their fellows quick of feeling for truth and reason'.[3] In each class there were a certain number of *aliens*, 'persons who are mainly led, not by their class spirit, but by a general *humane* spirit, by the love of human perfection',[4] and it was such people that Arnold was first addressing. In his preface to *Higher Schools and Universities in France*, he stated what one may

[1] Super, v, 36.
[2] *Culture and Anarchy*, Super, v, 235.
[3] Ibid. 205.   [4] Ibid. 146.

assume to be his conception of his own function as a writer:

Therefore we have always said that in this country the functions of a disinterested literary class—a class of non-political writers, having no organised and embodied set of supporters to please, simply setting themselves to observe and report faithfully, and looking for favour to those isolated persons only, scattered all through the community, whom such an attempt may interest—are of incalculable importance.[1]

Finally, we may try to see Arnold's 'puny warfare against the Philistines' in the perspective in which he himself saw it. Culture, for Arnold, was a striving after a perfection that would never be reached—'We shall die in the wilderness,' he wrote, 'but to have desired to enter it [the Promised Land], to have saluted it from afar, is already, perhaps, the best distinction among contemporaries.'[2] Perfection will never be reached; the virtue for Arnold lay in the struggle, in the striving. Much later in life he wrote: 'But we are always the better, all of us, for having aimed high, for having striven to see and know things as they really are, for having set ourselves to walk in the light of that knowledge, to help forward great designs, and to do good.'[3] The struggle would continue and each generation would have to meet its challenge. To the children of the future Arnold said:

But you, in your turn, with difficulties of your own, will then be mounting some new step in the arduous ladder whereby man climbs towards his perfection; towards that unattainable but irresistible lode-star, gazed after with earnest longing,

[1] *Works*, XII, 90.
[2] 'The Function of Criticism', Super, III, 285.
[3] 'Ecce, Convertimur ad Gentes', *Irish Essays, Works*, XI, 133.

and invoked with bitter tears; the longing of thousands of hearts, the tears of many generations.[1]

Of the considerable body of educational writings which Arnold produced we have chosen to print in full the introduction to the *Popular Education of France*, which Arnold later published as a separate essay, 'Democracy'; *A French Eton;* his article, 'The Twice-Revised Code'; some selections from the annual reports which he submitted as part of his work as a school inspector; and, finally, extracts from his speech on the occasion of his retirement. On the principle that a student may well wish, and indeed should be encouraged, to read a work in its entirety, we have chosen, except in the case of the reports, to include complete works rather than to extend the field by quoting more briefly from various essays and books. As it happens, such is the consistency of Arnold's point of view that the works we have chosen, read in conjunction especially with his letters and *Culture and Anarchy*, form an excellent starting-point for appreciating the essence of his educational thought.

Moreover, this selection, we feel, can fulfil three distinct but interrelated functions. First, these works of Arnold's can, for the student of education, give an insight into the quality and direction of the man's thinking on topics which he considered of urgency. For the student of literature, who knows only Arnold's poetry and literary criticism, the study of these writings will reveal another aspect of Arnold's work, and will help the student to see his literary criticism in a wider context; as Dover Wilson said, Arnold 'was indeed all of a piece'. Secondly, these writings deal with and

[1] *A French Eton*, Super, II, 325.

illuminate issues of historical interest, both in the realm of ideas and in that of educational practice; and clearly they demonstrate Arnold's urgent involvement in the controversy of his own day. What is perhaps so interesting and exciting about Arnold's involvement in such practical issues as the Revised Code is that it ensues from his more general thinking, and the reader is constantly made aware of the principles behind his objections and opinions.[1] The third function that is served by this selection is that it cannot but provoke the reader to look again, a hundred years after much of it was written, at the difficulties which, as we have said, Arnold foresaw would be ours. The difficulties are to a large extent the same as those which exercised Arnold —What is the function of a school? How can it help 'the humanisation of man in society'? In what way should the State provide education for its citizens? and so on. It is a fascinating and enlightening exercise to consider whether Arnold's faith, shared by many Victorians, in education, and especially middle-class education, has been justified. What adjectives, one wonders, would Arnold now apply to the middle class? Would he see it as a transformed middle class? Would he continue to view society in the same class terms? Certainly, one feels that were he alive he would now be, as he was a century ago, urgently and actively involved in the controversies which centre on secondary education. It is an irony which Arnold would perhaps have appreciated that the problems which now exercise us about secondary education stem in part from the fact that we too are in a state of transition and face the results of his

---

[1] Arnold's reservations about Kay-Shuttleworth's pamphlet on the Revised Code of 1861 were couched in a characteristic way: 'The matter is hardly enough treated in its first principles for my taste.'

successful pleas for the provision of effective middle-class education.

It remains for us to introduce briefly each work included in this selection. Enough has been said in the general introduction for the student to be able to set 'Democracy' and *A French Eton* in the context of Arnold's thinking; the other two works require a more detailed introduction.

'Democracy'

When, in 1858, the Royal Commission, under the chairmanship of the Duke of Newcastle, was appointed to 'consider and report what Measures, if any, are required for the Extension of sound and cheap elementary Instruction to all Classes of the People', Matthew Arnold was invited to become an assistant commissioner. Together with Mark Pattison, he was to report upon conditions on the Continent; ultimately it was decided that this responsibility should be for reporting upon elementary schooling in France, the French cantons of Switzerland, and Holland. Arnold was abroad for four months during 1859, and presented his report during the early part of 1860.

By December 1860 we find him writing to his sister, 'I have at last got the Commissioner's distinct leave to publish my Report, with additions, as a book'.[1] The most important difference was the introduction which he added and subsequently published independently as the essay 'Democracy', in *Mixed Essays* (1879). The report, when published as a book with the introduction, was called *The Popular Education of France*, and was published in 1861.

[1] *Letters*, I, 127.

The essay 'Democracy' represents the position to which Arnold's contemplation of the technical matters of education led him, and is essential to an understanding of his political and educational thinking.

'A French Eton'

A French Eton was likewise, as the text reveals, a result of Arnold's visit as an assistant commissioner for the Newcastle Commission. It is also, rather tenuously perhaps, related to a controversy that was current while he was preparing his report on the elementary education in France, and was involved with his objection to the Revised Code. In May 1860, that master of polemics, Matthew Higgins, published in the *Cornhill*, under the pseudonym of 'Paterfamilias', an attack on the quality of education which the major public schools, and in particular Eton, were offering. As a result of the controversy which ensued, the Clarendon Commission was appointed in 1861 to enquire into the conduct of the nine great public schools.

What Arnold did when he published the three articles which were to become *A French Eton* in *Macmillan's Magazine* (September 1863, February 1864, and May 1864), was to use the occasion of the public interest in secondary education for his own purpose. The debate concerned the secondary education provided by the public schools for the few; Arnold extended the area of discussion, and, in a book of which he said, 'I have written nothing better', made his eloquent plea for effective secondary education for the English middle classes.

'*The Twice-Revised Code*'

This essay is Arnold's major contribution to the controversy surrounding the introduction of the Revised Code in 1862. The building of schools, the training of pupil-teachers and the payment of 'augmentations' for certificated teachers—all three, through the agency of the National Society and the British and Foreign School Society, received financial aid from the Committee of the Privy Council on Education: in 1839 this amounted to £30,000; in 1861, over £800,000. In 1853 the major part of the grant was modified by a capitation grant related essentially to the number of pupils in any school.

Such aid was radically changed by Robert Lowe, M.P., vice-president of the Committee of Council from 1859 to 1864, in a minute tabled in the Commons on 29 July 1861. The essential revision was that grants should henceforth be related to the number of pupils able to satisfy the inspectors (who thereby became examiners) in reading, writing, and arithmetic: 'Every scholar attending more than 200 times in the morning or afternoon, for whom 8s. is claimed, forfeits 2s. 8d. for failure to satisfy the inspector in reading, 2s. 8d. in writing, and 2s. 8d. in arithmetic.'[1]

Arnold's reaction to the revision was one of deep revulsion, but his position as Inspector called for delicate discretion; nevertheless, he was not prepared to stifle his own voice, and indeed was prepared to lose his job. 'If', he wrote to his wife on 28 March 1862, 'thrown on the world I daresay we should be on our legs again before very long. Any way, I think I owed as much as this to a cause in which I have now a deep

[1] Article 48, Revised Code, chapter II, section I, para. 44.

interest, and always shall have, even if I cease to serve it officially.'

In November 1861, Kay-Shuttleworth brought out an eighty-page pamphlet—one of many—but Arnold's own broadside was delayed by other calls on his time. On 13 February 1862, Lowe introduced the Revised Code, further modified, to the House of Commons.[1] His strategy was double-barrelled: on the one hand, he played the whole thing down—'I beg the House not to over-estimate the importance of this question...it really will be found to turn on the point simply of annual grants'; Disraeli's reply was quite clear: 'It appears to me that this is not a small subject, but a great—a very great subject', and, again, 'I say it is a great subject, and one of the greatest importance'. On the other hand, Lowe presented the Revised Code as, indeed, a 'great subject', as, in effect, the watershed between a 'tentative, provisional, and preliminary' system of education and a 'definite, precise, and final' system.

His rationale of the Revised Code was rooted in the notion of an efficient return for investment, and in a narrow view of education: 'Our business is to promote instruction.' The condition on which the grant had been given, hitherto, was that the Inspector should be satisfied 'with the state of the school generally', but the Inspectors had led everyone up the garden path; they had not only fostered the myth that ninety per cent of the children in school were excellently or fairly taught, but had also suffered from the disease of Platonism: their comments on schools had been abstract where they should have been concrete and 'they deal in impalpable essences, such as "the moral

[1] The whole of his long speech deserves close attention for its rhetorical devices. See *Hansard*, February 1862, cols 191–242.

atmosphere," the "tone"...' Their metaphysical talk
had been put out of countenance, said Lowe, by the
rigorous and precise findings of the Commissioners who
collected evidence for the Newcastle Commission:
these 'authorities'—Lowe's word—had found that
'only one fourth are taught thoroughly well to read,
write and cipher'. Lowe's answer was clear: 'I do not
deny that quality is a very important thing, but when I
come to a final system I cannot but think that quantity
is, perhaps, more important.' In order to ensure due
quantity, the grant must be made to 'depend on conditions which insure good education' and 'we must
appeal to the passions of the human mind—we must
enlist hope and fear to work for us'. Speaking of the
growth of the teaching profession and the employment
of less well-qualified teachers, he insisted that 'collateral
and independent proof that such teachers do their duty
...is only to be found in a system of individual examination'. As for the opinions of the teachers themselves,
these he dismissed as subversive rumblings; the tone of
Lowe's performance is consistently paternalistic and
domineering, not to say grossly insensitive: 'Children',
he says, 'between six and seven years of age...may
fairly be called upon to answer on examination.'

Such was the man, such were the ideas that Arnold
felt impelled to attack; in the event, when 'The Twice-
Revised Code' appeared in *Fraser's Magazine* of
March 1862, such was its success that it was reprinted
as a pamphlet and widely distributed in influential
circles. The title, incidentally, may owe something to
Disraeli's observation, that 'We have now before us not
only the Revised Code, but a Revision of the Revised
Code'. Arnold's preoccupation with the effects of the
Code is evident throughout his annual *Reports on*

Elementary Schools (see below, pp. 203–38), and is also voiced in his pseudonymous letter to the *Daily News* of 25 March 1862,[1] the day of the Commons debate on the Code, and in 'The Code out of Danger', published in the *London Review*, 10 May 1862.[2]

The Code cast a shadow over Arnold's subsequent work in the Inspectorate, and as F. S. Marvin observes: 'He did not live to see the complete official endorsement of his view, the abolition of the system, which followed in the nineties. This long struggle and disappointment, only slightly tempered towards the end, give the reports their personal interest and pathos.'[3]

Extracts from Arnold's 'Reports on Elementary Schools 1852–1882'

Arnold's reports occupy an important place in the history of English education: they represent the first expression of a supremely civilised mind's response to first-hand observation of democratic education in practice. It is their conjunction of extensive, sustained, direct contact with the minute (and often mean and sorry) particularities, and of an exceptionally urbane, serious and cultured mind that also distinguishes them as unique. Of the great Victorians, J. S. Mill, T. H. Huxley, George Eliot and Dickens all had profound and pertinent things to say, in their several ways, about education, but only Arnold saw the schools at first hand over a long period of time, and related his quotidian experiences to his growing philosophy: the reports are therefore, in a distinctive sense, a 'criticism of life'.

[1] Reprinted in Super, II, 244.
[2] Reprinted ibid. 247.
[3] M. Arnold, *Reports on Elementary Schools 1852–1882*, ed. F. S. Marvin (1908), p. xvii.

English education over the past hundred years has been characterised by an odd and distressing dichotomy—we mean the separations between refined philosophical depth and expansiveness, on the one hand, and the work of the classroom on the other. The English, with their incorrigible and still resolute mistrust of ideas, have been further confirmed in their mistrust of, or indifference to, educational philosophising, by the distance—social and intellectual—between the philosopher's study and the classroom.

At a time when these divisions are mercifully breaking down, it seems timely to reprint at least a part of Arnold's reports, documents in which one sees the mind of *Essays in Criticism* and *Culture and Anarchy* examining, appraising, and modifying the education of the people. The reports were published twice after Arnold's death: in an edition by Sir Francis Sandford in 1889, and again in an enlarged edition, with useful appendices (appendix K, for instance, gives verbatim the Revised Code of Minutes and Regulations of the Committee of the Privy Council on Education, 1862), by F. S. Marvin, in 1908. Both editions are now difficult to come by, and the frustrations caused by their scarcity are part of our present reasons for including fairly extensive selections from them.

We have based our selection on three particular aspects of Arnold's thinking. First the rôle of the Inspectorate; this can be usefully and properly translated into more general terms, for present purposes, as the rôle of those, whoever and whatever they may be, whose first duty it is to provoke responsible thinking about education and to maintain standards. This rôle, we suggest, is not now the exclusive prerogative of the Inspectorate. Second, Arnold's persistent conception of the school as a humanising and civilising agency, with some reference to the deleterious effects of the Revised Code. Again, we suggest, it is not unwarranted now to recognise similar pressures in our society which are driving us toward a utilitarian or professional conception of education—the tendency, for example, to judge a school on its examination results. Finally, and perhaps most important, the thoughts of Arnold on the education, status, and rôle of teachers. The quality of education, Arnold insists, must rest on the quality of the teachers: his notions of what constitutes adequate quality are such as we still need to ponder. If the relatively brief selection that we have made impels some of our readers to seek out the full text of Arnold's *Reports* we shall feel well rewarded.

Arnold's Speech on his Retirement

This speech was given on the occasion of a farewell presentation to him by the teachers of Westminster, on 12 November 1886. It was printed the following day in the *Pall Mall Gazette* and in *The Times*. The full text is given in Fraser Neiman's edition of *Essays, Letters, and Reviews by Matthew Arnold* (1960), pp. 306–11.

On 13 November 1886 he wrote to his daughter, Lucy: 'I have had a horrid week with my speech to the Westminster teachers. You know how a thing of that kind worries me. However, last night it came off, and very well The affection and responsiveness of the teachers was touching...'[1] In fact there were eight interjections of 'Hear, hear', eight outbursts of laughter and eleven breaks for cheers.

[1] *Letters*, II, 351–2.

Asterisks in the texts refer to Arnold's footnotes; superior figures refer to the Notes, which will be found on pp. 244–55.

DEMOCRACY

I know that, since the Revolution, along with
many dangerous, many useful powers of Government have been weakened.[1]

BURKE (1770)

In giving an account of education in certain countries of
the Continent, I have often spoken of the State and its
action in such a way as to offend, I fear, some of my
readers, and to surprise others. With many Englishmen,
perhaps with the majority, it is a maxim that the State,
the executive power, ought to be entrusted with no more
means of action than those which it is impossible to
withhold from it; that the State neither would nor
could make a safe use of any more extended liberty;
would not, because it has in itself a natural instinct of
despotism, which, if not jealously checked, would
become outrageous; could not, because it is, in truth,
not at all more enlightened, or fit to assume a lead, than
the mass of this enlightened community.

No sensible man will lightly go counter to an opinion
firmly held by a great body of his countrymen. He will
take for granted, that for any opinion which has struck
deep root among a people so powerful, so successful,
and so well worthy of respect as the people of this
country, there certainly either are, or have been, good
and sound reasons. He will venture to impugn such an
opinion with real hesitation, and only when he thinks
he perceives that the reasons which once supported it
exist no longer, or at any rate seem about to disappear
very soon. For undoubtedly there arrive periods, when,
the circumstances and conditions of government having
changed, the guiding maxims of government ought to

4-2

change also. *J'ai dit souvent*, says Mirabeau,* admonishing the Court of France in 1790, *qu'on devait changer de manière de gouverner, lorsque le gouvernement n'est plus le même*. And these decisive changes in the political situation of a people happen gradually as well as violently. "In the silent lapse of events," says Burke,† writing in England twenty years before the French Revolution, "as material alterations have been insensibly brought about in the policy and character of governments and nations, as those which have been marked by the tumult of public revolutions."

I propose to submit to those who have been accustomed to regard all State-action with jealousy, some reasons for thinking that the circumstances which once made that jealousy prudent and natural have undergone an essential change. I desire to lead them to consider with me, whether, in the present altered conjuncture, that State-action, which was once dangerous, may not become, not only without danger in itself, but the means of helping us against dangers from another quarter. To combine and present the considerations upon which these two propositions are based, is a task of some difficulty and delicacy. My aim is to invite impartial reflection upon the subject, not to make a hostile attack against old opinions, still less to set on foot and fully equip a new theory. In offering, therefore, the thoughts which have suggested themselves to me, I shall studiously avoid all particular applications of them likely to give offence, and shall use no more illustration and development than may be indispensable to enable the reader to seize and appreciate them.

* *Correspondance entre le Comte de Mirabeau et le Comte de la Marck*, publiée par M. [Adolphe] de Bacourt, Paris, 1851, vol. ii, p. 143.   † Burke's *Works* (ed. of 1852), vol. iii, p. 115.

The dissolution of the old political parties which have governed this country since the Revolution of 1688 has long been remarked. It was repeatedly declared to be happening long before it actually took place, while the vital energy of these parties still subsisted in full vigour, and was threatened only by some temporary obstruction. It has been eagerly deprecated long after it had actually begun to take place, when it was in full progress, and inevitable. These parties, differing in so much else, were yet alike in this, that they were both, in a certain broad sense, *aristocratical* parties. They were combinations of persons considerable, either by great family and estate, or by Court favour, or lastly, by eminent abilities and popularity; this last body, however, attaining participation in public affairs only through a conjunction with one or other of the former. These connections, though they contained men of very various degrees of birth and property, were still wholly leavened with the feelings and habits of the upper class of the nation. They had the bond of a common culture; and, however their political opinions and acts might differ, what they said and did had the stamp and style imparted by this culture, and by a common and elevated social condition.

Aristocratical bodies have no taste for a very imposing executive, or for a very active and penetrating domestic administration. They have a sense of equality among themselves, and of constituting in themselves what is greatest and most dignified in the realm, which makes their pride revolt against the overshadowing greatness and dignity of a commanding executive. They have a temper of independence, and a habit of uncontrolled action, which makes them impatient of encountering, in the management of the interior concerns of the country, the machinery and regulations of a superior and peremptory power. The different parties amongst them, as they successively get possession of the government, respect this jealous disposition in their opponents, because they share it themselves. It is a disposition proper to them as great personages, not as ministers; and as they are great personages for their whole life, while they may probably be ministers but for a very short time, the instinct of their social condition avails more with them than the instinct of their official function. To administer as little as possible, to make its weight felt in foreign affairs rather than in domestic, to see in ministerial station rather the means of power and dignity than a means of searching and useful administrative activity, is the natural tendency of an aristocratic executive. It is a tendency which is creditable to the good sense of aristocracies, honourable to their moderation, and at the same time fortunate for their country, of whose internal development they are not fitted to have the full direction.

One strong and beneficial influence, however, the administration of a vigorous and high-minded aristocracy is calculated to exert upon a robust and sound people. I have had occasion, in speaking of Homer, to say very often, and with much emphasis, that he is *in the grand style*. It is the chief virtue of a healthy and uncorrupted aristocracy, that it is, in general, in this grand style. That elevation of character, that noble way of thinking and behaving, which is an eminent gift of nature to some individuals, is also often generated in whole classes of men (at least when these come of a strong and good race) by the possession of power, by the importance and responsibility of high station, by habitual dealing with great things, by being placed above the necessity of constantly struggling for little things. And it is the source of great virtues. It may go along with a not very quick or open intelligence; but it cannot well go along with a conduct vulgar and ignoble. A governing class imbued with it may not be capable of intelligently leading the masses of a people to the highest pitch of welfare for them; but it sets them an invaluable example of qualities without which no really high welfare can exist. This has been done for their nation by the best aristocracies. The Roman aristocracy did it; the English aristocracy has done it. They each fostered in the mass of the peoples they governed,— peoples of sturdy moral constitution and apt to learn such lessons,—a greatness of spirit, the natural growth of the condition of magnates and rulers, but not the natural growth of the condition of the common people. They made, the one of the Roman, the other of the English people, in spite of all the shortcomings of each, great peoples, peoples *in the grand style*. And this they did, while wielding the people according to their own notions, and in the direction which seemed good to them; not as servants and instruments of the people, but as its commanders and heads; solicitous for the good of their country, indeed, but taking for granted that of that good they themselves were the supreme judges, and were to fix the conditions.

The time has arrived, however, when it is becoming impossible for the aristocracy of England to conduct and wield the English nation any longer. It still, indeed, administers public affairs; and it is a great error to suppose, as many persons in England suppose, that it administers but does not govern. He who administers, governs,* because he infixes his own mark and stamps

* *Administrer, c'est gouverner*, says Mirabeau; *gouverner, c'est régner; tout se réduit là.*

45

his own character on all public affairs as they pass through his hands; and, therefore, so long as the English aristocracy administers the commonwealth, it still governs it. But signs not to be mistaken show that its headship and leadership of the nation, by virtue of the substantial acquiescence of the body of the nation in its predominance and right to lead, is nearly over. That acquiescence was the tenure by which it held its power; and it is fast giving way. The superiority of the upper class over all others is no longer so great; the willingness of the others to recognise that superiority is no longer so ready.

This change has been brought about by natural and inevitable causes, and neither the great nor the multitude are to be blamed for it. The growing demands and audaciousness of the latter, the encroaching spirit of democracy, are, indeed, matters of loud complaint with some persons. But these persons are complaining of human nature itself, when they thus complain of a manifestation of its native and ineradicable impulse. Life itself consists, say the philosophers, in the effort *to affirm one's own essence;*[2] meaning by this, to develop one's own existence fully and freely, to have ample light and air, to be neither cramped nor overshadowed. Democracy is trying *to affirm its own essence;* to live, to enjoy, to possess the world, as aristocracy has tried, and successfully tried, before it. Ever since Europe emerged from barbarism, ever since the condition of the common people began a little to improve, ever since their minds began to stir, this effort of democracy has been gaining strength; and the more their condition improves, the more strength this effort gains. So potent is the charm of life and expansion upon the living; the moment men are aware of them, they begin to desire them, and the more they have of them, the more they crave.

This movement of democracy, like other operations of nature, merits properly neither blame nor praise. Its partisans are apt to give it credit which it does not deserve, while its enemies are apt to upbraid it unjustly. Its friends celebrate it as the author of all freedom. But political freedom may very well be established by aristocratic founders; and, certainly, the political freedom of England owes more to the grasping English barons than to democracy. Social freedom,—equality, —that is rather the field of the conquests of democracy. And here what I must call the injustice of its enemies comes in. For its seeking after equality, democracy is often, in this country above all, vehemently and scornfully blamed; its temper contrasted with that worthier temper which can magnanimously endure social distinctions; its operations all referred, as of course, to the stirrings of a base and malignant envy. No doubt there is a gross and vulgar spirit of envy, prompting the hearts of many of those who cry for equality. No doubt there are ignoble natures which prefer equality to liberty. But what we have to ask is, when the life of democracy is admitted as something natural and inevitable, whether this or that product of democracy is a necessary growth from its parent stock, or merely an excrescence upon it. If it be the latter, certainly it may be due to the meanest and most culpable passions. But if it be the former, then this product, however base and blameworthy the passions which it may sometimes be made to serve, can in itself be no more reprehensible than the vital impulse of democracy is in itself reprehensible; and this impulse is, as has been shown, identical with the ceaseless vital effort of human nature itself.

Now, can it be denied, that a certain approach to

equality, at any rate a certain reduction of signal inequalities, is a natural, instinctive demand of that impulse which drives society as a whole,—no longer individuals and limited classes only, but the mass of a community,—to develop itself with the utmost possible fullness and freedom? Can it be denied, that to live in a society of equals tends in general to make a man's spirits expand, and his faculties work easily and actively; while, to live in a society of superiors, although it may occasionally be a very good discipline, yet in general tends to tame the spirits and to make the play of the faculties less secure and active? Can it be denied, that to be heavily overshadowed, to be profoundly insignificant, has, on the whole, a depressing and benumbing effect on the character? I know that some individuals react against the strongest impediments, and owe success and greatness to the efforts which they are thus forced to make. But the question is not about individuals. The question is about the common bulk of mankind, persons without extraordinary gifts or exceptional energy, and who will ever require, in order to make the best of themselves, encouragement and directly favouring circumstances. Can any one deny, that for these the spectacle, when they would rise, of a condition of splendour, grandeur, and culture, which they cannot possibly reach, has the effect of making them flag in spirit, and of disposing them to sink despondingly back into their own condition? Can any one deny, that the knowledge how poor and insignificant the best condition of improvement and culture attainable by them must be esteemed by a class incomparably richer-endowed, tends to cheapen this modest possible amelioration in the account of those classes also for whom it would be relatively a real progress, and to disenchant their imaginations with it? It seems to me impossible to deny this. And therefore a philosophic observer,* with no love for democracy, but rather with a terror of it, has been constrained to remark, that "the common people is more uncivilised in aristocratic countries than in any others;" because there "the lowly and the poor feel themselves, as it were, overwhelmed with the weight of their own inferiority." He has been constrained to remark,† that "there is such a thing as a manly and legitimate passion for equality, prompting men to desire to be, *all* of them, in the enjoyment of power and consideration." And, in France, that very equality, which is by us so impetuously decried, while it has by no means improved (it is said) the upper classes of French society, has undoubtedly given to the lower classes, to the body of the common people, a self-respect, an enlargement of spirit, a consciousness of counting for something in their country's action, which has raised them in the scale of humanity. The common people, in France, seems to me the soundest part of the French nation. They seem to me more free from the two opposite degradations of multitudes, brutality and servility, to have a more developed human life, more of what distinguishes elsewhere the cultured classes from the vulgar, than the common people in any other country with which I am acquainted.

I do not say that grandeur and prosperity may not be

---

* M. [Alexis] de Tocqueville. See his *Démocratie en Amérique* (edit. of 1835), vol. i, p. 11. "Le peuple est plus grossier dans les pays aristocratiques que partout ailleurs. Dans ces lieux, où se rencontrent des hommes si forts et si riches, les faibles et les pauvres se sentent comme accablés de leur bassesse; ne découvrant aucun point par lequel ils puissent regagner l'égalité, ils désespèrent entièrement d'eux-mêmes, et se laissent tomber au-dessous de la dignité humaine."

† *Démocratie en Amérique*, vol. i, p. 60.

attained by a nation divided into the most widely distinct classes, and presenting the most signal inequalities of rank and fortune. I do not say that great national virtues may not be developed in it. I do not even say that a popular order, accepting this demarcation of classes as an eternal providential arrangement, not questioning the natural right of a superior order to lead it, content within its own sphere, admiring the grandeur and highmindedness of its ruling class, and catching on its own spirit some reflex of what it thus admires, may not be a happier body, as to the eye of the imagination it is certainly a more beautiful body, than a popular order, pushing, excited, and presumptuous; a popular order, jealous of recognising fixed superiorities, petulantly claiming to be as good as its betters, and tastelessly attiring itself with the fashions and designations which have become unalterably associated with a wealthy and refined class, and which, tricking out those who have neither wealth nor refinement, are ridiculous. But a popular order of that old-fashioned stamp exists now only for the imagination. It is not the force with which modern society has to reckon. Such a body may be a sturdy, honest, and sound-hearted lower class; but it is not a democratic people. It is not that power, which at the present day in all nations is to be found existing; in some, has obtained the mastery; in others, is yet in a state of expectation and preparation.

The power of France in Europe is at this day mainly owing to the completeness with which she has organised democratic institutions. The action of the French State is excessive; but it is too little understood in England that the French people has adopted this action for its own purposes, has in great measure attained those purposes by it, and owes to its having done so the chief part of its influence in Europe. The growing power in Europe is democracy; and France has organised democracy with a certain indisputable grandeur and success. The ideas of 1789 were working everywhere in the eighteenth century; but it was because in France the State adopted them that the French Revolution became an historic epoch for the world, and France the lode-star of Continental democracy. Her airs of superiority and her overweening pretensions come from her sense of the power which she derives from this cause. Every one knows how Frenchmen proclaim France to be at the head of civilisation, the French army to be the soldier of God, Paris to be the brain of Europe, and so on. All this is, no doubt, in a vein of sufficient fatuity and bad taste; but it means, at bottom, that France believes she has so organised herself as to facilitate for all members of her society full and free expansion; that she believes herself to have remodelled her institutions with an eye to reason rather than custom, and to right rather than fact; it means, that she believes the other peoples of Europe to be preparing themselves, more or less rapidly, for a like achievement, and that she is conscious of her power and influence upon them as an initiatress and example. In this belief there is a part of truth and a part of delusion. I think it is more profitable for a Frenchman to consider the part of delusion contained in it; for an Englishman, the part of truth.

It is because aristocracies almost inevitably fail to appreciate justly, or even to take into their mind, the instinct pushing the masses towards expansion and fuller life, that they lose their hold over them. It is the old story of the incapacity of aristocracies for ideas,—the secret of their want of success in modern epochs.

The people treats them with flagrant injustice, when it denies all obligation to them. They can, and often do, impart a high spirit, a fine ideal of grandeur, to the people; thus they lay the foundations of a great nation. But they leave the people still the multitude, the crowd; they have small belief in the power of the ideas which are its life. Themselves a power reposing on all which is most solid, material, and visible, they are slow to attach any great importance to influences impalpable, spiritual, and viewless. Although, therefore, a disinterested looker-on might often be disposed, seeing what has actually been achieved by aristocracies, to wish to retain or replace them in their preponderance, rather than commit a nation to the hazards of a new and untried future; yet the masses instinctively feel that they can never consent to this without renouncing the inmost impulse of their being; and that they should make such a renunciation cannot seriously be expected of them. Except on conditions which make its expansion, in the sense understood by itself, fully possible, democracy will never frankly ally itself with aristocracy; and on these conditions perhaps no aristocracy will ever frankly ally itself with it. Even the English aristocracy, so politic, so capable of compromises, has shown no signs of being able so to transform itself as to render such an alliance possible. The reception given by the Peers[3] to the bill for establishing life-peerages was, in this respect, of ill omen. The separation between aristocracy and democracy will probably, therefore, go on still widening.

And it must in fairness be added, that as in one most important part of general human culture,—openness to ideas and ardour for them,—aristocracy is less advanced than democracy, to replace or keep the latter under the tutelage of the former would in some respects be actually unfavourable to the progress of the world. At epochs when new ideas are powerfully fermenting in a society, and profoundly changing its spirit, aristocracies, as they are in general not long suffered to guide it without question, so are they by nature not well fitted to guide it intelligently.

In England, democracy has been slow in developing itself, having met with much to withstand it, not only in the worth of the aristocracy, but also in the fine qualities of the common people. The aristocracy has been more in sympathy with the common people than perhaps any other aristocracy. It has rarely given them great umbrage; it has neither been frivolous, so as to provoke their contempt, nor impertinent, so as to provoke their irritation. Above all, it has in general meant to act with justice, according to its own notions of justice. Therefore the feeling of admiring deference to such a class was more deep-rooted in the people of this country, more cordial, and more persistent, that in any people of the Continent. But, besides this, the vigour and high spirit of the English common people bred in them a self-reliance which disposed each man to act individually and independently; and so long as this disposition prevails through a nation divided into classes, the predominance of an aristocracy, of the class containing the greatest and strongest individuals of the nation, is secure. Democracy is a force in which the concert of a great number of men makes up for the weakness of each man taken by himself; democracy accepts a certain relative rise in their condition, obtainable by this concert for a great number, as something desirable in itself, because though this is undoubtedly far below grandeur, it is yet a good deal above insignificance. A very strong, self-reliant people neither easily learns to act in concert, nor easily brings itself to regard any middling good, any good short of the best, as an object ardently to be coveted and striven for. It keeps its eye on the grand prizes, and these are to be won only by distancing competitors, by getting before one's comrades, by succeeding all by one's self; and so long as a people works thus individually, it does not work democratically. The English people has all the qualities which dispose a people to work individually; may it never lose them! A people without the salt of these qualities, relying wholly on mutual co-operation, and proposing to itself second-rate ideals, would arrive at the pettiness and stationariness of China. But the English people is no longer so entirely ruled by them as not to show visible beginnings of democratic action; it becomes more and more sensible to the irresistible seduction of democratic ideas, promising to each individual of the multitude increased self-respect and expansion with the increased importance and authority of the multitude to which he belongs, with the diminished preponderance of the aristocratic class above him.

While the habit and disposition of deference are thus dying out among the lower classes of the English nation, it seems to me indisputable that the advantages which command deference, that eminent superiority in high feeling, dignity, and culture, tend to diminish among the highest class. I shall not be suspected of any inclination to underrate the aristocracy of this country. I regard it as the worthiest, as it certainly has been the most successful, aristocracy of which history makes record. If it has not been able to develop excellences which do not belong to the nature of an aristocracy, yet it has been able to avoid defects to which the nature of an aristocracy is peculiarly prone. But I cannot read the history of the flowering time of the English aristocracy, the eighteenth century, and then look at this aristocracy in our own century, without feeling that there has been a change. I am not now thinking of private and domestic virtues, of morality, of decorum. Perhaps with respect to these there has in this class, as in society at large, been a change for the better. I am thinking of those public and conspicuous virtues by which the multitude is captivated and led,—lofty spirit, commanding character, exquisite culture. It is true that the advance of all classes in culture and refinement may make the culture of one class, which, isolated, appeared remarkable, appear so no longer; but exquisite culture and great dignity are always something rare and striking, and it is the distinction of the English aristocracy, in the eighteenth century, that not only was their culture something rare by comparison with the rawness of the masses, it was something rare and admirable in itself. It is rather that this rare culture of the highest class has actually somewhat declined,* than that it has come to look less by juxtaposition with the augmented culture of other classes.

Probably democracy has something to answer for in this falling off of her rival. To feel itself raised on high, venerated, followed, no doubt stimulates a fine nature to keep itself worthy to be followed, venerated, raised on high; hence that lofty maxim, *noblesse oblige*. To feel its

* This will appear doubtful to no one well acquainted with the literature and memoirs of the last century. To give but two illustrations out of a thousand. Let the reader refer to the anecdote told by Robert Wood in his *Essay on the Genius of Homer* (London, 1775), p. vii, and to Lord Chesterfield's *Letters* (edit. of 1845), vol. i, pp. 115, 143; vol. ii, p. 54; and then say, whether the culture there indicated as the culture of a *class* has maintained itself at that level.

culture something precious and singular, makes such a nature zealous to retain and extend it. The elation and energy thus fostered by the sense of its advantages, certainly enhances the worth, strengthens the behaviour, and quickens all the active powers of the class enjoying it. *Possunt quia posse videntur.* The removal of the stimulus a little relaxes their energy. It is not so much that they sink to be somewhat less than themselves, as that they cease to be somewhat more than themselves. But, however this may be, whencesoever the change may proceed, I cannot doubt that in the aristocratic virtue, in the intrinsic commanding force of the English upper class, there is a diminution. Relics of a great generation are still, perhaps, to be seen amongst them, surviving exemplars of noble manners and consummate culture; but they disappear one after the other, and no one of their kind takes their place. At the very moment when democracy becomes less and less disposed to follow and to admire, aristocracy becomes less and less qualified to command and to captivate.

On the one hand, then, the masses of the people in this country are preparing to take a much more active part than formerly in controlling its destinies; on the other hand, the aristocracy (using this word in the widest sense, to include not only the nobility and landed gentry, but also those reinforcements from the classes bordering upon itself, which this class constantly attracts and assimilates), while it is threatened with losing its hold on the rudder of government, its power to give to public affairs its own bias and direction, is losing also that influence on the spirit and character of the people which it long exercised.

I know that this will be warmly denied by some persons. Those who have grown up amidst a certain state of things, those whose habits, and interests, and affections, are closely concerned with its continuance, are slow to believe that it is not a part of the order of nature, or that it can ever come to an end. But I think that what I have here laid down will not appear doubtful either to the most competent and friendly foreign observers of this country, or to those Englishmen who, clear of all influences of class or party, have applied themselves steadily to see the tendencies of their nation as they really are. Assuming it to be true, a great number of considerations are suggested by it; but it is my purpose here to insist upon one only.

That one consideration is: On what action may we rely to replace, for some time at any rate, that action of the aristocracy upon the people of this country, which we have seen exercise an influence in many respects elevating and beneficial, but which is rapidly, and from inevitable causes, ceasing? In other words, and to use a short and significant modern expression which every one understands, what influence may help us to prevent the English people from becoming, with the growth of democracy, *Americanised?* I confess I am disposed to answer: On the action of the State.

I know what a chorus of objectors will be ready. One will say: Rather repair and restore the influence of aristocracy. Another will say: It is not a bad thing, but a good thing, that the English people should be Americanised. But the most formidable and the most widely entertained objection, by far, will be that which founds itself upon the present actual state of things in another country; which says: Look at France! there you have a signal example of the alliance of democracy with a powerful State-action, and see how it works.

This last and principal objection I will notice at once.

I have had occasion to touch upon the first already, and upon the second I shall touch presently. It seems to me, then, that one may save one's self from much idle terror at names and shadows if one will be at the pains to remember what different conditions the different character of two nations must necessarily impose on the operation of any principle. That which operates noxiously in one, may operate wholesomely in the other; because the unsound part of the one's character may be yet further inflamed and enlarged by it, the unsound part of the other's may find in it a corrective and an abatement. This is the great use which two unlike characters may find in observing each other. Neither is likely to have the other's faults, so each may safely adopt as much as suits him of the other's qualities. If I were a Frenchman I should never be weary of admiring the independent, individual, local habits of action in England, of directing attention to the evils occasioned in France by the excessive action of the State; for I should be very sure that, say what I might, the part of the State would never be too small in France, nor that of the individual too large. Being an Englishman, I see nothing but good in freely recognising the coherence, rationality, and efficaciousness which characterise the strong State-action of France, of acknowledging the want of method, reason, and result which attend the feeble State-action of England; because I am very sure that, strengthen in England the action of the State as one may, it will always find itself sufficiently controlled. But when either the *Constitutionnel*[4] sneers at the do-little talkativeness of parliamentary government, or when the *Morning Star*[5] inveighs against the despotism of a centralised administration, it seems to me that they lose their labour, because they are hardening themselves against dangers to which they are neither of them liable. Both the one and the other, in plain truth,

> "Compound for sins they are inclined to,
> By damning those they have no mind to."[6]

They should rather exchange doctrines one with the other, and each might thus, perhaps, be profited.

So that the exaggeration of the action of the State, in France, furnishes no reason for absolutely refusing to enlarge the action of the State in England; because the genius and temper of the people of this country are such as to render impossible that exaggeration which the genius and temper of the French rendered easy. There is no danger at all that the native independence and individualism of the English character will ever belie itself, and become either weakly prone to lean on others, or blindly confiding in them.

English democracy runs no risk of being over-mastered by the State; it is almost certain that it will throw off the tutelage of aristocracy. Its real danger is, that it will have far too much its own way, and be left far too much to itself. "What harm will there be in that?" say some; "are we not a self-governing people?" I answer: "We have never yet been a *self-governing democracy*, or anything like it." The difficulty for democracy is, how to find and keep high ideals. The individuals who compose it are, the bulk of them, persons who need to follow an ideal, not to set one; and one ideal of greatness, high feeling, and fine culture, which an aristocracy once supplied to them, they lose by the very fact of ceasing to be a lower order and becoming a democracy. Nations are not truly great solely because the individuals composing them are numerous, free, and active; but they are great when these numbers, this freedom, and this activity are employed in the service of an ideal higher than that of an ordinary man, taken by himself. Our society is probably destined to become much more democratic; who or what will give a high tone to the nation then? That is the grave question.

The greatest men of America, her Washingtons, Hamiltons, Madisons, well understanding that arisocratical institutions are not in all times and places possible; well perceiving that in their Republic there was no place for these; comprehending, therefore, that from these that security for national dignity and greatness, an ideal commanding popular reverence, was not to be obtained, but knowing that this ideal was indispensable, would have been rejoiced to found a substitute for it in the dignity and authority of the State. They deplored the weakness and insignificance of the executive power as a calamity. When the inevitable course of events has made our self-government something really like that of America, when it has removed or weakened that security for national dignity, which we possessed in *aristocracy*, will the substitute of the *State* be equally wanting to us? If it is, then the dangers of America will really be ours; the dangers which come from the multitude being in power, with no adequate ideal to elevate or guide the multitude.

It would really be wasting time to contend at length, that to give more prominence to the idea of the State is now possible in this country, without endangering liberty. In other countries the habits and dispositions of the people may be such that the State, if once it acts, may be easily suffered to usurp exorbitantly; here they certainly are not. Here the people will always sufficiently keep in mind that any public authority is a trust delegated by themselves, for certain purposes, and with certain limits; and if that authority pretends to an absolute, independent character, they will soon enough (and very rightly) remind it of its error. Here there can be no question of a paternal government, of an irresponsible executive power, professing to act for the people's good, but without the people's consent, and, if necessary, against the people's wishes; here no one dreams of removing a single constitutional control, of abolishing a single safeguard for securing a correspondence between the acts of government and the will of the nation. The question is, whether, retaining all its power of control over a government which should abuse its trust, the nation may not now find advantage in voluntarily allowing to it purposes somewhat ampler, and limits somewhat wider within which to execute them, than formerly; whether the nation may not thus acquire in the State an ideal of high reason and right feeling, representing its best self, commanding general respect, and forming a rallying-point for the intelligence and for the worthiest instincts of the community, which will herein find a true bond of union.

I am convinced that if the worst mischiefs of democracy ever happen in England, it will be, not because a new condition of things has come upon us unforeseen, but because, though we all foresaw it, our efforts to deal with it were in the wrong direction. At the present time, almost every one believes in the growth of democracy, almost every one talks of it, almost every one laments it; but the last thing people can be brought to do is to make timely preparation for it. Many of those who, if they would, could do most to forward this work of preparation, are made slack and hesitating by the belief that, after all, in England, things may probably never go very far; that it will be possible to keep much

more of the past than speculators say. Others, with a
more robust faith, think that all democracy wants is
vigorous putting-down; and that, with a good will and
strong hand, it is perfectly possible to retain or restore
the whole system of the Middle Ages. Others, free from
the prejudices of class and position which warp the
judgement of these, and who would, I believe, be the
first and greatest gainers by strengthening the hands
of the State, are averse from doing so by reason of
suspicions and fears, once perfectly well-grounded, but,
in this age and in the present circumstances, well-
grounded no longer.

I speak of the middle classes. I have already shown
how it is the natural disposition of an aristocratical
class to view with jealousy the development of a considerable State-power. But this disposition has in
England found extraordinary favour and support in
regions not aristocratical,—from the middle classes;
and, above all, from the kernel of these classes, the
Protestant Dissenters. And for a very good reason. In
times when passions ran high, even an aristocratical
executive was easily stimulated into using, for the
gratification of its friends and the abasement of its
enemies, those administrative engines which, the
moment it chose to stretch its hand forth, stood ready
for its grasp. Matters of domestic concern, matters of
religious profession and religious exercise, offered a
peculiar field for an intervention gainful and agreeable
to friends, injurious and irritating to enemies. Such an
intervention was attempted and practised. Government
lent its machinery and authority to the aristocratical
and ecclesiastical party, which it regarded as its best
support. The party which suffered comprised the flower
and strength of that middle class of society, always very

flourishing and robust in this country. That powerful class, from this specimen of the administrative activity of government, conceived a strong antipathy against all intervention of the State in certain spheres. An active, stringent administration in those spheres, meant at that time a High Church and Prelatic administration in them, an administration galling to the Puritan party and to the middle class; and this aggrieved class had naturally no proneness to draw nice philosophical distinctions between State-action in these spheres, as a thing for abstract consideration, and State-action in them as they practically felt it and supposed themselves likely long to feel it, guided by their adversaries. In the minds of the English middle class, therefore, State-action in social and domestic concerns became inextricably associated with the idea of a Conventicle Act,[7] a Five-Mile Act, an Act of Uniformity. Their abhorrence of such a State-action as this they extended to State-action in general; and, having never known a beneficent and just State-power, they enlarged their hatred of a cruel and partial State-power, the only one they had ever known, into a maxim that no State-power was to be trusted, that the least action, in certain provinces, was rigorously to be denied to the State, whenever this denial was possible.

Thus that jealousy of an important, sedulous, energetic executive, natural to grandees unwilling to suffer their personal authority to be circumscribed, their individual grandeur to be eclipsed, by the authority and grandeur of the State, became reinforced in this country by a like sentiment among the middle classes, who had no such authority or grandeur to lose, but who, by a hasty reasoning, had theoretically condemned for ever an agency which they had practically found at times oppressive. *Leave us to ourselves!* magnates and middle classes alike cried to the State. Not only from those who were full and abounded went up this prayer, but also from those whose condition admitted of great amelioration. Not only did the whole repudiate the physician, but also those who were sick.

For it is evident, that the action of a diligent, an impartial, and a national government, while it can do little to better the condition, already fortunate enough, of the highest and richest class of its people, can really do much, by institution and regulation, to better that of the middle and lower classes. The State can bestow certain broad collective benefits, which are indeed not much if compared with the advantages already possessed by individual grandeur, but which are rich and valuable if compared with the make-shifts of mediocrity and poverty. A good thing meant for the many cannot well be so exquisite as the good things of the few; but it can easily, if it comes from a donor of great resources and wide power, be incomparably better than what the many could, unaided, provide for themselves.

In all the remarks which I have been making, I have hitherto abstained from any attempt to suggest a positive application of them. I have limited myself to simply pointing out in how changed a world of ideas we are living; I have not sought to go further, and to discuss in what particular manner the world of facts is to adapt itself to this changed world of ideas. This has been my rule so far; but from this rule I shall here venture to depart, in order to dwell for a moment on a matter of practical institution, designed to meet new social exigencies: on the intervention of the State in public education.

The public secondary schools of France, decreed by

the Revolution and established under the Consulate, are said by many good judges to be inferior to the old colleges. By means of the old colleges and of private tutors, the French aristocracy could procure for its children (so it is said, and very likely with truth) a better training than that which is now given in the lyceums. Yes; but the boon conferred by the State, when it founded the lyceums, was not for the aristocracy; it was for the vast middle class of Frenchmen. This class, certainly, had not already the means of a better training for its children, before the State interfered. This class, certainly, would not have succeeded in procuring by its own efforts a better training for its children, if the State had not interfered. Through the intervention of the State this class enjoys better schools for its children, not than the great and rich enjoy (that is not the question), but than the same class enjoys in any country where the State has not interfered to found them. The lyceums may not be so good as Eton or Harrow; but they are a great deal better than a *Classical and Commercial Academy*.[8]

The aristocratic classes in England may, perhaps, be well content to rest satisfied with their Eton and Harrow. The State is not likely to do better for them. Nay, the superior confidence, spirit, and style, engendered by a training in the great public schools, constitute for these classes a real privilege, a real engine of command, which they might, if they were selfish, be sorry to lose by the establishment of schools great enough to beget a like spirit in the classes below them. But the middle classes in England have every reason not to rest content with their private schools; the State can do a great deal better for them. By giving to schools for these classes a public character, it can bring the instruction in them under a criticism which the stock of knowledge and judgement in our middle classes is not of itself at present able to supply. By giving to them a national character, it can confer on them a greatness and a noble spirit, which the tone of these classes is not of itself at present adequate to impart. Such schools would soon prove notable competitors with the existing public schools; they would do these a great service by stimulating them, and making them look into their own weak points more closely. Economical, because with charges uniform and under severe revision, they would do a great service to that large body of persons who, at present, seeing that on the whole the best secondary instruction to be found is that of the existing public schools, obtain it for their children from a sense of duty, although they can ill afford it, and although its cost is certainly exorbitant. Thus the middle classes might, by the aid of the State, better their instruction, while still keeping its cost moderate. This in itself would be a gain; but this gain would be slight in comparison with that of acquiring the sense of belonging to great and honourable seats of learning, and of breathing in their youth the air of the best culture of their nation. This sense would be an educational influence for them of the highest value. It would really augment their self-respect and moral force; it would truly fuse them with the class above, and tend to bring about for them the equality which they are entitled to desire.

So it is not State-action in itself which the middle and lower classes of a nation ought to deprecate; it is State-action exercised by a hostile class, and for their oppression. From a State-action reasonably, equitably, and nationally exercised, they may derive great benefit; greater, by the very nature and necessity of things, than can be derived from this source by the class above them. For the middle or lower classes to obstruct such a State-action, to repel its benefits, is to play the game of their enemies, and to prolong for themselves a condition of real inferiority.

This, I know, is rather dangerous ground to tread upon. The great middle classes of this country are conscious of no weakness, no inferiority; they do not want any one to provide anything for them. Such as they are, they believe that the freedom and prosperity of England are their work, and that the future belongs to them. No one esteems them more than I do; but those who esteem them most, and who most believe in their capabilities, can render them no better service than by pointing out in what they underrate their deficiencies, and how their deficiencies, if unremedied, may impair their future. They want culture and dignity; they want ideas. Aristocracy has culture and dignity; democracy has readiness for new ideas, and ardour for what ideas it possesses. Of these, our middle class has the last only: ardour for the ideas it already possesses. It believes ardently in liberty, it believes ardently in industry; and, by its zealous belief in these two ideas, it has accomplished great things. What it has accomplished by its belief in industry is patent to all the world. The liberties of England are less its exclusive work than it supposes; for these, aristocracy has achieved nearly as much. Still, of one inestimable part of liberty, liberty of thought, the middle class has been (without precisely intending it) the principal champion. The intellectual action of the Church of England upon the nation has been insignificant; its social action has been great. The social action of Protestant Dissent, that genuine product of the English middle class, has not been civilising; its positive intellectual action has been insignificant; its negative intellectual action,—in so far as by strenuously maintaining for itself, against persecution, liberty of conscience and the right of free opinion, it at the same time maintained and established this right as a universal principle,—has been invaluable. But the actual results of this negative intellectual service rendered by Protestant Dissent,—by the middle class,—to the whole community, great as they undoubtedly are, must not be taken for something which they are not. It is a very great thing to be able to think as you like; but, after all, an important question remains: *what* you think. It is a fine thing to secure a free stage and no favour; but, after all, the part which you play on that stage will have to be criticised. Now, all the liberty and industry in the world will not ensure these two things: a high reason and a fine culture. They may favour them, but they will not of themselves produce them; they may exist without them. But it is by the appearance of these two things, in some shape or other, in the life of a nation, that it becomes something more than an independent, an energetic, a successful nation,—that it becomes a *great* nation.

In modern epochs the part of a high reason, of ideas, acquires constantly increasing importance in the conduct of the world's affairs. A fine culture is the complement of a high reason, and it is in the conjunction of both with character, with energy, that the ideal for men and nations is to be placed. It is common to hear remarks on the frequent divorce between culture and character, and to infer from this that culture is a mere varnish, and that character only deserves any serious attention. No error can be more fatal. Culture without character is, no doubt, something frivolous, vain, and weak; but character without culture is, on the other hand, something raw, blind, and dangerous. The most interesting, the most truly glorious peoples, are those in which the alliance of the two has been effected most successfully, and its result spread most widely. This is why the spectacle of ancient Athens has such profound interest for a rational man; that is the spectacle of the culture of a *people*. It is not an aristocracy, leavening with its own high spirit the multitude which it wields, but leaving it the unformed multitude still; it is not a democracy, acute and energetic, but tasteless, narrow-minded, and ignoble; it is the middle and lower classes in the highest development of their humanity that these classes have yet reached. It was the *many* who relished those arts, who were not satisfied with less than those monuments. In the conversations recorded by Plato, or even by the matter-of-fact Xenophon, which for the free yet refined discussion of ideas have set the tone for the whole cultivated world, shopkeepers and tradesmen of Athens mingle as speakers. For any one but a pedant, this is why a handful of Athenians of two thousand years ago are more interesting than the millions of most nations our contemporaries. Surely, if they knew this, those friends of progress, who have confidently pronounced the remains of the ancient world to be so much lumber, and a classical education an aristocratic impertinence, might be inclined to reconsider their sentence.

The course taken in the next fifty years by the middle classes of this nation will probably give a decisive turn to its history. If they will not seek the alliance of the State for their own elevation, if they go on exaggerating their spirit of individualism, if they persist in their jealousy of all governmental action, if they cannot learn that the antipathies and the shibboleths of a past age are now an anachronism for them—that will not prevent them, probably, from getting the rule of their country for a season, but they will certainly *Americanise* it. They will rule it by their energy, but they will deteriorate it by their low ideals and want of culture. In the decline of the aristocratical element, which in some sort supplied an ideal to ennoble the spirit of the nation and to keep it together, there will be no other element present to perform this service. It is of itself a serious calamity for a nation that its tone of feeling and grandeur of spirit should be lowered or dulled. But the calamity appears far more serious still when we consider that the middle classes, remaining as they are now, with their narrow, harsh, unintelligent, and unattractive spirit and culture, will almost certainly fail to mould or assimilate the masses below them, whose sympathies are at the present moment actually wider and more liberal than theirs. They arrive, these masses, eager to enter into possession of the world, to gain a more vivid sense of their own life and activity. In this their irrepressible development, their natural educators and initiators are those immediately above them, the middle classes. If these classes cannot win their sympathy or give them their direction, society is in danger of falling into anarchy.

Therefore, with all the force I can, I wish to urge upon the middle classes of this country, both that they might be very greatly profited by the action of the State, and also that they are continuing their opposition to such action out of an unfounded fear. But at the same time I say that the middle classes have the right, in admitting the action of government, to make the condition that this government shall be one of their own adoption, one that they can trust. To ensure this is now in their own power. If they do not as yet ensure this, they ought to do so, they have the means of doing so. Two centuries ago they had not; now they have. Having this security, let them now show themselves jealous to keep the action of the State equitable and rational, rather than to exclude the action of the State altogether. If the State acts amiss, let them check it, but let them no longer take it for granted that the State cannot possibly act usefully.

The State—but what is *the State?* cry many. Speculations on the idea of a State abound, but these do not satisfy them; of that which is to have practical effect and power they require a plain account. The full force of the term, *the State,* as the full force of any other important term, no one will master without going a little deeply, without resolutely entering the world of ideas; but it is possible to give in very plain language an account of it sufficient for all practical purposes. The State is properly just what Burke called it—*the nation in its collective and corporate character.* The State is the representative acting-power of the nation; the action of the State is the representative action of the nation. Nominally emanating from the Crown, as the ideal unity in which the nation concentrates itself, this action, by the constitution of our country, really emanates from the ministers of the Crown. It is common to hear the depreciators of State-action run through a string of ministers' names, and then say: "Here is really your *State;* would you accept the action of these men as your own representative action? In what respect is their judgement on national affairs likely to be any better than that of the rest of the world?" In the first place I answer: Even supposing them to be originally no better or wiser

than the rest of the world, they have two great advantages from their position: access to almost boundless
means of information, and the enlargement of mind
which the habit of dealing with great affairs tends to
produce. Their position itself, therefore, if they are men
of only average honesty and capacity, tends to give them
a fitness for acting on behalf of the nation superior to
that of other men of equal honesty and capacity who
are not in the same position. This fitness may be yet
further increased by treating them as persons on whom,
indeed, a very grave responsibility has fallen, and from
whom very much will be expected;—nothing less than
the representing, each of them in his own department,
under the control of Parliament, and aided by the
suggestions of public opinion, the collective energy and
intelligence of his nation. By treating them as men on
whom all this devolves to do, to their honour if they
do it well, to their shame if they do it ill, one probably
augments their faculty of well-doing; as it is excellently
said: "To treat men as if they were better than they are,
is the surest way to *make* them better than they are." But
to treat them as if they had been shuffled into their
places by a lucky accident, were most likely soon to be
shuffled out of them again, and meanwhile ought to
magnify themselves and their office as little as possible;
to treat them as if they and their functions could without much inconvenience be quite dispensed with, and
they ought perpetually to be admiring their own incon-
ceivable good fortune in being permitted to discharge
them;—this is the way to paralyse all high effort
in the executive government, to extinguish all lofty
sense of responsibility; to make its members either
merely solicitous for the gross advantages, the
emolument and self-importance, which they derive

from their offices, or else timid, apologetic, and self-mistrustful in filling them; in either case, formal and inefficient.

But in the second place I answer: If the executive government is really in the hands of men no wiser than the bulk of mankind, of men whose action an intelligent man would be unwilling to accept as representative of his own action, whose fault is that? It is the fault of the nation itself, which, not being in the hands of a despot or an oligarchy, being free to control the choice of those who are to sum up and concentrate its action, controls it in such a manner that it allows to be chosen agents so little in its confidence, or so mediocre, or so incompetent, that it thinks the best thing to be done with them is to reduce their action as near as possible to a nullity. Hesitating, blundering, unintelligent, inefficacious, the action of the State may be; but, such as it is, it is the collective action of the nation itself, and the nation is responsible for it. It is our own action which we suffer to be thus unsatisfactory. Nothing can free us from this responsibility. The conduct of our affairs is in our own power. To carry on into its executive proceedings the indecision, conflict, and discordance of its parliamentary debates, may be a natural defect of a free nation, but it is certainly a defect; it is a dangerous error to call it, as some do, a perfection. The want of concert, reason, and organisation in the State, is the want of concert, reason, and organisation in the collective nation.

Inasmuch, therefore, as collective action is more efficacious than isolated individual efforts, a nation having great and complicated matters to deal with must greatly gain by employing the action of the State. Only, the State-power which it employs should be a power which really represents its best self, and whose action its intelligence and justice can heartily avow and adopt; not a power which reflects its inferior self, and of whose action, as of its own second-rate action, it has perpetually to be ashamed. To offer a worthy initiative, and to set a standard of rational and equitable action,—this is what the nation should expect of the State; and the more the State fulfils this expectation, the more will it be accepted in practice for what in idea it must always be. People will not then ask the State, what title it has to commend or reward genius and merit, since commendation and reward imply an attitude of superiority, for it will then be felt that the State truly acts for the English nation; and the genius of the English nation is greater than the genius of any individual, greater even than Shakspeare's genius, for it includes the genius of Newton also.

I will not deny that to give a more prominent part to the State would be a considerable change in this country; that maxims once very sound, and habits once very salutary, may be appealed to against it. The sole question is, whether those maxims and habits are sound and salutary at this moment. A yet graver and more difficult change,—to reduce the all-effacing prominence of the State, to give a more prominent part to the individual,—is imperiously presenting itself to other countries. Both are the suggestions of one irresistible force, which is gradually making its way everywhere, removing old conditions and imposing new, altering long-fixed habits, undermining venerable institutions, even modifying national character: *the modern spirit*.

Undoubtedly we are drawing on towards great changes; and for every nation the thing most needful is to discern clearly its own condition, in order to know in what particular way it may best meet them. Openness and flexibility of mind are at such a time the first of virtues. *Be ye perfect*, said the Founder of Christianity;[9] *I count not myself to have apprehended*, said its greatest Apostle.[10] Perfection will never be reached; but to recognise a period of transformation when it comes, and to adapt themselves honestly and rationally to its laws, is perhaps the nearest approach to perfection of which men and nations are capable. No habits or attachments should prevent their trying to do this; nor indeed, in the long run, can they. Human thought, which made all institutions, inevitably saps them, resting only in that which is absolute and eternal.

A FRENCH ETON
OR
MIDDLE-CLASS EDUCATION
AND THE STATE

> Forgetting those things which are behind, and
> reaching forth unto those things which are
> before.
>
> ST. PAUL

A lively and acute writer,[11] whom English society,
indebted to his vigilance for the exposure of a thousand
delinquents, salutes with admiration as its Grand
Detective, some time ago called public attention to the
state of the "College of the Blessed Mary" at Eton. In
that famous seat of learning, he said, a vast sum of
money was expended on education, and a beggarly
account of empty brains was the result. Rich endowments were wasted; parents were giving large sums to
have their children taught, and were getting a most
inadequate return for their outlay. Science, among those
venerable towers in the vale of the Thames, still adored
her Henry's holy shade; but she did very little else.
These topics, handled with infinite skill and vivacity,
produced a strong effect. Public attention, for a
moment, fixed itself upon the state of secondary instruction in England. The great class, which is interested in
the improvement of this, imagined that the moment was
come for making the first step towards that improvement. The comparatively small class, whose children are
educated in the existing public schools, thought that
some inquiry into the state of these institutions might do
good. A Royal Commission[12] was appointed to report

upon the endowments, studies, and management of the nine principal public schools of this country—Eton, Winchester, Westminster, Charterhouse, St. Paul's, Merchant Taylors', Harrow, Rugby, and Shrewsbury.

Eton was really the accused, although eight co-respondents were thus summoned to appear with Eton; and in Eton the investigation now completed will probably produce most reform. The reform of an institution which trains so many of the rulers of this country is, no doubt, a matter of considerable import-ance. That importance is certainly lessened if it is true, as the *Times* tells us, that the real ruler of our country is "The People," although this potentate does not absolutely transact his own business, but delegates that function to the class which Eton educates. But even those who believe that Mirabeau, when he said, *He who administers, governs*, was a great deal nearer the truth than the *Times*, and to whom, therefore, changes at Eton seem indeed matter of great importance, will hardly be disposed to make those changes very sweep-ing. If Eton does not teach her pupils profound wisdom, we have Oxenstiern's word for it that the world is governed by very little wisdom. Eton, at any rate, teaches her aristocratic pupils virtues which are among the best virtues of an aristocracy—freedom from affecta-tion, manliness, a high spirit, simplicity. It is to be hoped that she teaches something of these virtues to her other pupils also, who, not of the aristocratic class themselves, enjoy at Eton the benefit of contact with aristocracy. For these other pupils, perhaps, a little more learning as well, a somewhat stronger dose of ideas, might be desirable. Above all, it might be desirable to wean them from the easy habits and profuse notions of expense which Eton generates—habits and notions graceful enough in the lilies of the social field, but inconvenient for its future toilers and spinners. To convey to Eton the knowledge that the wine of Champagne does not water the whole earth, and that there are incomes which fall below 5,000*l*. a year, would be an act of kindness towards a large class of British parents, full of proper pride, but not opulent. Let us hope that the courageous social reformer who has taken Eton in hand may, at least, reap this reward from his labours. Let us hope he may succeed in somewhat reducing the standard of expense at Eton, and let us pronounce over his offspring the prayer of Ajax:—"O boys, may you be cheaper-"educated than your father, but in other respects like "him; may you have the same loving care for the im-"provement of the British officer, the same terrible eye "upon bullies and jobbers, the same charming gaiety in "your frolics with the 'Old Dog Tray;'—but may all "these gifts be developed at a lesser price!"

But I hope that large class which wants the improvement of secondary instruction in this country—secondary instruction, the great first stage of a liberal education, coming between elementary instruction, the instruction in the mother tongue and in the simplest and indispensable branches of knowledge on the one hand, and superior instruction, the instruction given by universities, the second and finishing stage of a liberal education, on the other—will not imagine that the appointment of a Royal Commission to report on nine existing schools can seriously help it to that which it wants. I hope it will steadily say to the limited class whom the reform of these nine schools (if they need reform) truly concerns—*Tua res agitur*. These nine schools are by their constitution such that they profess to reach but select portions of the multitudes that are claiming secondary instruction; and, whatever they might profess, being nine, they *can* only reach select portions. The exhibition which the Royal Commissioners have given us of these schools is indeed very interesting; I hope it will prove very useful. But, for the champions of the true cause of secondary instruction, for those interested in the thorough improvement of this most important concern, the centre of interest is not there. Before the English mind, always prone to throw itself upon details, has by the interesting Report of the Public School Commissioners been led completely to throw itself upon what, after all, in this great concern of secondary instruction, is only a detail, I wish to show, with all the clearness and insistence I can, where the centre of interest really lies.

To see secondary instruction treated as a matter of national concern, to see any serious attempt to make it both commensurate with the numbers needing it and of good quality, we must cross the Channel. The Royal Commissioners have thought themselves precluded, by the limits of their instructions, from making a thorough inquiry into the system of secondary instruction on the Continent. I regret that they did not trust to the vast importance of the subject for procuring their pardon even if they somewhat extended their scope, and made their survey of foreign secondary instruction exact. This they could have done only by investing qualified persons with the commission to seek, in their name, access to the foreign schools. These institutions must be seen at work, and seen by experienced eyes, for their operation to be properly understood and described. But to see them at work the aid of the public authorities abroad is requisite; and foreign governments, most prompt in giving this aid to accredited emissaries, are by no means disposed to extend it to the chance inquirer.

In 1859 I visited France, authorised by the Royal Commissioners who were then inquiring into the state of popular education in England, to seek, in their name, information respecting the French primary schools. I shall never cease to be grateful for the cordial help afforded to me by the functionaries of the French Government for seeing thoroughly the objects which I came to study. The higher functionaries charged with the supervision of primary instruction have the supervision of secondary instruction also; and their kindness enabled me occasionally to see something of the secondary schools—institutions which strongly attracted my interest, but which the Royal Commissioners had not authorised me to study, and which the French Minister of Public Instruction had not directed his functionaries to show me. I thus saw the Lyceum, or public secondary school, of Toulouse—a good specimen of its class. To make clear to the English reader what this class of institutions is, with a view of enabling him to see, afterwards, what is the problem respecting secondary instruction which we in this country really have to solve, I will describe the Toulouse Lyceum.

Toulouse, the chief city of the great plain of Languedoc, and a place of great antiquity, dignity, and importance, has one of the principal lyceums to be found out of Paris. But the chief town of every French department has its lyceum, and the considerable towns of every department have their communal colleges, as the chief town has its lyceum. These establishments of secondary instruction are attached to academies, local centres of the Department of Public Instruction at

Paris, of which there are sixteen in France. The head of an academy is called its "rector," and his chief ministers are called "academy-inspectors." The superintendence of all public instruction (under the general control of the Minister of Public Instruction at Paris) was given by M. Guizot's[13] education-law to the academies; that of primary instruction has been, in great measure, taken away from them and given to the prefects; that of secondary or superior instruction still remains to them. Toulouse is the seat of an academy of the first class, with a jurisdiction extending over eight departments; its rector, when I was there in 1859, was an ex-judge of the Paris Court of Cassation, M. Rocher, a man of about sixty, of great intelligence, courtesy, and knowledge of the world. Ill-health had compelled him to resign his judgeship, and the Minister of Public Instruction, his personal friend, had given him the rectorate of Toulouse, the second in France in point of rank, as a kind of dignified retreat. The position of rector in France much resembles that of one of our heads of houses at Oxford or Cambridge. M. Rocher placed me under the guidance of his academy-inspector, M. Peyrot; and M. Peyrot, after introducing me to the primary inspectors of Toulouse, and enabling me to make arrangements with them for visiting the primary schools of the city and neighbourhood, kindly took me over the lyceum, which is under his immediate supervision.

A French lyceum is an institution founded and maintained by the State, with aid from the department and commune. The communal colleges are founded and maintained by the commune, with aid from the State. The Lyceum of Toulouse is held in large and somewhat gloomy buildings, in the midst of the city; old ecclesiastical buildings have in a number of towns been converted by the Government into public-school premises. We were received by the *proviseur*, M. Seignette. The provisor is the chief functionary—the head master—of a French lyceum; he does not, however, himself teach, but manages the business concerns of the school, administers its finances, and is responsible for its general conduct and discipline; his place is one of the prizes of French secondary instruction, and the provisor, having himself served a long apprenticeship as a teacher, has all the knowledge requisite for superintending his professors. He, like the professors, has gone through the excellent normal school out of which the functionaries of secondary instruction are taken, and has fulfilled stringent conditions of training and examination. Three chaplains—Roman Catholic priests—have the charge of the religious instruction of the lyceum; a Protestant minister, however, is specially appointed to give this instruction to pupils whose parents are of the reformed faith, and these pupils attend, on Sundays, their own Protestant places of worship. The lyceum has from three to four hundred scholars; it receives both boarders and day-scholars. In every lyceum which receives boarders there are a certain number of *bourses*, or public scholarships, which relieve their holders from all cost for their education. The school has three great divisions, each with its separate schoolrooms and playground. The playgrounds are large courts, planted with trees. Attached to the institution, but in a separate building, is a school for little boys from six to twelve years of age, called the *Petit Collège;* here there is a garden as well as a playground, and the whole school-life is easier and softer than in the lyceum, and adapted to the tender years of the scholars. In the *Petit Collège*, too, there are both boarders and day-scholars.

The schoolrooms of the lyceum were much like our schoolrooms here; large bare rooms, looking as if they had seen much service, with their desks browned and battered, and inscribed with the various carvings of many generations of schoolboys. The cleanliness, order, and neatness of the passages, dormitories, and sick-rooms were exemplary. The dormitories are vast rooms, with a teacher's bed at each end; a light is kept burning in them all the night through. In no English school have I seen any arrangements for the sick to compare with those of the Toulouse Lyceum. The service of the *infirmary*, as it is called, is performed by Sisters of Charity. The aspect and manners of these nurses, the freshness and airiness of the rooms, the whiteness and fragrance of the great stores of linen which one saw ranged in them, made one almost envy the invalids who were being tended in such a place of repose.

In the playground the boys—dressed, all of them, in the well-known uniform of the French schoolboy— were running, shouting, and playing, with the animation of their age; but it is not by its playgrounds and means of recreation that a French lyceum, as compared with the half-dozen great English public schools, shines. The boys are taken out to walk, as the boys at Winchester used to be taken out to *hills;* but at the end of the French schoolboy's walk there are no *hills* on which he is turned loose. He learns and practices gymnastics more than our schoolboys do; and the court in which he takes his recreation is somewhat more spacious and agreeable than we English are apt to imagine a *court* to be; but it is a poor place indeed—poor in itself and poor in its resources—compared with the *playing-fields* of

Eton, or the *meads* of Winchester, or the *close* of Rugby.

Of course I was very desirous to see the boys in their schoolrooms, and to hear some of the lessons; but M. Peyrot and M. Seignette, with all the good-will in the world, were not able to grant to an unofficial visitor permission to do this. It is something to know what the programme of studies in a French lyceum is, though it would be far more interesting to know how that programme is practically carried out. But the programme itself is worth examining: it is the same for every lyceum in France. It is fixed by the Council of Public Instruction in Paris, a body in which the State, the Church, the French Academy, and the scholastic profession, are all represented, and of which the Minister of Public Instruction is president. The programme thus fixed is promulgated by the Minister's authority, and every lyceum is bound to follow it. I have before me that promulgated by M. Guizot in 1833; the variations from it, up to the present day, are but slight. In the sixth, or lowest class, the boys have to learn French, Latin, and Greek Grammar, and their reading is Cornelius Nepos and Phaedrus, and, along with the fables of Phaedrus, those of La Fontaine. For the next, or fifth class, the reading is Ovid in Latin, Lucian's Dialogues and Isocrates in Greek, and *Télémaque* in French.[14] For the fourth, besides the authors read in the classes below, Virgil in Latin and Xenophon in Greek, and, in French, Voltaire's *Charles XII*. For the third, Sallust and Cicero are added in Latin, Homer and Plutarch's *Moralia* in Greek; in French, Voltaire's *Siècle de Louis XIV.*, Massillon's *Petit Carême*, Boileau, and extracts from Buffon. For the second class (our fifth form), Horace, Livy, and Tacitus, in Latin; in

84

Greek, Sophocles and Euripides, Plato and Demosthenes; in French, Bossuet's *Histoire Universelle*, and Montesquieu's *Grandeur et Décadence des Romains*. The highest class (our sixth form) is divided into two, a rhetoric and a philosophy class; this division—which is important, and which is daily becoming, with the authorities of French Public Instruction, an object of greater importance—is meant to correspond to the direction, literary or scientific, which the studies of the now adult scholar are to take. In place of the Pindar, Thucydides, Lucan, and Molière, of the rhetoric class, the philosophy class has chemistry, physics, and the higher mathematics. Some instruction in natural science finds a place in the school-course of every class; in the lower classes, instruction in the elements of human physiology, zoology, botany, and geology; in the second class (fifth form), instruction in the elements of chemistry. To this instruction in natural science two or three hours a week are allotted. About the same time is allotted to arithmetic, to special instruction in history and geography, and to modern languages; these last, however, are said to be in general as imperfectly learnt in the French public schools as they are in our own. Two hours a week are devoted to the correction of composition. Finally, the New Testament, in Latin or Greek, forms a part of the daily reading of each class.

On this programme I will make two remarks, suggested by comparing it with that of any of our own public schools. It has the scientific instruction and the study of the mother-tongue which our school-course is without, and is often blamed for being without. I believe that the scientific instruction actually acquired by French schoolboys in the lower classes is very little, but still a boy with a taste for science finds in this instruction an element which keeps his taste alive; in the special class at the head of the school it is more considerable, but not, it is alleged, sufficient for the wants of this special class, and plans for making it more thorough and systematic are being canvassed. In the study of the mother-tongue the French school-boy has a more real advantage over ours; he does certainly learn something of the French language and literature, and of the English our schoolboy learns nothing. French grammar, however, is a better instrument of instruction for boys than English grammar, and the French literature possesses prose works, perhaps even poetical works, more fitted to be used as classics for schoolboys than any which English literature possesses. I need not say that the fitness of works for this purpose depends on other considerations than those of the genius alone, and of the creative force, which they exhibit.

The regular school-lessons of a lyceum occupy about twenty-two hours in the week, but among these regular school-lessons the lessons in modern languages are not counted. The lessons in modern languages are given out of school-hours; out of school-hours, too, all the boarders work with the masters at preparing their lessons; each boarder has thus what we call a private tutor, but the French schoolboy does not, like ours, pay extra for his private tutor: the general charge for board and instruction covers this special tuition.

Now I come to the important matter of school-fees. These are all regulated by authority; the scale of charges in every lyceum and communal college must be seen and sanctioned by the academy-inspector in order to have legality. A day-scholar in the Toulouse Lyceum pays, in the lowest of the three great divisions of the school, 110 f. (4*l*. 8*s*. 4*d*.) a year; in the second division he pays 135f. (5l. 8s. 4d.); in the third and highest division, 180f. (7l. 4s. 2d.). If he wishes to share in the special tuition of the boarders, he pays from 2l. to 4l. a year extra. Next, for the boarders. A boarder pays, for his whole board and instruction, in the lowest division, 800f. (32l.) a year; in the second division, 850f. (34l.); in the highest division, 900f. (36l.). In the scientific class the charge is 2l. extra. The payments are made quarterly, and always in advance. Every boarder brings with him an outfit (*trousseau*) valued at 500f. (20l.): the sum paid for his board and instruction covers, besides, all expense for keeping good this outfit, and all charges for washing, medical attendance, books, and writing materials. The meals, though plain, are good, and they are set out with a propriety and a regard for appearances which, when I was a boy, graced no school-dinners that I ever saw; just as, I must say, even in the normal schools for elementary teachers, the dinner-table in France contrasted strongly, by its clean cloth, arranged napkins, glass, and general neatness of service, with the stained cloth, napkinless knives and forks, jacks and mugs, hacked joints of meat, and stumps of loaves, which I have seen on the dinner-table of normal schools in England. With us it is always the individual that is filled, and the public that is sent empty away.

Such may be the cheapness of public school educa-tion, when the education is treated as a matter of public economy, to be administered upon a great scale, with rigid system and exact superintendence, in the interest of the pupil and not in the interest of the school-keeper.*

* *L'administration des lycées est complètement étrangère à toute idée de spéculation et de profit*, says the Toulouse prospectus which lies before me; "A lyceum is managed not in the least as a matter of speculation or profit;" and this is not a mere advertising puff, for the public is the real proprietor of the lyceums, which it has

But many people, it will be said, have no relish for such cast-iron schooling. Well, then, let us look at a French school not of the State-pattern—a school without the guarantees of State-management, but, also, without the uniformity and constraint which this management introduces.

A day or two after I had seen the Toulouse Lyceum, I started for Sorèze. Sorèze is a village in the department of the Tarn, a department bordering upon that in which Toulouse stands; it contains one of the most successful private schools in France, and of this school, in 1859, the celebrated Father Lacordaire was director. I left Toulouse by railway in the middle of the day; in two hours I was at Castelnaudary, an old Visigoth place, on a hill rising out of the great plain of Languedoc, with immense views towards the Pyrenees on one side and the Cevennes on the other. After rambling about the town for an hour, I started for Sorèze in a vehicle exactly like an English coach; I was outside with the driver, and the other places, inside and outside, were occupied by old pupils of the Sorèze school, who were going there for the annual *fête*, the *Speeches*, to take place the next day. They were, most of them, young men from the universities of Toulouse and Montpellier; two or three were settled in Paris, but, happening to be just then at their homes, at Béziers or Narbonne, they had come over like the rest: they seemed a good set, all of them, and their attachment to their old school and master was more according to one's notions of English school-life than French. We had to cross the *Montagne Noire*, an outlier of the Cevennes; the elevation was not

founded for the education of its youth, and for that object only; the directors of the lyceum are simple servants of the public, employed by the public at fixed salaries.

great, but the air, even on the 18th of May in Languedoc, was sharp, the vast distance looked grey and chill,
and the whole landscape was severe, lonely, and deso-
late. Sorèze is in the plain on the other side of the
Montagne Noire, at the foot of gorges running up into
the Cevennes; at the head of these gorges are the basins
from which the *Canal du Midi*—the great canal uniting
the Mediterranean with the Atlantic—is fed. It was
seven o'clock when we drove up the street, shaded with
large trees, of Sorèze; my fellow-travellers showed me
the way to the school, as I was obliged to get away early
the next morning, and wanted, therefore, to make my
visit that evening. The school occupies the place of an
old abbey, founded in 757 by Pepin the Little; for
several hundred years the abbey had been in the possession of the Dominicans, when, in Louis the Sixteenth's
reign, a school was attached to it. In this school the
king took great interest, and himself designed the dress
for the scholars. The establishment was saved at the
Revolution by the tact of the Dominican who was then
at its head; he resumed the lay dress, and returned, in
all outward appearance, to the secular life, and his
school was allowed to subsist. Under the Restoration
it was one of the most famous and most aristocratic
schools in France, but it had much declined when
Lacordaire, in 1854, took charge of it. I waited in the
monastic-looking court (much of the old abbey remains
as part of the present building) while my card, with a
letter which the Papal Nuncio at Paris, to whom I had
been introduced through Sir George Bowyer's kindness, had obtained for me from the Superior of the
Dominicans, was taken up to Lacordaire; he sent down
word directly that he would see me; I was shown across
the court, up an old stone staircase, into a vast corridor;

a door in this corridor was thrown open, and in a large bare room, with no carpet or furniture of any kind, except a small table, one or two chairs, a small bookcase, a crucifix, and some religious pictures on the walls, Lacordaire, in the dress of his order, white-robed, hooded, and sandalled, sat before me.

The first public appearance of this remarkable man was in the cause of education. The Charter of 1830 had promised liberty of instruction; liberty, that is, for persons outside the official hierarchy of public instruction to open schools. This promise M. Guizot's celebrated school law of 1833 finally performed; but, in the meantime, the authorities of public instruction refused to give effect to it. Lacordaire and M. de Monta-lembert[15] opened in Paris, on the 7th of May, 1831, an independent free school, of which they themselves were the teachers; it was closed in a day or two by the police, and its youthful conductors were tried before the Court of Peers and fined. This was Lacordaire's first public appearance; twenty-two years later his last sermon in Paris was preached in the same cause; it was a sermon on behalf of the schools of the Christian Brethren. During that space of twenty-two years he had run a conspicuous career, but on another field than that of education; he had become the most renowned preacher in Europe, and he had re-established in France, by his energy, conviction, and patience, the religious orders banished thence since the Revolution. Through this career I cannot now attempt to follow him; with the heart of friendship and the eloquence of genius, M. de Montalembert has recently written its history; but I must point out two characteristics which distinguished him in it, and which created in him the force by which, as an educator, he worked, the force by which he most impressed and commanded the young. One of these was his passion for firm order, for solid government. He called our age an age "which does "not know how to obey—*qui ne sait guère obéir*." It is easy to see that this is not so absolutely a matter of reproach as Lacordaire made it; in an epoch of transition society may and must say to its governors, "Govern me according to my spirit, if I am to obey you." One cannot doubt that Lacordaire erred in making absolute devotion to the Church (*malheur à qui trouble l'Église!*) the watch-word of a gifted man in our century; one cannot doubt that he erred in affirming that "the "greatest service to be rendered to Christianity in our "day was to do something for the revival of the mediaeval "religious orders." Still, he seized a great truth when he proclaimed the intrinsic weakness and danger of a state of anarchy; above all, when he applied this truth in the moral sphere he was incontrovertible, fruitful for his nation, especially fruitful for the young. He dealt vigorously with himself, and he told others that the first thing for them was to do the same; he placed character above everything else. "One may have spirit, "learning, even genius," he said, "and not *character;* for "want of character our age is the age of miscarriages. Let "us form Christians in our schools, but, first of all, let us "form Christians in our own hearts; the one great thing "is *to have a life of one's own.*"

Allied to this characteristic was his other—his passion, in an age which seems to think that progress can be achieved only by our herding together and making a noise, for the antique discipline of retirement and silence. His plan of life for himself, when he first took orders, was to go and be a village curé in a remote province in France. M. de Quélen, the Archbishop of

Paris, kept him in the capital as chaplain to the Convent of the Visitation; he had not then commenced the *conférences* which made his reputation; he lived perfectly isolated and obscure, and he was never so happy. "It is with delight," he wrote at this time, "that "I find my solitude deepening round me; 'one can do "nothing without solitude,' is my grand maxim. A man "is formed from within, and not from without. To "withdraw and be with oneself and with God, is the "greatest strength there can be in the world." It is impossible not to feel the serenity and sincerity of these words. Twice he refused to edit the *Univers;* he refused a chair in the University of Louvain. In 1836, when his fame filled France, he disappeared for five years, and these years he passed in silence and seclusion at Rome. He came back in 1841 a Dominican monk; again, at Notre Dame, that eloquence, that ineffable *accent*, led his countrymen and foreigners captive; he achieved his cherished purpose of re-establishing in France the religious orders. Then once more he disappeared, and after a short station at Toulouse consigned himself, for the rest of his life, to the labour and obscurity of Sorèze. "One of the great consolations of my present "life," he writes from Sorèze, "is, that I have now God "and the young for my sole companions." The young, with their fresh spirit, as they instinctively feel the presence of a great character, so, too, irresistibly receive an influence from souls which live habitually with God.

Lacordaire received me with great kindness. He was above the middle height, with an excellent countenance; great dignity in his look and bearing, but nothing ascetic; his manners animated, and every gesture and movement showing the orator. He asked me to dine with him the next day, and to see the school festival, the *fête des anciens élèves;* but I could not stop. Then he ordered lights, for it was growing dark, and insisted on showing me all over the place that evening. While we were waiting for lights he asked me much about Oxford; I had already heard from his old pupils that Oxford was a favourite topic with him, and that he held it up to them as a model of everything that was venerable. Lights came, and we went over the establishment; the school then contained nearly three hundred pupils —a great rise since Lacordaire first came in 1854, but not so many as the school has had in old days. It is said that Lacordaire at one time resorted so frequently to expulsion as rather to alarm people.

Sorèze, under his management, chiefly created interest by the sort of competition which it maintained with the lyceums, or State schools. A private school, in France, cannot be opened without giving notice to the public authorities; the consent of these authorities is withheld if the premises of the proposed school are improper, or if its director fails to produce a certificate of probation and a certificate of competency—that is, if he has not served for five years in a secondary school, and passed the authorised public examination for secondary teachers. Finally, the school is always subject to State-inspection, to ascertain that the pupils are properly lodged and fed, and that the teaching contains nothing contrary to public morality and to the laws; and the school may be closed by the public authorities on an inspector's report, duly verified. Still, for an establishment like the Sorèze school, the actual State-interference comes to very little; the Minister has the power of dispensing with the certificate of probation, and holy orders are accepted in the place of the certifi-

cate of competency (the examination in the seminary
being more difficult than the examination for this latter).
In France the State (Machiavel as we English think it),
in naming certain matters as the objects of its supervision in private schools, means what it says, and does
not go beyond these matters; and, for these matters, the
name of a man like Lacordaire serves as a guarantee,
and is readily accepted as such.

All the boys at Sorèze are boarders, and a boarder's
expenses here exceed by about 8*l.* or 10*l.* a year his
expenses at a lyceum. The programme of studies differs
little from that of the lyceums, but the military system
of these State schools Lacordaire repudiated. Instead
of the vast common dormitories of the lyceums, every
boy had his little cell to himself; that was, after all, as it
seemed to me, the great difference. But immense stress
was laid, too, upon physical education, which the
lyceums are said too much to neglect. Lacordaire
showed me with great satisfaction the stable, with more
than twenty horses, and assured me that all the boys
were taught to ride. There was the *salle d'escrime*, where
they fenced, the armoury full of guns and swords, the
shooting gallery, and so on. All this is in our eyes a
little fantastic, and does not replace the want of cricket
and football in a good field, and of freedom to roam over
the country out of school-hours; in France, however, it
is a good deal; and then twice a week all the boys used
to turn out with Lacordaire upon the mountains, to
their great enjoyment as the Sorèze people said, the
Father himself being more vigorous than any of them.
And the old abbey school has a small park adjoining it,
with the mountains rising close behind, and it has
beautiful trees in its courts, and by no means the dismal
barrack-look of a lyceum. Lacordaire had a staff of

more than fifty teachers and helpers, about half of these being members of his own religious order—Dominicans; all co-operated in some way or other in conducting the school. Lacordaire used never to give school-lessons himself, but scarcely a Sunday passed without his preaching in the chapel. The highest and most distinguished boys formed a body called *the Institute*, with no governing powers like those of our sixth form, but with a sort of common-room to themselves, and with the privilege of having their meals with Lacordaire and his staff. I was shown, too, a *Salle d'Illustres*, or Hall of Worthies, into which the boys are introduced on high days and holidays; we should think this fanciful, but I found it impressive. The hall is decorated with busts of the chief of the former scholars, some of them very distinguished. Among these busts was that of Henri de Larochejaquelein (who was brought up here at Sorèze),[16] with his noble, speaking countenance, his Vendean hat, and the heart and cross on his breast. There was, besides, a theatre for public recitations. We ended with the chapel, in which we found all the school assembled; a Dominican was reading to them from the pupil an edifying life of a scapegrace converted to seriousness by a bad accident, much better worth listening to than most sermons. When it was over, Lacordaire whispered to me to ask if I would stay for the prayers or go at once. I stayed; they were very short and simple; and I saw the boys disperse afterwards. The gaiety of the little ones and their evident fondness for the *Père* was a pretty sight. As we went out of chapel, one of them, a little fellow of ten or eleven, ran from behind us, snatched, with a laughing face, Lacordaire's hand, and kissed it; Lacordaire smiled, and patted his head. When I read the other day in M. de Montalembert's book how Lacordaire had said, shortly before his death, " I have always tried to serve God, the Church, "and our Lord Jesus Christ; besides these, I have loved "—oh, dearly loved!—children and young people," I thought of this incident.

Lacordaire knew absolutely nothing of our great English schools, their character, or recent history; but then no Frenchman, except a very few at Paris who know more than anybody in the world, knows anything about anything. However, I have seen few people more impressive; he was not a great modern thinker, but a great Christian orator of the fourth century, born in the nineteenth; playing his part in the nineteenth century not so sucessfully as he would have played it in the fourth, but still nobly. I would have given much to stay longer with him, as he kindly pressed me; I was tempted, too, by hearing that it was likely he would make a speech the next day. Never did any man so give one the sense of his being a natural orator, perfect in ease and simplicity; they told me that on Sunday, when he preached, he hardly ever went up into the pulpit, but spoke to them from his place " *sans façon*." But I had an engagement to keep at Carcassonne at a certain hour, and I was obliged to go. At nine I took leave of Lacordaire and returned to the village inn, clean, because it is frequented by the relations of pupils. There I supped with my fellow-travellers, the old scholars; charming companions they proved themselves. Late we sat, much *vin de Cahors* we drank, and great friends we became. Before we parted, one of them, the Béziers youth studying at Paris, with the amiability of his race assured me (God forgive him!) that he was well acquainted with my poems. By five the next morning I had started to return to Castelnaudary. Recrossing the

Montagne Noire in the early morning was very cold work, but the view was inconceivably grand. I caught the train at Castelnaudary, and was at Carcassonne by eleven; there I saw a school, and I saw the old *city* of Carcassonne. I am not going to describe either the one or the other, but I cannot forbear saying, Let everybody see the *cité de Carcassonne*. It is, indeed, as the anti-quarians call it, the Middle Age Herculaneum. When you first get sight of the old city, which is behind the modern town—when you have got clear of the modern town, and come out upon the bridge over the Aude, and see the walled *cité* upon its hill before you—you rub your eyes and think that you are looking at a vignette in *Ivanhoe*.

Thus I have enabled, as far as I could, the English reader to see what a French lyceum is like, and what a French private school, competing with a lyceum, is like. I have given him, as far as I could, the facts; now for the application of these facts. What is the problem respecting secondary instruction which we in this country have to solve? What light do these facts throw upon that problem?

For the serious thinker, for the real student of the question of secondary instruction, the problem respect-ing secondary instruction which we in England have to solve is this:—Why cannot we have throughout England—as the French have throughout France, as the Germans have throughout Germany, as the Swiss have throughout Switzerland, as the Dutch have through Holland—schools where the children of our middle and professional classes may obtain, at the rate of from 20*l.* to 50*l.* a year, if they are boarders, at the rate of from 5*l.* to 15*l.* a year if they are day-scholars, an education of as good quality, with as good guarantees, social character, and advantages for a future career in the world, as the education which French children of the corresponding class can obtain from institutions like that of Toulouse or Sorèze?

There is the really important question. It is vain to meet it by propositions which may, very likely, be true, but which are quite irrelevant. "Your French Etons," I am told, "are no Etons at all; there is nothing like an "Eton in France." I know that. Very likely France is to be pitied for having no Etons, but I want to call attention to the substitute, to the compensation. The English public school produces the finest boys in the world; the Toulouse Lyceum boy, the Sorèze College boy, is not to be compared with them. Well, let me grant all that too. But then there are only some five or six schools in England to produce this specimen-boy; and they cannot produce him cheap. Rugby and Winchester produce him at about 120*l.* a year; Eton and Harrow (and the Eton school-boy is perhaps justly taken as the most perfect type of this highly-extolled class) cannot produce him for much less than 200*l.* a year. *Tantae molis erat Romanam condere gentem*—such a business is it to produce an article so superior. But for the common wear and tear of middling life, and at rates tolerable for middling people, what do we produce? What do we produce at 30*l.* a year? What is the character of the schools which undertake for us this humbler, but far more widely-interesting production? Are they as good as the Toulouse Lyceum and the Sorèze College? That is the question.

Suppose that the recommendations of the Public School Commissioners bring about in the great public schools all the reforms which a judicious reformer

could desire;—suppose that they produce the best
possible application of endowments, the best possible
mode of election to masterships; that they lead to a
wise revision of the books and subjects of study, to a
reinforcing of the mathematics and of the modern
languages, where these are found weak; to a perfecting,
finally, of all boarding arrangements and discipline:
nothing will yet have been done towards providing for
the great want—the want of a secondary instruction at
once reasonably cheap and reasonably good. Suppose
that the recommendations of the Commissioners
accomplish something even in this direction—suppose
that the cost of educating a boy at Rugby is reduced to
about 100*l.* a year, and the cost of educating a boy at
Eton to about 150*l.* a year—no one acquainted with the
subject will think it practicable, or even, under present
circumstances, desirable, to effect in the cost of education in these two schools a greater reduction than this.
And what will this reduction amount to? A boon—in
some cases a very considerable boon—to those who now
frequent these schools. But what will it do for the great
class now in want of proper secondary instruction?
Nothing: for in the first place these schools are but two,
and are full, or at least sufficiently full, already; in the
second place, if they were able to hold all the boys in
England, the class I speak of would still be excluded
from them—excluded by a cost of 100*l.* or 150*l.* just as
much as by a cost of 120*l.* or 200*l.* A certain number
of the professional class, with incomes quite inadequate
to such a charge, will, for the sake of the future
establishment of their children, make a brave effort, and
send them to Eton or Rugby at a cost of 150*l.* or 100*l.*
a year. But they send them there already, even at the
existing higher rate. The great mass of middling people,

with middling incomes, not having for their children's future establishment in life plans which make a public school training indispensable, will not make this effort, will not pay for their children's schooling a price quite disproportionate to their means. They demand a lower school-charge—a school-charge like that of Toulouse or Sorèze.

And they find it. They have only to open the *Times*. There they read advertisement upon advertisement,[17] offering them, "conscientiously offering" them, in almost any part of England which suits their con-venience, "Education, 20*l.* per annum, no extras. Diet "unlimited, and of the best description. The education "comprises Greek, Latin, and German, French by a "resident native, mathematics, algebra, mapping, globes, "and all the essentials of a first-rate commercial edu-"cation." Physical, moral, mental, and spiritual—all the wants of their children will be sedulously cared for. They are invited to an "Educational Home," where "discipline is based upon moral influence and emula-"tion, and every effort is made to combine home-"comforts with school-training. Terms inclusive and "moderate." If they have a child with an awkward temper, and needing special management, even for this particular child the wonderful operation of the laws of supply and demand, in this great commercial country, will be found to have made perfect provision. "Un-"manageable boys or youths (up to twenty years) are "made perfectly tractable and gentlemanly in one year "by a clergyman near town, whose peculiarly persuasive "high moral and religious training at once elevates," &c. And all this, as I have said, is provided by the simple, natural operation of the laws of supply and demand, without, as the *Times* beautifully says, "the fetters of

"endowment and the interference of the executive."
Happy country! happy middle classes! Well may the
Times congratulate them with such fervency; well may
it produce dithyrambs, while the newspapers of less-
favoured countries produce only leading articles; well
may it declare that the fabled life of the Happy Islands
is already beginning amongst us.

But I have no heart for satire, though the occasion
invites it. No one, who knows anything of the subject,
will venture to affirm that these "educational homes"
give, or can give, that which they "conscientiously offer."
No one, who knows anything of the subject, will
seriously affirm that they give, or can give, an education
comparable to that given by the Toulouse and Sorèze
schools. And why? Because they want the securities
which, to make them produce even half of what they
offer, are indispensable—the securities of supervision
and publicity. By this time we know pretty well that to
trust to the principle of supply and demand to do for
us all that we want in providing education is to lean
upon a broken reed. We trusted to it to give us fit
elementary schools till its impotence became conspicuous; we have thrown it aside, and called upon
State-aid,[18] with the securities accompanying this, to
give us elementary schools more like what they should
be; we have thus founded in elementary education a
system still, indeed, far from perfect, but living and
fruitful—a system which will probably survive the most
strenuous efforts for its destruction. In secondary
education the impotence of this principle of supply and
demand is as signal as in elementary education. The
mass of mankind know good butter from bad, and
tainted meat from fresh, and the principle of supply and
demand, may, perhaps, be relied on to give us sound

meat and butter. But the mass of mankind do not so well know what distinguishes good teaching and training from bad; they do not here know what they ought to demand, and, therefore, the demand cannot be relied on to give us the right supply. Even if they knew what they ought to demand, they have no sufficient means of testing whether or no this is really supplied to them. Securities, therefore, are needed. The great public schools of England offer securities by their very publicity; by their wealth, importance, and connexions, which attract general attention to them; by their old reputation, which they cannot forfeit without disgrace and danger. The appointment of the Public School Commission is a proof, that to these moral securities for the efficiency of the great public schools may be added the material security of occasional competent supervision. I will grant that the great schools of the Continent do not offer the same moral securities to the public as Eton or Harrow. They offer them in a certain measure, but certainly not in so large measure: they have not by any means so much importance, by any means so much reputation. Therefore they offer, in far larger measure, the other security—the security of competent supervision. With them this supervision is not occasional and extraordinary, but periodic and regular; it is not explorative only; it is also, to a considerable extent, authoritative.

It will be said that between the "educational home" and Eton there is a long series of schools, with many gradations; and that in this series are to be found schools far less expensive than Eton, yet offering moral securities as Eton offers them, and as the "educational home" does not. Cheltenham, Bradfield, Marlborough, are instances which will occur to every one.[19] It is true that these schools offer securities; it is true that the mere presence, at the head of a school, of a distinguished master like Mr Bradley[20] is, perhaps, the best moral security which can be offered. But, in the first place, these schools are thinly scattered over the country; we have no provision for planting such schools where they are most wanted, or for insuring a due supply of them. Cheltenham, Bradfield, and Marlborough are no more a due provision for the Northumberland boy than the Bordeaux Lyceum is a due provision for the little Alsatian. In the second place, Are these schools cheap? Even if they were cheap once, does not their very excellence, in a country where schools at once good and cheap are rare, tend to deprive them of their cheapness? Marlborough was, I believe—perhaps it still is—the cheapest of them; Marlborough is probably just now the best-taught school in England; and Marlborough, therefore, has raised its school-charge. Marlborough was quite right in so doing, for Marlborough is an individual institution, bound to guard its own interests and to profit by its own successes, and not bound to provide for the general educational wants of the country. But what makes the school-charge of the Toulouse Lyceum remain moderate, however eminent may be the merits of the Toulouse masters, or the successes of the Toulouse pupils? It is that the Toulouse Lyceum is a public institution, administered in view of the general educational wants of France, and not of its own individual preponderance. And what makes (or made, alas!) the school-charge of the Sorèze College remain moderate, even with a most distinguished and attractive director, like Lacordaire, at its head? It was the organisation of a complete system of secondary schools throughout France, the abundant supply of institutions, with at once respectable guarantees and reasonable charges, fixing a general mean of school-cost which even the most successful private school cannot venture much to exceed.

After all, it is the "educational home," and not Brad-field or Marlborough, which supplies us with the nearest approach to that rate of charges which secondary instruction, if it is ever to be organised on a great scale, and to reach those who are in need of it, must inevitably adopt. People talk of the greater cheapness of foreign countries, and of the dearness of this; everything costs more here, they say, than it does abroad; good education, like everything else. I do not wish to dispute, I am willing to make some allowance for this plea; one must be careful not to make too much, however, or we shall find ourselves to the end of the chapter with a secondary instruction failing just where our present secondary instruction fails—a secondary instruction which, out of the multitude needing it, a few, and only a few, make sacrifices to get; the many, who do not like sacrifices, go without it. If we fix a school-charge varying from 25*l.* to 50*l.* a year, I am sure we have fixed the outside rate which the great body of those needing secondary instruction will ever pay. Sir John Coleridge analyses this body into "the clergy "of moderate or contracted incomes" (and that means the immense majority of the clergy), "officers of the army "and navy, medical men, solicitors, and gentry of large "families and small means." Many more elements might be enumerated. Why are the manufacturers left out? The very rich, among these, are to be counted by ones, the middling sort by hundreds. And when Sir John Coleridge[21] separates "tenant-farmers, small land-"holders, and retail tradesmen" into a class by themselves, and proposes to appropriate a separate class of schools for them, he carries the process of distinction and demarcation further than I can think quite desirable. But taking the constituent parts of the class requiring a liberal education as he assigns them, it seems to me certain that a sum ranging from 25*l*. to 50*l*. a year is as much as those whom he enumerates can in general be expected to pay for a son's education, and as much as they need be called upon to pay for a sound and valuable education, if secondary instruction were organised as it might be. It must be remembered, however, that a reduced rate of charge for boarders, at a good boarding-school, is not by any means the only benefit to the class of parents in question—perhaps not even the principal benefit—which the organisation of secondary instruction brings with it. It brings with it, also, by establishing its schools in proper numbers, and all over the country, facilities for bringing up many boys as day-scholars who are now brought up as boarders. At present many people send their sons to a boarding-school when they would much rather keep them at home, because they have no suitable school within reach. Opinions differ as to whether it is best for a boy to live at home or to go away to school, but there can be no doubt which of the two modes of bringing him up is the cheapest for his parents; and those (and they are many) who think that the continuation of home-life along with his schooling is far best for the boy himself, would enjoy a double benefit in having suitable schools made accessible to them.

But I must not forget that an institution, or rather a group of institutions, exists, offering to the middle classes, at a charge scarcely higher than that of the 20*l*. "educational home," an education affording considerable guarantees for its sound character. I mean the College of St. Nicholas, Lancing, and its affiliated schools. This institution certainly demands a word of notice here, and no word of mine, regarding Mr. Woodard and his labours,[22] shall be wanting in unfeigned interest and respect for them. Still, I must confess that, as I read Mr. Woodard's programme, and as I listened to an excellent sermon from the Dean of Chichester in recommendation of it, that programme and that sermon seemed to me irresistibly to lead towards conclusions which they did not reach, and the conclusions which they did reach were far from satisfying. Mr. Woodard says with great truth: "It may be asked, Why cannot "the shopkeeper-class educate their own children with- "out charity? It may be answered, Scarcely any class in "the country does educate its own children without "some aid. Witness the enormous endowments of our "Universities and public schools, where the sons of our "well-to-do people resort. Witness our national schools "supported by State grants, and by parochial and "national subscriptions. On the other hand, the lower "middle class" (Mr. Woodard might quite properly have said the middle class in general), "politically a "very important one, is dependent to a great extent for "its education on private desultory enterprise. This "class, in this land of education, gets *nothing* out of the "millions given annually for this purpose to every class "except themselves." In his sermon Dr. Hook spoke, in his cordial, manly way, much to the same effect.

This was the grievance; what was the remedy? That this great class should be rescued from the tender mercies of private desultory enterprise? That, in this land of education, it should henceforth get something out of the millions given annually for this purpose to

every class except itself? That in an age when "enormous endowments,"—the form which public aid took in
earlier ages, and taking which form public aid founded
in those ages the Universities and the public schools for
the benefit, along with the upper class, of this very
middle class which is now, by the irresistible course of
events, in great measure excluded from them—that in
an age, I say, when these great endowments, this
mediaeval form of public aid, have ceased, public
aid should be brought to these classes in that simpler
and more manageable form which in modern societies
it assumes—the form of public grants, with the guarantees of supervision and responsibility? The Universities
receive public grants; for—not to speak of the payment
of certain professors* by the State—that the State
regards the endowments of the Universities as in reality
public grants, it proves by assuming to itself the right
of interfering in the disposal of them; the elementary
schools receive public grants. Why, then, should not
our secondary schools receive public grants? But this
question Mr. Woodard (I do not blame him for it, he had
a special function to perform) never touches. He falls
back on an Englishman's favourite panacea—a sub-
scription. He has built a school at Lancing, and a
school at Shoreham, and he proposes to build a bigger
school than either at Balcombe. He asks for a certain
number of subscribers to give him contributions for a
certain number of years, at certain rates, which he has
calculated. I cannot see how, in this way, he will be
delivering English secondary instruction from the

* These professors are now nominally paid by the University;
but the University pays them in consideration of the remission to
her, by the State, of certain duties of greater amount than the
salaries which the State used to pay to these professors. They are
still, therefore, in fact, paid by the State.

hands of "private desultory enterprise." What English secondary instruction wants is these two things: sufficiency of provision to fit schools, sufficiency of securities for their fitness. Mr. Woodard proposes to establish one great school in Sussex, where he has got two already. What sort of a provision is this for that need which is, on his own showing, so urgent? He hopes, indeed, that "if the public will assist in raising this one "school, it will lead to a general extension of middle class "education all over England." But in what number of years? How long are we to wait first? And then we have to consider the second great point—that of *securities*. Suppose Mr. Woodard's hopes to be fulfilled—suppose the establishment of the Balcombe school to have led to the establishment of like schools all over England— what securities shall we have for the fitness of these schools? Sussex is not a very large and populous county, but, even if we limit ourselves to the ratio adopted for Sussex, of three of these schools to a county, that gives us 120 of them for England proper only, without taking in Wales. I have said that the eminence of the master may be in itself a sound security for the worth of a school; but, when I look at the number of these schools wanted, when I look at the probable position and emoluments of their teachers, I cannot think it reasonable to expect that all of them, or anything like all, will be provided with masters of an eminence to make all further guarantees unnecessary. But, perhaps, they will all be affiliated to the present institution at Lancing, and, in some degree, under its supervision? Well, then, that gives us, as the main regulative power of English secondary instruction, as our principal security for it, the Provost and Fellows of St. Nicholas College, Lancing. I have the greatest, the most sincere respect for Mr. Woodard and his coadjutors—I should be quite ready to accept Mr. Woodard's name as sufficient security for any school which he himself conducts—but I should hesitate, I confess, before accepting Mr. Woodard and his colleagues, or any similar body of private persons, as my final security for the right management of a great national concern, as the last court of appeal to which the interests of English secondary instruction were to be carried. Their constitution is too close, their composition too little national. Even if this or that individual were content to take them as his security, the bulk of the public would not. We saw this the other day, when imputations were thrown out against Lancing,[23] and our proposed security had to find security for itself. It had no difficulty in so doing; Mr. Woodard has, it cannot be repeated too often, governed Lancing admirably; all I mean is—and Mr. Woodard himself would probably be the first to agree with me—that, to command public confidence for a great national system of schools, one needs a security larger, ampler, more national, than any which, by the very nature of things, Mr. Woodard and his friends can quite supply.

But another and a very plausible security has been provided for secondary instruction by the zeal and energy of Mr. Acland and Dr. Temple;[24] I mean, the Oxford and Cambridge Middle Class Examinations. The good intentions and the activity of the promoters of these examinations cannot be acknowledged too gratefully; good has certainly been accomplished by them: yet it is undeniable that this security also is, in its present condition, quite insufficient. I write, not for the professed and practised educationist, but for the general reader; above all, for the reader of that class

which is most concerned in the question which I am
raising, and which I am most solicitous to carry with me
—the middle class. Therefore, I shall use the plainest
and most unprofessional language I can, in attempting
to show what the promoters of these University examinations try to do, what they have accomplished, wherein
they have failed. They try to make *security* do for us all
that we want in the improvement of our secondary
education. They accept the "educational homes" at
present scattered all over the country; they do not aim
at replacing them by other and better institutions; they
do not visit or criticise them; but they invite them to
send select pupils to certain local centres, and when the
pupils are there, they examine them, class them, and
give prizes to the best of them. Undoubtedly this action
of the Universities has given a certain amount of
stimulus to these schools, and has done them a certain
amount of good. But any one can see how far this action
falls, and must fall, short of what is required. Any one
can see that the examination of a few select scholars
from a school, not at the school itself, not preceded or
followed by an inspection of the school itself, affords
no solid security for the good condition of their school.
Any one can see that it is for the interest of an un-
scrupulous master to give all his care to his few
cleverest pupils, who will serve him as an advertisement,
while he neglects the common bulk of his pupils, whose
backwardness there will be nobody to expose. I will not,
however, insist too strongly on this last mischief,
because I really believe that, serious as is its danger, it
has not so much prevailed as to counterbalance the
benefit which the mere stimulus of these examinations
has given. All I say is, that this stimulus is an insufficient security. Plans are now broached for reinforcing

University examination by University inspection. There we get a far more solid security. And I agree with Sir John Coleridge, that a body fitter than the Universities to exercise this inspection could not be found. It is indispensable that it should be exercised in the name, and on the responsibility, of a great public body; therefore the Society of Arts,[25] which deserves thanks for its readiness to help in improving secondary instruction, is hardly, perhaps, from its want of weight, authority, and importance, qualified to exercise it: but whether it is exercised by the State, or by great and august corporations like Oxford and Cambridge, the value of the security is equally good; and learned corporations, like the Universities, have a certain natural fitness for discharging what is, in many respects, a learned function. It is only as to the power of the Universities to organise, equip, and keep working an efficient system of inspection for secondary schools that I am in doubt; organisation and regularity are as indispensable to this guarantee as weight and authority. Can the Universities organise and pay a body of inspectors to travel all over England, to visit, at least once in every year, the four or five hundred endowed schools of this country, and its unnumbered "educational homes;" can they supply a machinery for regulating the action of these gentlemen, giving effect to the information received from them, printing their reports, circulating them through the country? The French University could; but the French University was a department of State. If the English Universities cannot, the security of their inspection will be precarious; if they can, there can be no better.

No better *security*. But English secondary instruction wants, I said, two things: sufficient provision of good schools, sufficient security for these schools continuing good. Granting that the Universities may give us the second, I do not see how they are to give us the first. It is not enough merely to provide a staff of inspectors and examiners, and still to leave the children of our middle class scattered about through the numberless obscure endowed schools and "educational homes" of this country, some of them good,* many of them middling, most of them bad; but none of them great institutions, none of them invested with much consideration or dignity. What is wanted for the English middle class is *respected* schools, as well as *inspected* ones. I will explain what I mean.

The education of each class in society has, or ought to have, its ideal, determined by the wants of that class, and by its destination. Society may be imagined so uniform that one education shall be suitable for all its members; we have not a society of that kind, nor has any European country. We have to regard the condition of classes, in dealing with education; but it is right to take into account not their immediate condition only, but their wants, their destination—above all, their evident pressing wants, their evident proximate destination. Looking at English society at this moment, one may say that the ideal for the education of each of its classes to follow, the aim which the education of each

* A friendly critic, in the *Museum*, complains that my censure of private schools is too sweeping, that I set them all down, all without exception, as utterly bad,—he will allow me to point to these words as my answer. No doubt there are some masters of cheap private schools who are doing honest and excellent work; but no one suffers more than such men themselves do from a state of things in which, from the badness of the majority of these schools, a discredit is cast over them all, bad and good alike; no one would gain more by obtaining a public, trustworthy discrimination of bad from good, an authentic recognition of merit. The teachers of these schools would then have, in their profession, a career; at present they have none.

should particularly endeavour to reach, is different. Mr. Hawtrey,[26] whose admirable and fruitful labours at St. Mark's School entitle him to be heard with great respect, lays it down as an absolute proposition that the *family is the type of the school*. I do not think that is true for the schools of all classes alike. I feel sure my father, whose authority Mr. Hawtrey claims for this maxim, would not have laid it down in this absolute way. For the wants of the highest class—of the class which frequents Eton, for instance—not *school a family*, but rather *school a little world*, is the right ideal. I cannot concede to Mr. Hawtrey that, for the young gentlemen who go to Eton, our grand aim and aspiration should be, in his own words, "to make their boyhood a joyous "one, by gentle usage and friendly confidence on the "part of the master." Let him believe me, the great want for the children of luxury is not this sedulous tenderness, this smoothing of the rose-leaf for them; I am sure that, in fact, it is not by the predominance of the family and parental relation in its school-life that Eton is strongest: and it is well that this is so. It seems to me that, for the class frequenting Eton, the grand aim of education should be to give them those good things which their birth and rearing are least likely to give them: to give them (besides mere book-learning) the notion of a sort of republican fellowship, the practice of a plain life in common, the habit of self-help. To the middle class, the grand aim of education should be to give largeness of soul and personal dignity; to the lower class, feeling, gentleness, humanity. Here, at last, Mr. Hawtrey's ideal of the *family* as the type for the school, comes in its due place; for the children of poverty it is right, it is needful to set oneself first to "make their boyhood a joyous one, by gentle usage and

"friendly confidence on the part of the master;" for them
the great danger is not insolence from over-cherishing,
but insensibility from over-neglect. Mr. Hawtrey's
labours at St. Mark's have been excellent and fruitful,
just because he has here applied his maxim where it was
the right maxim to apply. Yet even in this sphere Mr.
Hawtrey's maxim must not be used too absolutely or
too long. Human dignity needs almost as much care as
human sensibility. First, undoubtedly, you must make
men feeling; but the moment you have done that, you
must lose no time in making them magnanimous. Mr.
Hawtrey will forgive me for saying that perhaps his danger
lies in pressing the spring of gentleness, of confidence,
of child-like docility, of "kindly feeling of the dependent
"towards the patron who is furthering his well-being" a
little too hard. The energy and manliness, which he
values as much as any one, run perhaps some little risk
of etiolating. At least, I think I can see some indications
of this danger in the reports—pleasing as in most
respects they are—of his boys' career in the world after
they have left school. He does so much for them at St.
Mark's, that he brings them to the point at which the
ideal of education changes, and the prime want for their
culture becomes identical with the prime want for the
culture of the middle classes. Their fibre has been
suppled long enough; now it wants fortifying.

To do Eton justice, she does not follow Mr. Hawtrey's
ideal; she does not supple the fibre of her pupils too
much; and, to do the parents of these pupils justice,
they have in general a wholesome sense of what their
sons do really most want, and are not by any means
anxious that school should over-foster them. But I am
afraid our middle classes have not quite to the same
degree this just perception of the true wants of their

offspring. They wish them to be comfortable at school, to be sufficiently instructed there, and not to cost much. Hence the eager promise of "home comforts" with school teaching, all on "terms inclusive and moderate," from the conscientious proprietor of the educational home. To be sure, they do not get what they wish. So long as human nature remains what it is, they never will get it, until they take some better security for it than a prospectus. But suppose they get the security of inspection exercised by the Universities, or by any other trustworthy authority. Some good such an inspection would undoubtedly accomplish; certain glaring specimens of charlatanism it might probably expose, certain gross cases of mishandling and neglect it might put a stop to. It might do a good deal for the school teaching, and something for the home comforts. It can never make these last what the prospectuses promise, what the parents who believe the prospectuses hope for, what they might even really have for their money; for only secondary instruction organised on a great and regular scale can give this at such cheap cost, and so to organise secondary instruction the inspection we are supposing has no power. But even if it had the power, if secondary instruction were organised on a great and regular scale, if it were a national concern, it would not be by ensuring to the offspring of the middle classes a more solid teaching at school, and a larger share of home comforts than they at present enjoy there (though certainly it would do this), that such a secondary instruction would confer upon them the greatest boon. Its greatest boon to the offspring of these classes would be its giving them great, honourable, public institutions for their nurture—institutions conveying to the spirit, at the time of life

when the spirit is most penetrable, the salutary influences of greatness, honour, and nationality—
influences which expand the soul, liberalise the mind,
dignify the character.

Such institutions are the great public schools of
England and the great Universities; with these influences, and some others to which I just now pointed,
they have formed the upper class of this country—a
class with many faults, with many shortcomings, but
imbued, on the whole, and mainly through these
influences, with a high, magnanimous, governing spirit,
which has long enabled them to rule, not ignobly, this
great country, and which will still enable them to rule
it until they are equalled or surpassed. These institutions had their origin in endowments; and the age of
endowments is gone. Beautiful and venerable as are
many of the aspects under which it presents itself, this
form of public establishment of education, with its
limitations, its preferences, its ecclesiastical character,
its inflexibility, its inevitable want of foresight, proved,
as time rolled on, to be subject to many inconveniences,
to many abuses. On the Continent of Europe a clean
sweep has in general been made of this old form of
establishment, and new institutions have arisen upon
its ruins. In England we have kept our great school and
college foundations, introducing into their system what
correctives and palliatives were absolutely necessary.
Long may we so keep them! but no such palliatives or
correctives will ever make the public establishment of
education which sufficed for earlier ages suffice for this,
nor persuade the stream of endowment, long since
failing and scanty, to flow again for our present needs
as it flowed in the middle ages. For public establishments modern societies have to betake themselves to

the State; that is, to *themselves in their collective and corporate character*. On the Continent, society has thus betaken itself to the State for the establishment of education. The result has been the formation of institutions like the Lyceum of Toulouse; institutions capable of great improvement, by no means to be extolled absolutely, by no means to be imitated just as they are; but institutions formed by modern society, with modern modes of operation, to meet modern wants; and in some important respects, at any rate, meeting those wants. These institutions give to a whole new class—to the middle class taken at its very widest—not merely an education for whose teaching and boarding there is valid security, but something—not so much I admit, but something—of the same enlarging, liberalising sense, the sense of belonging to a great and honourable public institution, which Eton and our three or four great public schools give to our upper class only, and to a small fragment broken off from the top of our middle class. That is where England is weak, and France, Holland, and Germany are strong. Education is and must be a matter of public establishment. Other countries have replaced the defective public establishment made by the middle ages for their education with a new one, which provides for the actual condition of things. We in England keep our old public establishment for education. That is very well; but then we must not forget to supplement it where it falls short. We must not neglect to provide for the actual condition of things.

I have no pet scheme to press, no crochet to gratify, no fanatical zeal for giving this or that particular shape to the public establishment of our secondary instruction. All I say is, that it is most urgent to give to the establishment of it a wider, a truly public character, and that only the State can give this. If the matter is but once fairly taken in hand, and by competent agency, I am satisfied. In this country we do not move fast; we do not organise great wholes all in a day. But if the State only granted for secondary instruction the sum which it originally granted for primary—20,000*l*. a year—and employed this sum in founding scholarships for secondary schools, with the stipulation that all the schools which sent pupils to compete for these scholarships should admit inspection, a beginning would have been made; a beginning which I truly believe would, at the end of ten years' time, be found to have raised the character of secondary instruction all through England. If more than this can be attempted at first, Sir John Coleridge, in his two excellent letters on this subject to the *Guardian*,[27] perfectly indicates the right course to take: indeed, one could wish nothing better than to commit the settlement of this matter to men of such prudence, moderation, intelligence, and public character as Sir John Coleridge. The four or five hundred endowed schools, whose collective operations now give so little result, should be turned to better account; amalgamation should be used, the most useful of these institutions strengthened, the most useless suppressed, the whole body of them treated as one whole, destined harmoniously to co-operate towards one end. What should be had in view is to constitute, in every county, at least one great centre of secondary instruction, with low charges, with the security of inspection, and with a public character. These institutions should bear some such title as that of *Royal Schools*, and should derive their support, mainly, of course, from school-fees, but partly, also, from endowments—their own, or those appropriated to them—and partly from scholarships supplied by public grants. Wherever it is possible, wherever, that is, their scale of charges is not too high, or their situation not too unsuitable, existing schools of good repute should be adopted as the *Royal Schools*. Schools such as Mr. Woodard's, such as King Edward's School at Birmingham, such as the Collegiate School at Liverpool, at once occur to one as suitable for this adoption; it would confer upon them, besides its other advantages, a public character which they are now without. Probably the very best medicine which could be devised for the defects of Eton, Harrow, and the other schools which the Royal Commissioners have been scrutinising, would be the juxtaposition, and, to a certain extent, the competition, of establishments of this kind. No wise man will desire to see root-and-branch work made with schools like Eton or Harrow, or to see them diverted from the function which they at present discharge, and, on the whole, usefully. Great subversive changes would here be out of place; it is an addition of new that our secondary instruction wants, not a demolition of old, or, at least, not of this old. But to this old I cannot doubt that the apparition and operation of this desirable new would give a very fruitful stimulus; as this new, on its part, would certainly be very much influenced and benefited by the old.

The repartition of the charge of this new secondary instruction, the mode of its assessment, the constitution of the bodies for regulating the new system, the proportion and character of functions to be assigned to local and to central authority respectively, these are matters of detail and arrangement which it is foreign to my business here to discuss, and, I hope, quite foreign to my disposition to haggle and wrangle about. They are to be settled upon a due consideration of circumstances, after an attentive scrutiny of our existing means of operation, and a discriminating review of the practice of other countries. In general, if it is agreed to give a public and coherent organisation to secondary instruction, few will dispute that its particular direction, in different localities, is best committed to local bodies, properly constituted, with a power of supervision by an impartial central authority, and of resort to this authority in the last instance. Of local bodies, bad or good, administering education, we have already plenty of specimens in this country; it would be difficult for the wit of man to devise a better governing body for its purpose than the trustees of Rugby School, or a worse governing body than the trustees of Bedford School.[28] To reject the bad in the examples offering themselves, to use the good, and to use it with just regard to the present purpose, is the thing needful. Undoubtedly these are important matters; but undoubtedly, also, it is not difficult to settle them properly; not difficult, I mean, for ordinary good sense, and ordinary good temper. The intelligence, fairness, and moderation which, in practical matters, our countrymen know so well how to exercise, make one feel quite easy in leaving these common-sense arrangements to them.

I am more anxious about the danger of having the whole question misconceived, of having false issues raised upon it. One of these false issues I have already noticed. People say: "After all, your Toulouse Lyceum "is not so good as Eton." But the Toulouse Lyceum is for the middle class, Eton for the upper class. I will allow that the upper class, amongst us, is very well taken care of, in the way of schools, already. But is the middle class? The Lyceum loses, perhaps, if compared with Eton;

but does it not gain if compared with the "Classical and "Commercial Academy?" And it is with this that the comparison is to be instituted. Again, the French Lyceum is reproached with its barrack life, its want of country air and exercise, its dismalness, its rigidity, its excessive supervision. But these defects do not come to secondary instruction from its connexion with the State; they are not necessary results of that connexion; they come to French secondary instruction from the common French and continental habitudes in the training of children and school-boys—habitudes that do not enough regard physical well-being and play. They may be remedied in France, and men's attention is now strongly drawn to them there; there has even been a talk of moving the Lyceums into the country, though this would have its inconveniences. But, at any rate, these defects need not attend the public establishment of secondary instruction in England, and assuredly, with our notions of training, they would not attend them. Again, it is said that France is a despotically-governed country, and that its Lyceums are a part of its despotism. But Switzerland is not a despotically-governed country, and it has its Lyceums just as much as France. Again, it is said that in France the Lyceums are the only schools allowed to exist, that this is monopoly and tyranny, and that the Lyceums themselves suffer by the want of competition. There is some exaggeration in this complaint, as the existence of Sorèze, and other places like Sorèze, testifies; still the restraints put upon private enterprise in founding schools in France, are, no doubt, mischievously strict; the refusal of the requisite authorisation for opening a private school is often vexatious; the Lyceums would really be benefited by the proximity of other, and sometimes rival, schools. But who supposes that any check would ever be put, in England, upon private enterprise in founding schools? Who supposes that the authorisation demanded in France for opening a private school would ever be demanded in England, that it would ever be possible to demand it, that it would ever be desirable? Who supposes that all the benefits of a public establishment of instruction are not to be obtained without it? It is for what it does itself that this establishment is so desirable, not for what it prevents others from doing. Its letting others alone does not prevent it from itself having a most useful work to do, and a work which can be done by no one else. The most zealous friends of free instruction upon the Continent feel this. One of the ablest of them, M. Dollfus, lately published in the *Revue Germanique* some most interesting remarks on the defects of the French school system, as at present regulated. He demands freedom for private persons to open schools without any authorisation at all. But does he contest the right of the State to have its own schools, to make a public establishment of instruction? So far from it, he treats this as a right beyond all contestation, as a clear duty. He treats as certain, too, the right of the State to inspect all private schools once opened, though he denies the right, and the good policy, of its putting the present obstacles in the way of opening them.

But there is a catchword which, I know, will be used against me. England is the country of cries and catchwords; a country where public life is so much carried on by means of parties must be. That English public life should be carried on as it is, I believe to be an excellent thing; but it is certain that all modes of life have their special inconveniences, and every sensible man, however much he may hold a particular way of life to be the best, and may be bent on adhering to it, will yet always be sedulous to guard himself against its inconveniences. One of these is, certainly, in English public life, the prevalence of cries and catchwords, which are very apt to receive an application, or to be used with an absoluteness, which do not belong to them; and then they tend to narrow our spirit and to hurt our practice. It is good to make a catchword of this sort come down from its stronghold of commonplace, to force it to move about before us in the open country, and to show us its real strength. Such a catchword as this: *The State had better leave things alone.* One constantly hears that as an absolute maxim; now, as an absolute maxim, it has really no force at all. The absolute maxims are those which carry to man's spirit their own demonstration with them; such propositions as, *Duty is the law of human life, Man is morally free*, and so on. The proposition, *The State had better leave things alone*, carries no such demonstration with it; it has, therefore, no absolute force; it merely conveys a notion which certain people have generalised from certain facts which have come under their observation, and which, by a natural vice of the human mind, they are then prone to apply absolutely. Some things the State had better leave alone, others it had better not. Is this particular thing one of these, or one of those?—that, as to any particular thing, is the right question. Now, I say, that education is one of those things which the State ought not to leave alone, which it ought to establish. It is said that in education given, wholly or in part, by the State, there is something eleemosynary, pauperising, degrading; that the self-respect and manly energy of those receiving it are likely to become impaired, as I have said that the manly energy of those who are too much made to feel their dependence upon a parental benefactor, is apt to become impaired. Well, now, is this so? Is a citizen's relation to the State that of a dependant to a parental benefactor? By no means; it is that of a member in a partnership to the whole firm. The citizens of a State, the members of a society, are really a partnership; "a "partnership," as Burke nobly says, "in all science, in all "art, in every virtue, in all perfection." [29] Towards this great final design of their connexion, they apply the aids which co-operative association can give them. This applied to education will, undoubtedly, give the middling person a better schooling than his own individual unaided resources could give him; but he is not thereby humiliated, he is not degraded; he is wisely and usefully turning his associated condition to the best account. Considering his end and destination, he is bound so to turn it; certainly he has a right so to turn it. Certainly he has a right—to quote Burke again—"to "a fair portion of all which society, *with all its combina-* "*tions of skill and force,* can do in his favour." Men in civil society have the right—to quote Burke yet once more (one cannot quote him too often)—as "to the "acquisitions of their parents and to the fruits of their "own industry," so also "*to the improvement of their* "*offspring, to instruction in life,* and to consolation in "death."

How vain, then, and how meaningless, to tell a man who, for the instruction of his offspring, receives aid from the State, that he is humiliated! Humiliated by receiving help for himself as an individual from himself in his corporate and associated capacity! help to which his own money, as a tax-payer, contributes, and for which, as a result of the joint energy and intelligence of the whole community in employing its powers, he him-

self deserves some of the praise! He is no more humiliated than one is humiliated by being on the foundation
of the Charterhouse or of Winchester, or by holding a
scholarship or a fellowship at Oxford or Cambridge.
Nay (if there be any humiliation here), not so much.
For the amount of benefaction, the amount of obligation, the amount, therefore, I suppose, of humiliation,
diminishes as the public character of the aid becomes
more undeniable. He is no more humiliated than when
he crosses London Bridge, or walks down the King's
Road, or visits the British Museum. But it is one of the
extraordinary inconsistencies of some English people in
this matter, that they keep all their cry of humiliation
and degradation for help which the State offers. A man
is not pauperised, is not degraded, is not oppressively
obliged, by taking aid for his son's schooling from Mr.
Woodard's subscribers, or from the next squire, or
from the next rector, or from the next ironmonger, or
from the next druggist; he is only pauperised when he
takes it from the State, when he helps to give it
himself!

This matter of State-intervention in the establishment of public instruction is so beset with misrepresen-
tation and misconception, that I must, before conclud-
ing, go into it a little more fully. I want the middle classes
(it is for them, above all, I write), the middle classes so
deeply concerned in this matter, so numerous, so right-
intentioned, so powerful, to look at the thing with
impartial regard to its simple reason and to its present
policy.

The State mars everything which it touches, say some.
It attempts to do things for private people, and private
people could do them a great deal better for themselves.

"The State," says the *Times*, "can hardly aid education
"without cramping and warping its growth, and
"mischievously interfering with the laws of its natural
"development." "Why should persons in Downing
"Street," asks Dr. Temple,[30] "be at all better qualified
"than the rest of the world for regulating these matters?"
Happily, however, this agency, at once so mischievous
and so blundering, is in our country little used. "In this
"country," says the *Times* again, "people cannot com-
"plain of the State, because the State never promised
"them anything, *but, on the contrary, always told them
"it could do them no good*. The result is, none are fed
"with false hopes." So it is, and so it will be to the
end. "This is something more than a system with us; *it
"is usage, it is a necessity*. We shall go on for ages doing
"as we have done."

Whether this really is so or not, it seems as if it *ought*
not to be so. "Government" says Burke (to go back to
Burke again),[31] "is a contrivance of human wisdom to
"provide for human wants. Men have a right that these
"wants should be provided for by this wisdom." We are a
free people, we have made our own Government. Our
own wisdom has planned our contrivance for providing
for our own wants. And what sort of a contrivance has
our wisdom made? According to the *Times*, a contrivance of which the highest merit is, that it candidly
avows its own impotency. It does not provide for our
wants, but then it "always told us" it could not provide
for them. It does not fulfil its function, but then it
"never fed us with false hopes" that it would. It is
perfectly useless, but perfectly candid. And it will always
remain what it is now; it will always be a contrivance
which contrives nothing: this with us "is usage, it is a
"necessity." Good heavens! what a subject for self-

congratulation! What bitterer satire on us and our institutions could our worst enemy invent?

Dr. Temple may well ask, "Why should persons in "Downing Street be at all better qualified than the rest "of the world for regulating such matters as education?" Why should not a sporting rector in Norfolk, or a fanatical cobbler in Northamptonshire, be just as good a judge of what is wise, equitable, and expedient in public education, as an Education Minister? Why, indeed? The Education Minister is a part of our contrivance for providing for our wants, and we have seen what that contrivance is worth. It might have been expected, perhaps, that in contriving a provision for a special want, we should have sought for some one with a special skill. But we know that our contrivance will do no good, so we may as well let Nimrod manage as Numa.[32]

From whence can have arisen, in this country, such contemptuous disparagement of the efficiency and utility of State-action? Whence such studied depreciation of an agency which to Burke, or, indeed, to any reflecting man, appears an agency of the greatest possible power and value? For several reasons. In the first place, the government of this country is, and long has been, in the hands of the aristocratic class. Where the aristocracy is a small oligarchy, able to find employment for all its members in the administration of the State, it is not the enemy, but the friend of State-action; for State action is then but its own action under another name, and it is itself directly aggrandised by all that aggrandises the State. But where, as in this country, the aristocracy is a very large class, by no means conterminous with the executive, but overlapping it and spreading far beyond it, it is the natural enemy rather than the friend of State-action; for only a small part of its members can directly administer the State, and it is not for the interest of the remainder to give to this small part an excessive preponderance. Nay, this small part will not be apt to seek it; for its interest in its order is permanent, while its interest in State-function is transitory, and it obeys an instinct which attaches it by preference to its order. The more an aristocracy has of that profound political sense by which the English aristocracy is so much distinguished, the more its members obey this instinct; and, by doing so, they signally display their best virtues, moderation, prudence, sagacity; they prevent fruitful occasions of envy, dissension, and strife; they do much to insure the permanence of their order, its harmonious action, and continued predominance. A tradition unfavourable to much State-action in home concerns (foreign are another thing) is thus insensibly established in the Government itself. This tradition, this essentially aristocratic sentiment, gains even those members of the Government who are not of the aristocratic class. In the beginning they are overpowered by it; in the end they share it. When the shepherd Daphnis first arrives in heaven, he naturally bows to the august traditions of his new sphere—*candidus insuetum miratur limen Olympi*. By the time the novelty of his situation has worn off, he has come to think just as the immortals do; he is now by conviction the foe of State-interference; the worthy Daphnis is all for letting things alone—*amat bonus otia Daphnis*.

Far from trying to encroach upon individual liberty, far from seeking to get everything into its own hands, such a Government has a natural and instinctive tendency to limit its own functions. It turns away from offers of increased responsibility or activity; it deprecates them. To propose increased responsibility and activity to an aristocratic Government is the worst possible way of paying one's court to it. The *Times* is its genuine mouthpiece, when it says that the business of Government, in domestic concerns, is negative—to prevent disorder, jobbery, and extravagance; that it need "have no notion of securing the future, not even "of regulating the present;" that it may and ought to "leave the course of events to regulate itself, and trust "the future to the security of the unknown laws of "human nature and the unseen influences of higher "powers." This is the true aristocratic theory of civil government: to have recourse as little as possible to State-action, to the collective action of the community; to leave as much as possible to the individual, to local government. And why? Because the members of an aristocratic class are preponderating individuals, with the local government in their hands. No wonder that they do not wish to see the State overshadowing them and ordering them about. Since the feudal epoch, the palmy time of local government, the State has overlaid individual action quite enough. Mr. Adderley[33] remembers with a sigh that "Houses of Correction were once "voluntary institutions." Go a little further back, and the court of justice was a voluntary institution; the gallows was a voluntary institution; voluntary, I mean, in Mr. Adderley's sense of the word voluntary—not depending on the State, but on the local government, on the lord of the soil, on the preponderating individual. The State has overlaid the feudal gallows, it has overlaid the feudal court of justice, it has overlaid the feudal House of Correction, and finally, says Mr. Adderley, "it has "overlaid our school-system." What will it do next?

In the aristocratic class, whose members mainly

collector and policeman—the hewer of wood and drawer of water to the community.

There is another cause also which indisposes the English middle class to increased action on the part of the State. M. Amédée Thierry, in his "History of the Gauls," observes, in contrasting the Gaulish and Germanic races, that the first is characterised by the instinct of intelligence and mobility, and by the preponderant action of individuals; the second, by the instinct of discipline and order, and by the preponderant action of bodies of men. This general law of M. Thierry's has to submit to many limitations, but there is a solid basis of truth in it. Applying the law to a people mainly of German blood like ourselves, we shall best perceive its truth by regarding the middle class of the nation. Multitudes, all the world over, have a good deal in common; aristocracies, all the world over, have a good deal in common. The peculiar national form and habit exist in the masses at the bottom of society in a loose, rudimentary, potential state; in the few at the top of society, in a state modified and reduced by various culture. The man of the multitude has not yet solidified into the typical Englishman; the man of the aristocracy has been etherealised out of him. The typical Englishman is to be looked for in the middle class. And there we shall find him, with a complexion not ill-suiting M. Thierry's law; with a spirit not very open to new ideas, and not easily ravished by them; not, therefore, a great enthusiast for universal progress, but with a strong love of discipline and order,—that is, of keeping things settled, and much as they are; and with a disposition, instead of lending himself to the onward-looking statesman and legislator, to act with bodies of men of his own kind, whose aims and efforts reach no further than his own. Poverty and hope make man the friend of ideals, therefore the multitude has a turn for ideals; culture and genius make man the friend of ideals, therefore the gifted or highly-trained few have a turn for ideals. The middle class has the whet neither of poverty nor of culture; it is not ill-off in the things of the body, and it is not highly trained in the things of the mind; therefore it has little turn for ideals: it is self-satisfied. This is a chord in the nature of the English middle class which seldom fails, when struck, to give an answer, and which some people are never weary of striking. All the variations which are played on the endless theme of *local self-government* rely on this chord. Hardly any local government is, in truth, in this country, exercised by the middle class; almost the whole of it is exercised by the aristocratic class. Every locality in France—that country which our middle class is taught so much to compassionate—has a genuine municipal government, in which the middle class has its due share; and by this municipal government all matters of local concern (schools among the number) are regulated; not a country parish in England has any effective government of this kind at all. But what is meant by the habit of local self-government, on which our middle class is so incessantly felicitated, is its habit of voluntary combination, in bodies of its own arranging, for purposes of its own choosing—purposes to be carried out within the limits fixed for a private association by its own powers. When the middle class is solemnly warned against State-interference, lest it should destroy "the habit of self-reliance and love of "local self-government," it is this habit, and the love of it, that are meant. When we are told that "nothing can be "more dangerous than these constant attempts on the "part of the Government to take from the people the "management of its own concerns," this is the sort of management of our own concerns that is meant; not the management of them by a regular local government, but the management of them by chance private associations. It is our habit of acting through these associations which, says Mr. Roebuck, saves us from being "a set of "helpless imbeciles, totally incapable of attending to our "own interests."[37] It is in the event of this habit being at all altered that, according to the same authority, "the "greatness of this country is gone."* And the middle class, to whom that habit is familiar and very dear, will never be insensible to language of this sort.

Finally, the English middle class has a strong practical sense and habit of affairs, and it sees that things managed by the Government are often managed ill. It sees them treated sometimes remissly, sometimes vexatiously; now with a paralysing want of fruitful energy, now with an over-busy fussiness, with rigidity, with formality, without due consideration of special circumstances. Here, too, it finds a motive disinclining it to trust State-action, and leading it to give a willing ear to those who declaim against it.

Now, every one of these motives of distrust is respectable. Every one of them has, or once had, a solid ground. Every one of them points to some virtue in those actuated by it, which is not to be suppressed, but to

* Mr. Roebuck, in his recent excellent speech at Sheffield,[38] has shown that in popular education, at any rate, he does not mean these maxims to apply without restriction. But perhaps it is a little incautious for a public man ever to throw out, without guarding himself, maxims of this kind; for, on the one hand, in this country such maxims are sure never to be lost sight of; on the other, but too many people are sure always to be prone to use them amiss, and to push their application much further than it ought to go.

find true conditions for its exercise. The English middle class was quite right in repelling State-action, when the State suffered itself to be made an engine of the High Church party to persecute Nonconformists. It gave an excellent lesson to the State in so doing. It rendered a valuable service to liberty of thought and to all human freedom. If State-action now threatened to lend itself to one religious party against another, the middle class would be quite right in again thwarting and confining it. But can it be said that the State now shows the slightest disposition to take such a course? Is such a course the course towards which the modern spirit carries the State? Does not the State show, more and more, the resolution to hold the balance perfectly fair between religious parties? The middle class has it in its own power, more than any other class, to confirm the State in this resolution. This class has the power to make it thoroughly sure—in organising, for instance, any new system of public instruction—that the State shall treat all religious persuasions with exactly equal fairness. If, instead of holding aloof, it will now but give its aid to make State-action equitable, it can make it so.

Again, as to the "habits of self-reliance and the love "of local self government." People talk of Government *interference*, Government *control*, as if State-action were necessarily something imposed upon them from without; something despotic and self-originated; something which took no account of their will, and left no freedom to their activity. Can any one really suppose that, in a country like this, State-action—in education, for instance—can ever be that, unless we choose to make it so? We can give it what form we will. We can make it our agent, not our master. In modern societies the agency of the State, in certain matters, is so indispensable, that it will manage, with or without our common consent, to come into operation somehow; but when it has introduced itself without the common consent—when a great body, like the middle class, will have nothing to say to it—then its course is indeed likely enough to be not straightforward, its operation not satisfactory. But, by all of us consenting to it, we remove any danger of this kind. By really agreeing to deal in our collective and corporate character with education, we can form ourselves into the best and most efficient of voluntary societies for managing it. We can make State-action upon it a genuine local government of it, the faithful but potent expression of our own activity. We can make the central Government that mere court of disinterested review and correction, which every sensible man would always be glad to have for his own activity. We shall have all our self-reliance and individual action still (in this country we shall always have plenty of them, and the parts will always be more likely to tyrannise over the whole than the whole over the parts), but we shall have had the good sense to turn them to account by a powerful, but still voluntary, organisation. Our beneficence will be "beneficence "acting *by rule*" (that is Burke's definition of law, as instituted by a free society,)[39] and all the more effective for that reason. Must this make us "a set of helpless "imbeciles, totally incapable of attending to our own "interests?" Is this "a grievous blow aimed at the inde-"pendence of the English character?" Is "English self-"reliance and independence" to be perfectly satisfied with what it produces already without this organisation? In middle-class education it produces, without it, the educational home and the classical and commercial academy. Are we to be proud of that? Are we to be satisfied with that? Is "the greatness of this country" to be seen in that? But it will be said that, awakening to a sense of the badness of our middle-class education, we are beginning to improve it. Undoubtedly we are; and the most certain sign of that awakening, of those beginnings of improvement, is the disposition to resort to a public agency, to "beneficence working *by rule*," to help us on faster with it. When we really begin to care about a matter of this kind, we cannot help turning to the most efficient agency at our disposal. Clap-trap and commonplace lose their power over us; we begin to see that, if State-action has often its inconveniences, our self-reliance and independence are best shown in so arranging our State-action as to guard against those inconveniences, not in forgoing State-action for fear of them. So it was in elementary education. Mr. Baines[40] says that this was already beginning to improve, when Government interfered with it. Why, it was because we were all beginning to take a real interest in it, beginning to improve it, that we turned to Government—to ourselves in our corporate character—to get it improved faster. So long as we did not care much about it, we let it go its own way, and kept singing Mr. Roebuck's fine old English stave about "self-reliance." We kept crying just as he cries now: "nobody has the same interest to "do well for a man as he himself has." That was all very pleasant so long as we cared not a rush whether the people were educated or no. The moment we began to concern ourselves about this, we asked ourselves what our song was worth. We asked ourselves how the bringing up of our labourers and artisans—they "doing for "themselves," and "nobody having the same interest to "do well for a man as he himself has"—was being done. We found it was being done detestably. Then we asked

ourselves whether casual, precarious, voluntary beneficence, or "beneficence acting by rule," was the better
agency for doing it better. We asked ourselves if we
could not employ our public resources on this concern,
if we could not make our beneficence act upon it by
rule, without losing our "habits of self-reliance," without "aiming a grievous blow at the independence of the
"English character." We found that we could; we began
to do it; and we left Mr. Baines to sing in the wilderness.

Finally, as to the objection that our State-action—
our "beneficence working by rule"—often bungles and
does its work badly. No wonder it does. The imperious
necessities of modern society force it, more or less, even
in this country, into play; but it is exercised by a class
to whose cherished instincts it is opposed—the aristocratic class; and it is watched by a class to whose
cherished prejudices it is opposed—the middle class. It
is hesitatingly exercised and jealously watched. It
therefore works without courage, cordiality, or belief
in itself. Under its present conditions it must work so,
and, working so, it must often bungle. But it need not
work so; and the moment the middle class abandons
its attitude of jealous aversion, the moment they frankly
put their hand to it, the moment they adopt it as an
instrument to do them service, it will work so no
longer. Then it will not bungle; then, if it is applied,
say, to education, it will not be fussy, baffling, and
barren; it will bring to bear on this concern the energy
and strong practical sense of the middle class itself.

But the middle class must make it do this. They must
not expect others to do the business for them. It is they
whose interest is concerned in its being done, and they
must do it for themselves. Why should the upper class
—the aristocratic class—do it for them? What motive—

except the distant and not very peremptory one of their general political sense, their instinct for taking the course which, for the whole country's sake, ought to be taken—have the aristocratic class to impel them to go counter to all their natural maxims, nay, and to all their seeming interest? They do not want new schools for their children. The great public schools of the country are theirs already. Their numbers are not such as to overflow these few really public schools; their fortunes are such as to make the expensiveness of these schools a matter of indifference to them. The Royal Commissioners, whose report has just appeared, do not, indeed, give a very brilliant picture of the book-learning of these schools. But it is not the book-learning (easy to be improved if there is a will to improve it) that this class make their first care; they make their first care the tone, temper, and habits generated in these schools. So long as they generate a public spirit, a free spirit, a high spirit, a governing spirit, they are not ill-satisfied. Their children are fitted to succeed them in the government of the country. Why should they concern themselves to change this state of things? Why should they create competitors for their own children? Why should they labour to endow another class with those great instruments of power—a public spirit, a free spirit, a high spirit, a governing spirit? Why should they do violence to that distaste for State-action, which, in an aristocratic class, is natural and instinctive, for the benefit of the middle class?

No; the middle class must do this work for themselves. From them must come the demand for the satisfaction of a want that is theirs. They must leave off being frightened at shadows. They may keep (I hope they always will keep) the maxim that self-reliance and independence are the most invaluable of blessings, that the great end of society is the perfecting of the individual, the fullest, freest, and worthiest development of the individual s activity. But that the individual may be perfected, that his activity may be worthy, he must often learn to quit old habits, to adopt new, to go out for himself, to transform himself. It was said, and truly said, of one of the most unwearied and successful strivers after human perfection that have ever lived—Wilhelm von Humboldt—that it was a joy to him to feel himself modified by the operation of a foreign influence. And this may well be a joy to a man whose centre of character and whose moral force are once securely established. Through this he makes growth in perfection. Through this he enlarges his being and fills up gaps in it; he unlearns old prejudices and learns new excellences; he makes advance towards inward light and freedom. Societies may use this means of perfection as well as individuals, and it is a characteristic (perhaps the best characteristic) of our age, that they are using it more and more. Let us look at our neighbour, France. What strikes a thoughtful observer most in modern France, is the great, wide breach which is being made in the old French mind; the strong flow with which a foreign thought is pouring in and mixing with it. There is an extraordinary increase in the number of German and English books read there, books the most unlike possible to the native literary growth of France. There is a growing disposition there to pull to pieces old stock French commonplaces, and to put a bridle upon old stock French habitudes. France will not, and should not, like some English liberals, run a-muck against State-action altogether; but she shows a tendency to control her excessive State-action, to reduce it within just limits where it has overpassed them, to make a larger part for free local activity and for individuals. She will not, and should not, like Sir Archibald Alison,[41] cry down her great Revolution as the work of Satan; but she shows more and more the power to discern the real faults of that Revolution, the real part of delusion, impotence, and transitoriness in the work of '89 or of '91, and to profit by that discernment.

Our middle class has secured for itself that centre of character and that moral force which are, I have said, the indispensable basis upon which perfection is to be founded. To securing them, its vigour in resisting the State, when the State tried to tyrannise over it, has contributed not a little. In this sense, it may be said to have made way towards perfection by repelling the State's hand. Now it has to enlarge and to adorn its spirit. I cannot seriously argue with those who deny that the independence and free action of the middle class is now, in this country, immutably secure; I cannot treat the notion of the State now overriding it and doing violence to it, as anything but a vain chimera. Well, then, if the State can (as it can) be of service to the middle class in the work of enlarging its mind and adorning its spirit, it will now make way towards perfection by taking the State's hand. State-action is not in itself unfavourable to the individual's perfection, to his attaining his fullest development. So far from it, it is in ancient Greece, where State-action was omnipresent, that we see the individual at his very highest pitch of free and fair activity. This is because, in Greece, the individual was strong enough to fashion the State into an instrument of his own perfection, to make it serve, with a thousand times his own power, towards his own ends. He was not enslaved by it, he did not annihilate it, but he used it. Where, in modern nations, the State has maimed and crushed individual activity, it has been by operating as an alien, exterior power in the community, a power not originated by the community to serve the common weal, but entrenched among them as a conqueror with a weal of its own to serve. Just because the vigour and sturdiness of the people of this country have prevented, and will always prevent, the State from being anything of this kind, I believe we, more than any modern people, have the power of renewing, in our national life, the example of Greece. I believe that we, and our American kinsmen, are specially fit to apply State-action with advantage, because we are specially sure to apply it voluntarily.

Two things must, I think, strike any one who attentively regards the English middle class at this moment. One is the intellectual ferment which is taking place, or rather, which is beginning to take place, amongst them. It is only in its commencement as yet; but it shows itself at a number of points, and bids fair to become a great power. The importance of a change, placing in the great middle class the centre of the intellectual life of this country, can hardly be over-estimated. I have been reproved for saying that the culture and intellectual life of our highest class seem to me to have somewhat flagged since the last century. That is my opinion, indeed, and all that I see and hear strengthens rather than shakes it. The culture of this class is not what it used to be. Their value for high culture, their belief in its importance, is not what it used to be. One may see it in the public schools, one may see it in the universities. Whence come the deadness, the want of intellectual life, the poverty of acquirement after years of schooling, which the Commissioners, in their remarkable and interesting report, show us so prevalent in our most distinguished public schools? What gives to play and amusement, both there and at the universities, their present overweening importance, so that home critics cry out: "The real studies of Oxford are its games," and foreign critics cry out: "At Oxford the "student is still the mere schoolboy"? The most experienced and acute of Oxford heads of houses told me himself, that when he spoke to an undergraduate the other day about trying for some distinguished scholarship, the answer he got was: "Oh, the men from the "great schools don't care for those things now; the men "who care about them are the men from Marlborough, "Cheltenham, and the second-rate schools." Whence, I say, does this slackness, this sleep of the mind, come, except from a torpor of intellectual life, a dearth of ideas, an indifference to fine culture or disbelief in its necessity, spreading through the bulk of our highest class, and influencing its rising generation? People talk as if the culture of this class had only changed; the Greek and Roman classics, they say, are no longer in vogue as they were in Lord Chesterfield's time. Well, if this class had only gone from one source of high culture to another; if only, instead of reading Homer and Cicero, it now read Goethe and Montesquieu;—but it does not; it reads the *Times* and the *Agricultural Journal*. And it devotes itself to practical life. And it amuses itself. It is not its rising generation only which loves play; never in all its history has our whole highest class shown such zeal for enjoying life, for amusing itself. It would be absurd to make this a matter of reproach against it. The triumphs of material progress multiply the means of material enjoyment; they attract all classes, more and more, to taste of this enjoyment; on

the highest class, which possesses in the amplest
measure these means, they must needs exercise this
attraction very powerfully. But every thoughtful
observer can perceive that the ardour for amusement
and enjoyment, often educative and quickening to a
toil-numbed working class or a strait-laced middle
class, whose great want is expansion, tends to become
enervative and weakening to an aristocratic class—a
class which must rule by superiority of all kinds,
superiority not to be won without contention of spirit
and a certain severity. I think, therefore, both that the
culture of our highest class has declined, and that this
declension, though natural and venial, impairs its
power.

Yet in this vigorous country everything has a wonderful ability for self-restoration, and he would be a bold
prophet who should deny that the culture of our highest
class may recover itself. But however this may be, there
is no doubt that a liberal culture, a fullness of intellectual
life, in the middle class, is a far more important matter,
a far more efficacious stimulant to national progress,
than the same powers in an aristocratic class. Whatever
may be its culture, an aristocratic class will always have
at bottom, like the young man in Scripture with great
possessions,[42] an inaptitude for ideas; but, besides this,
high culture or ardent intelligence, pervading a large
body of the community, acquire a breadth of basis, a
sum of force, an energy of central heat for radiating
further, which they can never possess when they
pervade a small upper class only.[43] It is when such a
broad basis is obtained, that individual genius gets its
proper nutriment, and is animated to put forth its best
powers; this is the secret of rich and beautiful epochs
in national life; the epoch of Pericles in Greece, the

epoch of Michael Angelo in Italy, the epoch of Shak-speare in England. Our actual middle class has not yet, certainly, the fine culture, or the living intelligence, which quickened great bodies of men at these epochs; but it has the forerunner, the preparer, the indispens-able initiator; it is traversed by a strong intellectual ferment. It is the middle class which has real mental ardour, real curiosity; it is the middle class which is the great reader; that immense literature of the day which we see surging up all round us,—literature the absolute value of which it is almost impossible to rate too humbly, literature hardly a word of which will reach, or deserves to reach, the future,—it is the middle class which calls it forth, and its evocation is at least a sign of a widespread mental movement in that class. Will this movement go on and become fruitful: will it conduct the middle class to a high and commanding pitch of culture and intelligence? That depends on the sensi-bility which the middle class has for *perfection;* that depends on its power to *transform itself.*

And it is not yet manifest how far it possesses this power. For—and here I pass to the second of those two things which particularly, I have said, strike any one who observes the English middle class just now—in its public action this class has hitherto shown only the power and disposition to *affirm itself*, not at all the power and disposition to *transform itself.* That, indeed, is one of the deep-seated instincts of human nature, but of vulgar human nature—of human nature not high-souled and aspiring after perfection—to esteem itself for what it is, to try to establish itself just as it is, to try even to impose itself with its stock of habitudes, petti-nesses, narrownesses, shortcomings of every kind, on the rest of the world as a conquering power. But nothing has really a right to be satisfied with itself, to be and remain itself, except that which has reached perfection; and nothing has the right to impose itself on the rest of the world as a conquering force, except that which is of higher perfection than the rest of the world. And such is the fundamental constitution of human affairs, that the measure of right proves also, in the end, the measure of power. Before the English middle class can have the right or the power to assert itself absolutely, it must have greatly perfected itself. It has been jokingly said of this class, that all which the best of it cared for was summed up in this alliterative phrase—*Business and Bethels:* and that all which the rest of it cared for was the *Business* without the *Bethels*. No such jocose and slighting words can convey any true sense of what the religion of the English middle class has really been to it; what a source of vitality, energy, and persistent vigour. "They "who wait on the Lord," says Isaiah, in words not less true than they are noble, "*shall renew their strength;*"[44] and the English middle class owes to its religion not only comfort in the past, but also a vast latent force of unworn life and strength for future progress. But the Puritanism of the English middle class, which has been so great an element of strength to them, has by no means brought them to perfection; nay, by the rigid mould in which it has cast their spirit, it has kept them back from perfection. The most that can be said of it is, that it has supplied a stable basis on which to build perfection; it has given them character, though it has not given them culture. But it is in making endless additions to itself, in the endless expansion of its powers, in endless growth in wisdom and beauty, that the spirit of the human race finds its ideal; to reach this ideal, culture is an indispensable aid, and that is the true value of culture. The life of aristocracies, with its large and free use of the world, its conversance with great affairs, its exemption from sordid cares, its liberation from the humdrum provincial round, its external splendour and refinement, is a kind of outward shadow of this ideal, a prophecy of it; and there lies the secret of the charm of aristocracies, and of their power over men's minds. In a country like England, the middle class, with its industry and its Puritanism, and nothing more, will never be able to make way beyond a certain point, will never be able to divide power with the aristocratic class, much less to win for itself a preponderance of power. While it only tries to affirm its actual self, to impose its actual self, it has no charm for men's minds, and can achieve no great triumphs. And this is all it attempts at present. The Conservative reaction, of which we hear so much just now, is in great part merely a general indisposition to let the middle-class spirit, working by its old methods, and having only its old self to give us, establish itself at all points and become master of the situation. Particularly on Church questions is this true. In this sphere of religion, where feeling and beauty are so all-important, we shrink from giving to the middle-class spirit, limited as we see it, with its sectarianism, its under-culture, its intolerance, its bitterness, its unloveliness, too much its own way. Before we give it quite its own way, we insist on its making itself into something larger, newer, more fruitful. This is what the recent Church Rate divisions really mean,[45] and the lovers of perfection, therefore, may accept them without displeasure. They are the voice of the nation crying to the *untransformed* middle class (if it will receive it) with a voice of thunder:[46] "The future is not yours!"

And let me say, in passing, that the indifference, so

irritating to some persons, with which European opinion has received the break-up of the old American Union has at bottom a like ground. I put the question of slavery on one side; so far as the resolution of that question depends on the issue of the conflict between the North and the South, every one may wish this party or that to prevail. But Mr. Bright[47] and Mr. Cobden[48] extol the old American Republic as something interesting and admirable in itself, and are displeased with those who are not afflicted at its disaster, and not jealous for its restoration. Mr. Bright is an orator of genius; Mr. Cobden is a man of splendid understanding. But why do they refuse to perceive, that, apart from all class-jealousy of aristocracies towards a democratic republic, there existed in the most impartial and thoughtful minds a profound dissatisfaction with the spirit and tendencies of the old American Union, a strong aversion to their unchecked triumph, a sincere wish for the disciplining and correcting of them? And what were the old United States but a colossal expression of the English middle-class spirit, somewhat more accessible to ideas there than here, because of the democratic air it breathed, much more arrogant and over-weening there than here, because of the absence of all check and counterpoise to it—but there, as here, full of rawness, hardness, and imperfection; there, as here, greatly needing to be liberalised, enlarged, and ennobled, before it could with advantage be suffered to assert itself absolutely? All the energy and success in the world could not have made the United States admirable so long as their spirit had this imperfection. Even if they had overrun the whole earth, their old national style would have still been detestable, and Mr. Beecher would have still been a heated barbarian.[49] But they could not thus triumph, they could not make their rule thus universal, so long as their spirit was thus imperfect. They had not power enough over the minds of men. Now they are transforming their spirit in the furnace of civil war; with what success we shall in due time see. But the lovers of perfection in America itself ought to rejoice—some of them, no doubt, do rejoice—that the national spirit should be compelled, even at any cost of suffering, to transform itself, to become something higher, ampler, more gracious. To be glad that it should be compelled thus to transform itself, that it should not be permitted to triumph untransformed, is no insult, no unkindness; it is a homage to perfection. It is a religious devotion to that providential order which forbids the final supremacy of imperfect things. God keeps tossing back to the human race its failures, and commanding it to try again.

In the Crusade of Peter the Hermit, where the hosts that marched were not filled after the usual composition of armies, but contained along with the fighters whole families of people—old men, women, and children, swept by the universal torrent of enthusiasm towards the Holy Land—the marches, as might have been expected, were tedious and painful. Long before Asia was reached, long before even Europe was half traversed, the little children in that travelling multitude began to fancy, with a natural impatience, that their journey must surely be drawing to an end; and every evening, as they came in sight of some town which was the destination of that day's march, they cried out eagerly to those who were with them, "*Is this Jerusalem?*" No, poor children, not this town, nor the next, nor yet the next, is Jerusalem; Jerusalem is far off, and it needs time, and strength, and much endurance to reach it.

Seas and mountains, labour and peril, hunger and thirst, disease and death, are between Jerusalem and you.

So, when one marks the ferment and stir of life in the middle class at this moment, and sees this class impelled to take possession of the world, and to assert itself and its own actual spirit absolutely, one is disposed to exclaim to it, " *Jerusalem is not yet.* Your present spirit is "not Jerusalem, is not the goal you have to reach, the "place you may be satisfied in." And when one says this, they sometimes fancy that one has the same object as others who say the same to them; that one means that they are to yield themselves to be moulded by some existing force, their rival; that one wishes Nonconformity to take the law from actual Anglicanism, and the middle class from the present governing class; that one thinks Anglicanism Jerusalem, and the English aristocratic class Jerusalem.

I do not mean, or wish, or think this, though many, no doubt, do. It is not easy for a reflecting man, who has studied its origin, to feel any vehement enthusiasm for Anglicanism; Henry the Eighth and his parliaments have taken care of that. One may esteem it as a beneficent social and civilising agent. One may have an affection for it from life-long associations, and for the sake of much that is venerable and interesting which it has inherited from antiquity. One may cherish gratitude to it—and here, I think, Mr. Goldwin Smith,[50] who fights against it the battle of the Nonconformists with so much force and so much ability, is a little ungrateful —for the shelter and basis for culture which this, like other great nationally established forms of religion, affords; those who are born in them can get forward on their road, instead of always eyeing the ground on which they stand disputing about it. But actual

Anglicanism is certainly not Jerusalem, and I should be sorry to think it the end which Nonconformity and the middle class are to reach. The actual governing class, again, the English aristocratic class (in the widest sense of the word *aristocratic*)—I cannot wish that the rest of the nation, the new and growing part of the nation, should be transformed in spirit exactly according to the image of that class. The merits and services of that class no one rates higher than I do; no one appreciates higher than I do the value of the relative standard of elevation, refinement and grandeur, which they have exhibited; no one would more strenuously oppose the relinquishing of this for any lower standard. But I cannot hide from myself that while modern societies increasingly tend to find their best life in a free and heightened spiritual and intellectual activity, to this tendency aristocracies offer at least a strong passive resistance, by their eternal prejudices, their incurable dearth of ideas. In modern, rich, and industrial societies, they tend to misplace the ideal for the classes below them; the immaterial chivalrous ideal of high descent and honour is, by the very nature of the case, of force only for aristocracies themselves; the immaterial modern ideal of spiritual and intellectual perfection through culture, they have not to communicate. What they can and do communicate is the material ideal of splendour of wealth, and weight of property. And this ideal is the ideal truly operative upon our middle classes at this moment. To be as rich as they can, that they may reach the splendour of wealth and weight of property, and, with time, the importance, of the actual heads of society, is their ambition. I do not blame them, or the class from which they get their ideal; all I say is, that the good ideal for humanity, the true Jerusalem, is an ideal more spiritual than splendid wealth and boundless property, an ideal in which more can participate. The beloved friends of humanity have been those who made it feel its ideal to be in the things of the mind and spirit, to be in an internal condition separable from wealth and accessible to all—men like St. Francis, the ardent bridegroom of poverty; men like the great personages of antiquity, almost all of them, as Lacordaire was so fond of saying, poor. Therefore, that the middle class should simply take its ideal from the aristocratic class, I do not wish. That the aristocratic class should be able absolutely to assert itself, and its own spirit, is not my desire. No, no; they are not Jerusalem.

The truth is, the English spirit has to accomplish an immense evolution; nor, as that spirit at this moment presents itself in any class or description amongst us, can one be perfectly satisfied with it, can one wish it to prevail just as it is.

But in a transformed middle class, in a middle class raised to a higher and more genial culture, we may find, not perhaps Jerusalem, but, I am sure, a notable stage towards it. In that great class, strong by its numbers, its energy, its industry, strong by its freedom from frivolity, not by any law of nature prone to immobility of mind, actually at this moment agitated by a spreading ferment of mind, in that class, liberalised by an ampler culture, admitted to a wider sphere of thought, living by larger ideas, with its provincialism dissipated, its intolerance cured, its pettinesses purged away,—what a power there will be, what an element of new life for England! Then let the middle class rule, then let it affirm its own spirit, when it has thus perfected itself.

And I cannot see any means so direct and powerful for developing this great and beneficent power as the public establishment of schools for the middle class. By public establishment they may be made cheap and accessible to all. By public establishment they may give securities for the culture offered in them being really good and sound, and the best that our time knows. By public establishment they may communicate to those reared in them the sense of being brought in contact with their country, with the national life, with the life of the world; and they will expand and dignify their spirits by communicating this sense to them. I can see no other mode of institution which will offer the same advantages in the same degree.

I cannot think that the middle class will be much longer insensible to its own evident interests. I cannot think that, for the pleasure of being complimented on their self-reliance by Lord Fortescue[51] and the *Times*, they will much longer forego a course leading them to their own true dignity instead of away from it. I know that with men who have reached or passed the middle of life, the language and habits of years form a network round the spirit through which it cannot easily break; and among the elder leaders of the middle class there are men whom I would give much to persuade—men of weight and character, like Mr. Baines, men of character and culture too, like Mr. Miall[52]—whom I must not, I fear, hope to persuade. But among the younger leaders of this class—even of that part of it where resistance is most to be apprehended, among the younger Dissenting ministers, for instance—there exists, I do believe, a disposition not fixedly averse to the public establish-ment of education for the middle classes—a willingness, at any rate, to consider a project of this kind on its merits. Amongst them particularly is the ferment and expansion of mind, of which I have spoken, perceptible;

their sense of the value of culture, and their culture itself, increases every day. Well, the old bugbear which scares us all away from the great confessed means of best promoting this culture—the religious difficulty, as it is called—is potent only so long as these gentlemen please. It rests solely with themselves to procure the public establishment of secondary instruction upon a perfectly equitable basis as regards religious differences. If its establishment is suffered to fix itself in private hands, those hands will be the clergy's. It is to the honour of the clergy—of their activity, of their corporate spirit, of their sense of a pressing want—that this should be so. But in that case the dominant force in settling the teaching in these schools will be clerical. Their organisation will be ecclesiastical. Mr Woodard tells us so himself; and indeed he (very naturally) makes a merit of it. This is not what the Dissenters want, neither is it what the movement of the modern spirit tends to. But when instruction has once been powerfully organised in this manner, it is very difficult for the State afterwards to interfere for the purpose of giving effect to the requirements of the modern spirit. It is met by vested interests—by legitimate vested interests—not to be conciliated without great delay and difficulty. It is not easy for the State to impose a conscience clause on primary schools, when the establishment of those schools has been for the most part made by the clergy. It is not easy to procure the full benefits of the national universities to Nonconformists, when Anglicanism has got a vested interest in the colleges. Neither will it be easy hereafter, in secondary instruction, to settle the religious difficulty equitably, if the establishment of that instruction shall have been effected by private bodies in which clerical influence predominates.

I hope the middle class will not much longer delay to take a step on which its future value and dignity and influence so much depend. By taking this step they will indirectly confer a great boon upon the lower class also. This obscure embryo, only just beginning to move, travailing in labour and darkness, so much left out of account when we celebrate the glories of our Atlantis, now and then, by so mournful a glimpse, showing itself to us in Lambeth, or Spitalfields, or Dorsetshire; this immense working class, now so without a practicable passage to all the joy and beauty of life, for whom in an aristocratic class, which is unattainable by them, there is no possible ideal, for whom in a middle class, narrow, ungenial, and unattractive, there is no adequate ideal, will have, in a cultured, liberalised, ennobled, transformed middle class, a point towards which it may hopefully work, a goal towards which it may with joy direct its aspirations.

Children of the future, whose day has not yet dawned, you, when that day arrives, will hardly believe what obstructions were long suffered to prevent its coming! You who, with all your faults, have neither the aridity of aristocrats, nor the narrow-mindedness of middle classes, you, whose power of simple enthusiasm is your great gift, will not comprehend how progress towards man's best perfection—the adorning and ennobling of his spirit—should have been reluctantly undertaken; how it should have been for years and years retarded by barren commonplaces, by worn-out clap-traps. You will wonder at the labour of its friends in proving the self-proving; you will know nothing of the doubts, the fears, the prejudices they had to dispel; nothing of the outcry they had to encounter; of the fierce protestations of life from policies which were dead and did not know it, and the shrill querulous upbraiding from publicists in their dotage. But you, in your turn, with difficulties of your own, will then be mounting some new step in the arduous ladder whereby man climbs towards his perfection; towards that unattainable but irresistible lode-star, gazed after with earnest longing, and invoked with bitter tears; the longing of thousands of hearts, the tears of many generations.

THE TWICE-REVISED CODE

The Archbishop of Canterbury said a few months ago at Maidstone,[53] that the Revised Code, lately promulgated by the Committee of Council on Education, must at last stand or fall according to the verdict pronounced upon it by the *common sense of the country*. His Grace could not have said a truer thing. But the common sense of the country finds itself at some loss for clear data to guide it in coming to a verdict. The system of our Education Department bristles with details so numerous, so minute, and so intricate, that any one not practically conversant with this system has great difficulty in mastering them, and, by failing to master them, may easily be led into error.* With a certain amount of trouble, however, even the details of our Council Office system may of course be mastered. But such an amount of trouble the general public will not take. From this cause the pamphlet of a master of the subject—of the founder of our public elementary education, Sir James Shuttleworth[54]—fails, it seems to us, perfectly to meet the occasion with which it has to deal. For readers already familiar with the subject, for school-managers, school-teachers, school-inspectors, it is admirable: for the general reader it is somewhat too copious. For this last, it goes too much into detail; it presupposes more acquaintance with the subject than he is likely to possess. Every member of Parliament,

* For want of this practical acquaintance, a writer so able and so exact as Dr. Vaughan bases an argument upon the assertion that a low certificate from the Committee of Council does not at present entitle its holder to any grant of money.[55] The assertion and the argument from it are alike erroneous.

every one who has to *discuss* the new Code, should read Sir James Shuttleworth's pamphlet. Every one who is disposed to go deeply into the subject should read it. For those who are not disposed to do this, who desire only to know the essential facts of the case, so as to be able to form an opinion upon it, a simpler statement is required,—a statement dealing less with the details of the subject and more with its *rationale*.

Such a statement we here propose to attempt. We propose, at this last moment before the Parliamentary discussion comes,[56] to show the general reader—1. What it is that the Revised Code will actually do; 2. Why its authors are trying to do this; 3. What is the merit of their design in itself, and what, moreover, is the prospect of its accomplishing what it intends. And we shall notice, in conclusion, the changes in his original scheme which have just been propounded by Mr. Lowe, and examine the value and importance of these.

1.—What the Revised Code will actually *do*, is to reduce considerably the grants at present contributed by the State towards the support of schools for the poor. This is what it will certainly and indisputably do. It may do other things besides, but about its doing these other things there is much dispute; about its effecting a reduction of existing grants there is no dispute. The reduction may be more or less great; Sir James Shuttleworth, the best of authorities on such a matter, estimates it at two-fifths, or £175,000 a year, of the money now annually paid; Archdeacon Sinclair,[57] representing the National Society, estimates it at forty per cent (the same thing). Even Mr. Lowe admits that there will be a loss, although he declares such an estimate of it as the above to be exaggerated. It is possible that this estimate may not be exactly correct;

but that the reduction will be considerable, no one who has any real acquaintance with the subject denies. It is probably safe to reckon it at nearly two-fifths of the present annual grant.

The heads of a public department are not, in general, the persons most forward in proposing to contract the operations of their own department, and to reduce its expenditure. Of any such want of self-denying disinterestedness the heads of our Education Department cannot be accused. They have propounded a scheme which—while it dismays and discourages the supporters of that system of State-aid to public education, which the infinite zeal and adroitness of Sir James Shuttleworth, the infinite moderation and sagacity of Lord Lansdowne,[58] founded in this country with so much difficulty—delights and animates all the bitterest adversaries of that system. It is from these adversaries, almost as much surprised as rejoiced, that the framers of the Revised Code have received the warmest approval. A clergyman, well known in the North Midland Counties for his uncompromising opposition to all State-interference in national education, procured from a Yorkshire meeting, filled with ardent Voluntaries who shared his own opinions, a vote of entire adhesion to the new Code. Mr. Crossley, member for the West Riding, an Independent and a Voluntary, declared at an Education Conference lately held, that 'the new Minute of the Privy Council had given fresh heart and life to the opponents of the system.' Those members of the late Education Commission who, though not refusing to sign their names to the recommendations of their fellow Commissioners, signed them with the reservation that to the principle of State-intervention in this matter they were still opposed, confess that while the action of the majority of their own body was at variance with their wishes, the present action of the Committee of Council is quite in conformity with them. 'It is a step in the right direction,' says Mr. Miall. 'The penny will become a halfpenny, the halfpenny will become a farthing, and the farthing nothing at all.'

We will not stop here to ask how it is that the Education Department should itself have promulgated a Code such as those most hostile to the very existence of that department would have been glad to promulgate had they possessed the power. The secretary who drew up the new Code should have been Mr. Miall;[59] the vice-president who defended it should have been Mr. Baines.[60] But this is a mere question of persons. What we are here concerned to ask, what the general reader will care to know is, on what grounds the reduction to be effected by the new Code is proposed; why its authors have been, as they profess, induced to make it.

2.—These grounds are the following. 'The duty of a State in public education is,' it is said,[61] 'when clearly defined, to obtain the greatest possible quantity of reading, writing, and arithmetic for the greatest number.' These are, so far as the State is concerned, 'the education of the people.' To obtain the greatest possible quantity of these is 'the requirement of a State'; and to attempt to give this greatest possible quantity is 'to attempt to give as much as the State can be expected to give.' To give this is 'the one thing which the elementary schools of the State are bound to do, just as the one thing a brewer is bound to do is to make good beer.' But the State has hitherto given more than this. It has paid for a machinery of instruction extending itself to many other things besides this. It has thus been paying for discipline, for civilization, for religious and moral training, for a superior instruction to clever and forward children—all of them matters quite out of its province to pay for: it has not exclusively kept its grants for the matters exclusively meriting them, the reading, writing, and arithmetic.

In thus acting, the State has of course been extravagant. But not only has it been extravagant, inasmuch as it has been paying for what it had no business to pay for: by attending to this it has relaxed its attention to those elementary matters which alone concerned it. These have suffered in consequence. While inspectors were reporting on the tone and general influence of a school, on the discipline and behaviour of the children, on the geography and history of the first class, the indispensable elements, the reading, writing, and arithmetic, were neglected.

The Education Commission reported[62] 'that the children attend long enough to afford an opportunity of teaching them to read, write, and cipher; but that a large proportion of them, in some districts, do not even learn to read; that they do not write well; and that they learn their arithmetic in such a way as to be of little practical use in after life.' They declared their opinion that, 'even under the present conditions of school age and attendance, it would be possible for at least *three-fifths* of the children on the books of the schools to learn to read and write without conscious difficulty, and to perform such arithmetical operations as occur in the ordinary business of life.' They came to the conclusion that 'the existing system has hitherto educated successfully only one-fourth of its pupils.' Seven-twentieths of the present body of scholars in our State-aided schools ought to read, write, and cipher well, who do not.

At the same time, the Commissioners bore the strongest testimony to the superiority of these schools in discipline, in method, in general instruction, to all elementary schools not aided by the State.

Well then, it was said, here has the State been creating a system which 'suits admirably in all points but one, but that one unfortunately is *the education of the people.*' It was proposed to cure the error by paying solely for the reading, writing, and arithmetic actually taught, and by lowering the standard of instruction. The 'principles involved in the Code which are really worth contending for, are', it was declared, '*payment by results*; requiring all managers to make their own terms with teachers, and *the lowering the standard of popular education.*'

But we must remark here that another 'principle' also was said to be 'involved' in the new Code, along with these principles of payment by results and lowering the standard of popular education. This other principle is no less than—what do our readers think?— 'the *extending more widely the area and benefit* of popular education.' This, they will naturally say, is a most important addition. This 'principle' is undoubtedly, if it be involved in the new Code, one well 'worth contending for.' And it therefore urgently behoves us to be well assured whether it is really involved in the new Code or no; for we may be very sure that the two points on which, in the House of Commons, the framers of the Code will chiefly rely for winning to it the support of the country gentlemen, and indeed of that large body of members with fair intentions but without special acquaintance with the subject, whose votes must decide the fate of the new scheme, will be these—1. That the Code will repress the exorbitant pretensions of schoolmasters, and reduce the over-ambitious instruction of their highest classes; 2. *That it will carry instruction into the 'waste places' of the country*, and, in Dr. Vaughan's words, 'extend the advantages of education, to a certain though limited amount, to a larger number than heretofore.'

Now the plain truth is, that to hold out this expectation that the new Code will extend the advantages of education to the waste places of the country, to places too poor or too neglected to obtain these advantages under the present system, is to hold out an expectation utterly and entirely delusive. Its framers should be challenged to prove *how* the new Code will do this. We hope they will be pressed very closely on this point. The present system, they will keep saying—Mr. Lowe said it the other day[63]—leaves untouched many of the most necessitous places in the country; it helps most those who can best help themselves. True, let them be answered, this is a just reproach to bring against the old system; *only show us how your new system will in this respect do better*. 'Somebody or other must gain', it is said, 'by a redistribution in which so many are said to lose.' But this is not a case of *redistribution*, but of reduction. Two-fifths of the sum at present contributed by the State to the support of schools for the poor are to be suddenly taken away. Why *must* 'somebody or other,' among the maintainers of such schools, gain by this? On the contrary, Archdeacon Sinclair declares, '*everybody* loses.' And so far are the 'waste places' of the country from gaining, that they will be among the heaviest losers. We assert this deliberately; let the framers of the Revised Code disprove it if they can. Take the very type of a 'waste place:' some remote rural village in Wiltshire or Nottinghamshire, with a school of about forty children; the school of this place would obtain from the Committee of Council under the Revised Code annual assistance to the amount of £10; at the present moment it can obtain from them, without having to fulfil one condition which it would not have to fulfil under the Revised Code, and the attendance of the scholars being reckoned as precisely the same in both cases—it can obtain £30. Let the country gentleman who complains that the present system leaves poor and remote districts untouched, while it lavishes its aid on wealthy centres of population, and who hopes for some amendment in this respect from the new Code, behold the amendment which he will actually obtain!

The principles really involved in the new Code remain, therefore, those stated above—*payment by results*, those results being understood to be good reading, good writing, and good arithmetic, the proper 'requirement of a State' from the schools which it aids; and the lopping off of all payments hitherto made for anything else. In other words, *reduction* and a *prize-scheme*.

The proposal of the Royal Commissioners had been very different. They had proposed two grants; one of them to be paid, as at present, for the general maintenance of the school and its machinery if these were such as to deserve maintaining at all; in other words, 'in consideration of the discipline, efficiency, and general character of the school,'—of all those matters not touched by an individual examination of the scholars in reading, writing, and arithmetic,—duly attested by the inspector; the other, like the new sole grant established by the Revised Code, to be paid in direct reward of proficiency, proved by examination, of individual scholars in the three branches of instruction, supposed to be suffering—'in consideration of the attainment of a certain degree of knowledge in reading, writing, and arithmetic.' Thus the Royal Commissioners proposed two grants: a *maintenance-grant* and a *prize-grant*. But the money for one of these grants they proposed to raise by a rate. An education-rate it is, or is supposed to be, impossible at present to introduce in this country; so one of the two grants proposed by the Commissioners the Privy Council authorities resolved to abandon. They selected for sacrifice that one which from all their own previous practice and traditions they might have been expected to retain, the *maintenance-grant;* a contribution, not in the nature of prizes for the proficiency, in certain subjects, of individual scholars, but in the nature of assistance towards the payment of teachers, towards the general support of the school. They adopted, as henceforth their sole grant, that one which was new and foreign to their traditions and practice, the *prize-grant.* No aid was henceforth to be given towards the maintenance of teachers, the support of the school, in consideration of the school's 'discipline, efficiency, and general character;' but in consideration of each examination successfully passed before the inspector, by scholars fulfilling certain conditions of age and attendance, in reading, writing, and arithmetic, a certain reward was to be paid. This was called payment by results; and the reduction of two-fifths on the total contribution of the State will arise from limiting the State's contribution to a payment for reading, writing, and arithmetic only, and only for proved proficiency in these.

It is sometimes alleged, indeed, that the aid of the State will still, under the Revised Code, be partly given in consideration of the 'discipline, efficiency, and general character' of the school, inasmuch as on the inspector's unfavourable report of these, one-half of the grant which we have called the prize-grant may be stopped. But this allegation is really, when closely looked into, quite illusory; as illusory as the allegation that the new Code will carry instruction into the waste places of the country, now neglected. It amounts to this; that the elementary schools of England, already mulcted by the new Code of two-fifths of the sum which they formerly received for maintaining their discipline, efficiency, and good general character, may be mulcted one and a half-fifth more, if, with their reduced rate of aid, they fail still to maintain these. This is not the old payment for maintaining these matters; it is a new penalty for not maintaining them. The sole objects judged worthy of the grants of the State are the reading, writing, and arithmetic; but of these grants part is forfeited if the objects no longer deemed worthy of State-grants are not provided for all the same. Singular encouragement for these latter! Religion, according to Mr. Lowe's latest revision of his plan, is to be *encouraged* in a similar manner; that is, some more of the grant is to be forfeited if the religious instruction is found to have been neglected. These forfeitures, however, will seldom be pronounced. Inspectors are, after all, human; and where so much aid has been stopped already, an inspector will probably try very hard not to see anything which might force him to stop more.

State-aid to popular education diminished in amount, and administered under the conditions of a prize-scheme for proved proficiency in reading, writing, and arithmetic, on the plea that the State has hitherto been paying for matters with which it has no concern, that 'the greatest quantity of reading, writing, and arith-

metic for the greatest number' is 'the requirement of
the State,' is, so far as the State is concerned, 'the
education of the people;' on the plea that this State-
requirement has hitherto been ill satisfied because
attention was not exclusively enough given to it, that it
will be satisfied better when attention is concentrated
upon it and withdrawn from supererogatory matters;
—this is in fact, stripped of all official details and plainly
expressed, the meaning of the original Revised Code.
We have now to examine the merit of these pleas.

3.—We will take the last plea first. It is founded on
the declaration of the Royal Commissioners that a very
large proportion of the scholars, even in inspected
schools, carry very little instruction away with them;
that even under the present conditions of school-age
and attendance a much greater number of children
might 'learn to read and write without conscious
difficulty, and to perform such arithmetical operations
as occur in the ordinary business of life;' that, in fact,
'so many as seven-twentieths of the children ought to
learn as much as this, even under the present conditions,
who do not.' Now, is this true? About the fact, that a
very large proportion of the scholars, even in inspected
schools, carry very little instruction away with them
when they leave school, there can be no doubt: the
inspectors themselves declare it; the Royal Commissioners are careful to assure us that they assert this on
the authority of the inspectors themselves, and not on
that of their own Assistant-Commissioners. But what
are we to say to the next assertion of the Royal Commissioners, that, this fact being granted, it is, even under
the present conditions of school-age and attendance,
remediable; that even now seven-twentieths of the
scholars ought to learn to read, write, and cipher much

better than they do? As to the truth of this second
assertion, there is by no means the same agreement.
School-teachers deny it, school-managers deny it, Sir
James Shuttleworth denies it, the most experienced of
the inspectors deny it. They declare the fact of the
ignorance in which so many poor children, after passing
through our elementary schools, still remain; but they
give an explanation of this fact which is not that of
the Royal Commissioners. 'We know this,' says Mr
Watkins,[64] '*and we know also the cause*. It is the short-
ness of school-life. You cannot cram into the space of
two or three years the instruction which ought to
occupy five or six. Yet this is what is being done now,
and must be done so long as the present inexorable demands of labour continue.' The Royal Commissioners,
however, will not admit such an explanation as this;
they attribute the ignorance complained of to other
causes; to the neglect of the lower classes of his school
by the master, to his over-ambitious teaching of the
higher classes, to his imperfect teaching of the elementary parts of instruction, reading, writing, and arithmetic, to all. They say that reading, writing, and
arithmetic might be much better taught than they are
now, and to a much greater number. Who is in the
right, and where lies the real truth in this matter?

Everything depends here upon a rigid exactitude in
the use of terms. And there has been, on the contrary,
much laxity. Sir James Shuttleworth and others have
shown with triumph, from the reports of the inspectors,
that a vastly greater proportion of scholars than that
given by the Commissioners, are returned as reading,
writing, and ciphering fairly or well. It has been
retorted with equal triumph that this only proves how
fallacious these reports of the inspectors are; for this

proportion, calculated from their reports, is quite inconsistent with the state of imperfect instruction known to exist, and indeed admitted elsewhere by the inspectors themselves. The truth is, the terms *fair* and *good*, when applied to the reading, writing, and arithmetic of our elementary schools, are not always used in precisely the same sense, and do not carry, to the minds of all who hear them used, precisely the same impression.

We wish to avoid all unnecessary detail, so we will illustrate this from the case of reading only. If, when we speak of a scholar reading fairly or well, we merely mean that reading in his accustomed lesson-book, his provincial tone and accent being allowed for, his want of home-culture and refinement being allowed for, some inevitable interruptions in his school attendance being allowed for, he gets through his task fairly or well, then a much larger proportion of scholars in our inspected schools than the one-fourth assigned by the Royal Commissioners, may be said to ready fairly or well. And this is what the inspectors mean when they return scholars as reading fairly or well. Such reading as this might honestly be said to meet sufficiently the requirement of the Commissioners that a scholar shall 'read without conscious difficulty.' Holding the Commissioners fast to this expression of theirs, we may safely assert that—whatever may be the value of their assertion that as many of the scholars as three-fifths *may be* taught, even under the present conditions of school age and attendance, to 'read without conscious difficulty'— the assertion that as few of the scholars as one-fourth *are actually* at present taught so to read is completely erroneous.

But the truth is, the Commissioners presently shift

their terms a little. In order to read *fairly* or *well*, it is no longer enough to read *without conscious difficulty;* it is necessary to read *in an intelligent manner*.

It is necessary, to use Dr. Vaughan's words, that the scholar shall be able to *read the Bible with intelligence;* it is necessary, to use the words of one of the ablest and most ardent of the Assistant-Commissioners—Mr. Fraser—that he shall be able to *read the newspaper with sufficient ease to be a pleasure to himself and to convey information to listeners*. The Commissioners, in adopting these words, no longer confine themselves to the requirement that the scholar shall *read without conscious difficulty*; they understand by fair or good reading something more than this. They abandon what may be called the scholastic and professional acceptation of these terms; they adopt the acceptation of them current in the world and among the educated classes.

Now if it is understood by the assertion that a child in an elementary school reads fairly or well, that he reads in an intelligent manner, that he can read the Bible with intelligence, that he can read the newspaper sufficiently well to be a pleasure to himself and his hearers, then no doubt the inspectors, in reporting so large a proportion of children in inspected schools as reading fairly or well, have asserted what is most untrue. If this is what is understood by reading fairly or well, the Commissioners, in declaring that not more than one-fourth of the children in inspected schools now read fairly or well, have asserted what is most true. Whether they are equally right in asserting that at least three-fifths of them *ought*, even under present conditions, to learn to read fairly or well in this sense, is quite another question.

But the inspectors have themselves given the clearest

proof that they at least do not use the terms *fairly* or *well* in this absolute sense. Mr. Norris,[65] who has been much quoted on this point, expressly tells us that the newspaper-test is one which he has applied only in his good schools, and that even these good schools failed to stand it. 'Where I found a school *much above par in reading*,' he says, 'I tested the *first class* by giving them a newspaper and telling them to read aloud some paragraph; but in not more than 20 out of 169 schools did I find a first class able to read a newspaper at sight.' He, at any rate, does not mean when he says that a poor child goes through his reading-lesson well or fairly, can read without conscious difficulty, that he is an *intelligent* reader, can *read the newspaper so as to give pleasure to himself and others*. He knows very well, as all persons know who are familiar with the poor and their life, and who do not take their standards from the life of the educated classes, that the goodness of a poor child's reading is something relative, that absolute standards are here out of place.

The Commissioners are certainly mistaken if they imagine that three-fifths of the children in our elementary schools can, under the present conditions, be brought to read *fairly* or *well* in the absolute sense, which, by slightly shifting their terms, they have come to attach to these words. What renders impossible the attainment by so many of a power so considerable—a power which is a real lasting acquirement for the whole life—is the utter want of care for books and knowledge in the homes from which the great majority of them come forth, to which the great majority of them return; in a word, the general want of civilization in themselves and in those among whom they pass their lives. It is the advance of them and their class in civilization which will

bring them nearer to this power, not the confining them
to reading-lessons, not the striking out lessons on
geography or history from the course of our elementary
schools. Intelligent reading—reading such as to give
pleasure to the reader himself and to his hearers—is a
very considerable acquirement; it is not very common
even among the children of the rich and educated class.
When children in this class possess it, they owe it not to
the assiduity with which they have been taught reading
and nothing but reading, but partly to natural aptitude,
far more to the civilizing and refining influences, the
current of older and educated people's ideas and knowledge, in the midst of which they have been brought up.
It may safely be said that the religious teaching and the
general information given in schools for the poor supply
—most imperfectly indeed, but still in some sort or
other supply—a kind of substitute for this current, the
loss of which would do harm to those mechanical parts
of instruction on which it is now proposed to lay
exclusive stress. Some remarks in the *Guardian* newspaper bring this out very well. 'Reading', it is there
said, 'is not a merely mechanical art; good reading
requires many of the qualities of good oratory; nor will
the most elaborate drill enable dullness and ignorance to
wear the appearance of intelligent skill. The *general
intellectual cultivation* which in late years we have all
been promoting in schools is the best preparation for
such reading as will please and interest reader and
hearer alike.' And the Commissioners themselves
quote the case of a school at Greenwich, in which
backward readers, kept to reading-lessons only, were
found to make less progress even in reading than others
equally backward whose lessons were of a more varied
cast. The most experienced inspectors, too, declare that

the schools in which the general instruction is best are precisely the schools in which the elementary instruction is best also.

The Commissioners, therefore, probably overestimated both the actual neglect of elementary instruction in schools for the poor, and the possible improvement in it which the creating a prize-grant exclusively for proficiency in this instruction might bring about. But after all, the Commissioners proposed still to keep what we have called the *maintenance-grant*—the grant by which aid is given to a school not as a mere machine for teaching reading, writing, and arithmetic, but as a living whole with complex functions, religious, moral, and intellectual. So far as a school by its full and efficient discharge of all these functions acts beneficially on the elementary instruction, the Commissioners helped it still so to act; for they proposed still to assist the school in the full and efficient discharge of all of them. But the same cannot be said of the framers of the Revised Code, who withdraw the subsidy altogether, and leave only a system of prizes for three particular subjects. Yet an advocate of this Code—the Assistant-Commissioner whom we have already quoted, Mr. Fraser—has published a pamphlet,[66] of which the whole scope is this—that the new Code really tends to promote the acquirement of general information in schools, certainly will not tend to discourage it, because (as we have already shown) good reading is impossible without general information and intelligence. Was there ever such reasoning heard of? If for the very object you have in view, good reading, cultivation in other subjects is necessary, why cut off all grants for these subjects in the hope of thereby getting better reading? How are you thus brought one step nearer to the end you have in view? How are you not rather pushed several steps farther back from it? The schools even with these auxiliary subjects encouraged by your grants have failed to produce reading good enough to satisfy you, and you hope, by discouraging these, to make them produce better. Thus it turns out that by persisting to teach just what you rebuke them for teaching, the schools are to produce the result which you desire! And when, in spite of your rebuke, in spite of the withdrawal of your grants, they have persisted in giving some general cultivation, as that without which good reading is impossible, you turn round and assure them that after all the best friends of this general cultivation are yourselves!

This plea, then, for the change introduced by the Revised Code—that elementary instruction has suffered from the undue attention given to higher instruction, that it will be amended by concentrating upon it the exclusive encouragement of the State—cannot stand. We pass to the other plea, that the State has hitherto been paying for matters with which it has no concern; that the requirement of the State from the schools which it aids is the greatest possible quantity of reading, writing, and arithmetic for the greatest number, and this alone.

Mr. Cumin, perhaps the cleverest of the Assistant-Commissioners, declares that the parents of our poor scholars care solely for good elementary instruction for their children, that they care nothing about the higher instruction generally superadded to this, that the higher instruction is due to the ambitiousness of the teacher or to the requirements of the Privy Council Office. A little more experience would have convinced Mr. Cumin that this is often by no means so. A little more experience would have shown him teachers and managers struggling with difficulty against the demand for ornamental accomplishments for their children by parents who imagine that these tend to make ladies and gentlemen of them; it would have shown him teachers excusing themselves for teaching geography in their lower classes by the plea that if they did not teach something of this kind the parents would remove their children to private schools which professed to teach more subjects; it would have shown him the scholars of the highest class themselves putting a pressure upon the master to teach them mathematics or French or even Latin. He would have found that one of the most successful baits by which private schools, more expensive and less efficient, draw scholars away from public schools, is the lure of a more ambitious programme. There is a great deal of folly in all this; but the source of it lies in something natural and respectable—the strong desire of the lower classes to raise themselves. The faults of the teachers themselves, so visible, so pardonable, and so little pardoned, proceed from this desire. It is by no means clear to us that this effort of the humbler classes towards a higher stage of civilization deserves no assistance from the State. It certainly requires direction, and the only way of obtaining the right to give it direction is to give it some assistance. The present, however, is an unpropitious time for dwelling on this topic. That tide of reactionary sentiment against everything supposed to be in the least akin to democracy which, in presence of the spectacle offered by America, is now sweeping over Europe, it is useless at this moment to try to stem. *Now is your hour and the power of darkness.*[67] Democracy, by its faults and extravagances, has almost deserved even so undiscriminating a reaction. But while forbearing at this inauspicious time to press the claims of the higher instruction of the lower classes upon State-encouragement,* let the friends of these claims steadily refuse to ignore them. When a writer in *Blackwood's Magazine*[68] contemptuously tells the parish schoolmaster that 'if he thinks that the men whom the State wants for "cutting and polishing" the little boys and girls of the labouring classes are those who claim a social equality with surgeons and lawyers, he very much mistakes the feeling of the country,' let us remind him that Coleridge, certainly no levelling Radical, desired 'a schoolmaster in every parish who in due time, and under condition of a faithful performance of his arduous duties, *should succeed to the pastorate*, so that both he and the pastor should be labourers in different compartments of the same field, *with such difference of rank as might be suggested in the names pastor and sub-pastor, or as now exists between rector and curate*'.[69] Let us repeat the wise admonition of M. de Rémusat[70] to the upper classes, uttered only the other day: 'Attaquez avec courage tous les problèmes de l'avenir de la société où le sort vous a placés, *en pénétrant avec intelligence et avec sympathie dans les sentiments qui l'animent et dans les pensées qui la guident, en formant avec elle ces liens de solidarité morale sans lesquels tous les avantages de l'éducation ou de la fortune excitent l'envie et ne donnent pas l'influence.*'

But, whatever may be the case as to the higher instruction, it is surely beyond a doubt that the 'discipline, efficiency, and general character' of its

---

* 'The poor man's child,' says the excellent President of the Wesleyan Education Committee, Mr Scott, in his letter to Lord Granville,' *deserves a better education than this new regulation will give.*'

elementary schools are 'requirements of a State,' as well as the successful teaching of reading, writing, and arithmetic. Yet for these, to which the Royal Commissioners expressly devoted a grant from the State, the Revised Code gives nothing. Two-fifths of the money which now goes to maintain these, it takes away, on the plea that even with this reduction good reading, writing, and arithmetic may be sufficiently encouraged; and that, when these have been sufficiently encouraged, the State has nothing more to do. Limit the State's duty, in the schools of the nation, to offering a capitation grant for every good reader, writer, and cipherer? You might as well limit the State's duty, in the prisons of the nation, to the offering a capitation grant for every reformed criminal! But in prisons, it will be said, the State has another interest besides the reformation of the criminal—the protection of society. We answer: And so, too, in schools the State has another interest besides the encouragement of reading, writing, and arithmetic —*the protection of society*. It has an interest in them so far as they keep children out of the streets, so far as they teach them—the dull as well as the clever—an orderly, decent, and human behaviour; so far as they civilize the neighbourhood where they are placed. It owes to its schools for the poor something more than *prizes*, it owes them *help for maintenance*. It owes them that very *subsidy* which Mr. Lowe is so indignant at now giving, and so impatient to withdraw. Whether this help is bestowed in the form of a contribution towards the payment of the teachers, or in that of a contribution towards the general expenses of the school, matters little. But for every school-machinery which is thrown out of gear, for every glimmer of civilization which is quenched, for every poor scholar who is no longer humanized, owing to a reduction, on the plea that reading, writing, and arithmetic are all the State ought to pay for in our present State-expenditure for elementary schools, the State will be directly responsible. It will be as responsible as it would be for the harm to society of any deterioration which should be brought about in our prison-system by a reduction, on the plea that reformed criminals are all the State ought to pay for in the present expenditure for prisons.

Lord Stanley said the other day at Leeds[71] that he should be satisfied 'if three-fourths of all those who attend day-schools could be sent out into the world knowing thoroughly how to read, write, and cipher; having acquired, in addition, those habits of order, discipline, and neatness, which a well-managed school gives, and having been taught the elementary truths of religion.' Well, the State, if the Revised Code is adopted, will do something towards giving Lord Stanley satisfaction. It will give prizes for the production of good reading, writing, and ciphering. But for the formation of 'those habits of order, discipline, and neatness, which a well-managed school gives,' it will give nothing. For the inculcation of the elementary truths of religion, it will give nothing. But these, say the advocates of the Revised Code, it is the clergyman's duty to see cared for. True, it is his duty; but what a course for the State, to put a clergyman's duty at variance with his interests! Instead of strengthening his hands, it creates a temptation for him to stimulate in his parish school the secular rather than the religious instruction, and then tells him that it is his duty to overcome this temptation! Why this is as if a highwayman, who puts his pistol to your head and demands your money or your life, were to tell you at the same time that you would be a very cowardly fellow if you did not resist him. 'I should like nothing better', you might answer, 'than to show a proper spirit, and to do my duty as a man; but I should like also not to have my brains blown out for doing it.'

But even supposing that, alarmed at discovering what grave evils will follow the withdrawal of a large amount of the aid now given to elementary schools, the framers of the Revised Code were to consent to increase their Capitation Grant, so that the amount of this aid should still remain the same, the Revised Code would yet remain open to the most serious objections. The partisans of the Code at first laid great stress on its economy. But it was soon evident that they must not base its excellence on its economy alone; for a Minute abolishing all grants whatever to education would have been more economical still, and therefore more excellent. Of late, therefore, they have changed their ground a little, and all the stress is now laid on the Code's *efficiency*. The concessions just announced somewhat diminish the reduction at first threatened. 'Lord Granville and Mr. Lowe do not', we are now told,[72] 'propose to diminish the grant, or to exclude one child from a share in it. But it will henceforth be *no work, no pay*.' 'I cannot promise', says Mr. Lowe, 'that the new scheme will be economical; but if it is not economical, it will be *efficient*.' 'I am not aware', says Dr. Vaughan, 'that a positive diminution of expenditure is a prominent object of the changes proposed.' But 'who shall complain,' he asks, 'if henceforth the State should say, "What I give, I choose to give as the reward of success; of success in teaching the rudiments?"' The State, we have said, owes to its elementary schools more than 'prizes for success in teaching the rudiments;' it is a social and political blunder to confine its duty towards such schools to the duty of offering these. If, however, under the name of 'prizes for success in teaching the rudiments,' it gives as much as it formerly gave under the name of 'grants in consideration of the discipline, efficiency, and general character' of schools, the bad consequences of this social and political blunder are no doubt lessened. They are not by any means removed; for it is idle to say that when the State proclaims 'success in teaching the rudiments' to be the sole object of its rewards, other matters, really of vital importance to the State—the humanizing of that multitude of children whose home-training is defective, who are very rude, ignorant, or dull, very unlikely to obtain prizes, and whom, therefore, under the operation of such a Prize-scheme as that proposed, '*it will not pay to teach;*'*—it is idle to say that this, that the forming those 'habits of order, discipline, and neatness,' the inculcating those 'elementary truths of religion,' which Lord Stanley wishes to be formed and inculcated, will not be made in some degree secondary, will not, therefore, to some extent suffer. But even if this were not so, even should the social and political blunder entirely disappear, a great administrative blunder would remain. The State would be forced to appropriate to the *supervision* of public education much too large a proportion of its whole grant for public education; a great deal of money would have to be spent in maintaining inspectors, which would be better spent in maintaining schools. This is the inconvenience of losing sight of the State's proper business. The State's proper business in popular education, is to help in the creation and

* The words of the Memorial read by a deputation from the Educational Societies to Lord Granville.

maintenance of the schools necessary; to cause fit local bodies to be appointed with the function of watching over these schools; and, finally, itself to exercise over these bodies and their performance of their functions, a general supervision. When it goes far beyond this, when it makes its aid a system of prizes requiring the most minute and detailed examinations; when it tries to test the acquirements of every individual child to whose instruction it contributes, it goes beyond its province; it invests itself with municipal, not imperial, functions, it creates an administrative expenditure which is excessive. It is as if (to revert to our old comparison of prisons) the State, proposing to support prisons by a capitation grant on reformed criminals, had to ascertain for what criminals the grant was due. The staff of officers to conduct this minute inquisition would absorb funds which might have provided prison-discipline enough to reform scores of criminals. Even at present the cost of inspection forms a very large item in the expenditure of the Committee of Council. Under the operation of the Prize-scheme proposed by the new Code, this cost would be doubled. 'The first piece of statesmanship we have had on this subject' would be guilty of this grave administrative blunder! The last remaining friends of 'voluntary energy and spontaneity' would create a mass of State-mechanism only to be paralleled in China! Examination, we are told, is now the rule of our public service. Yes; but where, except in China, is examination the rule not only for every public servant, but for all those to whom the public servant's action extends? Yet this is the rule which Mr. Lowe institutes, by examining—not his own inspectors before appointment—but every child in the schools which these inspectors visit. This is as if the

State undertook, not only to send the exciseman before the Civil Service Commissioners, but to send before them also all the people who drink beer!

Such are the merits of the Revised Code. It will not do what it proposes to do; it will not 'extend the advantages of education to a larger number than heretofore,' and it will not remove 'the unsatisfactory state of elementary instruction in inspected schools.' It will not make the distribution of the Parliamentary grant for education 'more general and more effective.' And, even were it to do what it proposes, the means by which it proposes to do this would still be objectionable; namely, the confining the State's part in popular education to the offering 'prizes for success in teaching the rudiments', and the compelling the State to institute, in order to test this success, an immense system of individual examination.

Concocted in the recesses of the Privy Council Office, with no advice asked from those practically conversant with schools, no notice given to those who largely support schools, this new scheme of the Council Office authorities—by which they abruptly revolutionize the system which they were appointed to administer, stab in the back the ward committed to their guardianship—has taken alike their friends and enemies by surprise. Their own inspectors, education-societies, school-managers, are astounded. Their enemies, while enjoying their triumph, can hardly believe that they have obtained it so easily. They cannot refrain from scornfully complimenting the Committee of Council on the facility with which it has yielded. 'We learnt with *equal surprise and satisfaction*,' say the Edinburgh Reviewers,[73] 'the prompt and radical remedy which the Lords of the Education Committee were already prepared (as it now appears) to apply to the evils and short-comings we had endeavoured to point out. The justification of our strictures is therefore complete, since the heads of the department are so conscious of these defects that they have since promulgated a Minute which rescinds the whole of their former code of regulations, and substitutes an entirely new system for that of 1846. All that we take to be proved at present is, that *the old system is irrevocably condemned by the very persons who have administered it.*' And the reviewers applaud the new plan proposed, because it will give 'greater liberty of action to managers, more self-reliance to teachers;' not caring to add that in their opinion it is a great pity managers should not be made yet more free, and teachers yet more self-reliant, by the abolition of all State-aid to them whatever.

But they accept the Revised Code as an instalment, as the 'commencement of the end' of a system of State-aid to national education, that palpable 'defiance of the laws of supply and demand.' The enemies of such a system are relieved to discover that their own maxims are now predominant in the Council Office; that the authorities there are indeed still encumbered with 'this system of which Sir James Shuttleworth was the author,' but that they are convinced that 'it is time to halt,' to 'arrest the growth for the future of this vested interest,' which, by making State-payments to school-masters, he created. They find Mr. Lingen,[74] the Secretary, himself deprecating any further extension of the system; apprehending that it must become unmanageable, enlarging on its administrative difficulties. Sir James Shuttleworth, who knows the details of this business at least as well as Mr. Lingen, makes very short work of these administrative difficulties. A more honourable and indefatigable public servant than Mr. Lingen does not exist; but the most indefatigable man sees difficulties in a course for which he has no love. Mr. Lingen's difficulties show the presence, in the heart of the Education Department, of this want of love for the very course which such a department is created to follow.

The present heads of this department would certainly never have instituted it. They cannot well abolish it outright, but they reduce its action as much as possible. They share in their hearts the feelings of those who think the existence of such a department opposed to English habits, and undesirable. Indeed, this existence is opposed to so great a body of English habits and English prejudices, that one wonders how it ever found means to establish itself. It found them, almost entirely, in the zeal and perseverance of one man, Sir James Shuttleworth. He has been taunted with not possessing the graces of style, the skill of the literary artist; but he possesses that which is perhaps almost as useful as these, and which those who taunt him do not always exhibit—a thorough knowledge of this subject of popular education. And how comes he to know it so well? Alas! there is no royal road to knowledge in these matters; he knows it in the only way by which this subject can ever be well known—he knows it because he loves it. Statesmen—and among them Lord Lansdowne deserves to be named the first—who perhaps did not share his zeal, were yet wise and open-minded enough to see the benefits which might be wrought by it. So, in the face of immense prejudice, of angry outcry, of vehement opposition, the Education Department was established. The good which it did, reconciled to it gradually even that body, which by its nature shares most strongly the popular prejudices on this matter, which had been warmest in its opposition, loudest in its outcry—the clergy. Because they have thus outgrown a vain prejudice, the clergy are now reproached with inconsistency, with being debauched by Government grants, with 'relying too little upon personal exertion,' with 'importunately petitioning for public alms.' The old cry, so hollow, yet to the heedless so plausible, is again raised: 'It is time that our schools should be thrown back upon that mode of maintenance which is the most independent.' Independent for whom? For those for whose sake these schools exist— the poor and their children? Is a poor man more independent by receiving help from his squire or his rector towards his child's education, than by receiving it from the State? Are his reasonable wishes as to the kind of that education more likely to be respected by his local, or by his imperial benefactor? To state a commonplace like this fully, is to refute it. Experience, the best of teachers, has convinced the clergy of the hollowness of this and other like commonplaces which once deluded them. Their schools have been dearer to them than their prejudices. As they saw the change gradually worked in the country by the Education Grant—as they began to perceive the benefits for the present and future of a steady current of communication opened, for help, sympathy, and guidance, between the Government of this country and the schools of the lower classes—their prejudices were dispersed or forgotten, and the system which it is now proposed to 'simplify' until it becomes, in Mr. Miall's words, 'nothing at all,' grew precious to them. Their attachment will probably even now save it from destruction. Their experience has been a truer guide to the clergy than has their enlightenment to organs of public opinion, such as the *Guardian* or the *Spectator*, most friendly to the improvement and gradual elevation of the lower classes, but so sensitive to the faults of the present system that they are disposed to welcome the Revised Code for attacking it. To such friends of the lower classes we may well say: *You know what you do.* It is because there is something *vital* in the connection established between the State and the lower classes by the old system, that this system—with all its complication, all its expensiveness, all its mistakes, with all the false taste of many of its schoolmasters and students, all their pretentiousness, all their sciolism, all their nonsense—was yet precious; it is because the Revised Code, by destroying—under the specious pleas of simplifying, of giving greater liberty of action to managers—this vital connection, takes the heart out of the old system, that it is so condemnable.

For it withdraws from popular education, so far as it can, all serious guidance, all initiatory direction by the State; it makes the action of the State upon this as mechanical, as little dynamical, as possible. It turns the inspectors into a set of registering clerks, with a mass of minute details to tabulate, such a mass as must, in Sir James Shuttleworth's words, 'necessarily withdraw their attention from the religious and general instruction, and from the moral features of the school.' In fact the inspector will just hastily glance round the school, and then he must fall to work at the 'log-books.' And this to ascertain the precise state of each individual scholar's reading, writing, and arithmetic. As if there might not be in a school most grave matters needing inspection and correction; as if the whole school might not be going wrong, at the same time that a number of individual scholars might carry off prizes for reading, writing, and arithmetic![75] It is as if the generals of an army,—for the inspectors have been the veritable generals of the educational army,—were to have their duties limited to inspecting the men's cartouch-boxes.[76] The organization of the army is faulty;—inspect the cartouch-boxes! The camp is ill-drained, the men are ill-hutted, there is danger of fever and sickness. Never mind; inspect the cartouch-boxes! But the whole discipline is out of order, and needs instant reformation:— no matter; inspect the cartouch-boxes! But the army is beginning a general movement, and that movement is a false one; it is moving to the left when it should be moving to the right: it is going to a disaster! That is not your business; inspect, inspect the cartouch-boxes!

'But what was to be done?' cry Mr. Lowe and his friends. 'It was impossible for us,' says Mr. Lowe, 'to remain quiet under the actual imputations cast upon the system.' 'Not being able to avail itself of the suggestion of a county rate, nor yet, *in the face of a recent exposure, to ask Parliament for a large increase of the grant*, all the Committee of Council could do', say Mr. Lowe's friends, 'was to do as it has done, to *economize;* and it is in its economies that the Minute differs from the report of the Royal Commissioners.' Not quite so; it differs from it, radically, in the principle on which it makes its grants, in that it makes its grants for reading, writing, and arithmetic only, while the Royal Commissioners proposed to make theirs partly for these, but partly also for the 'discipline, efficiency, and general character' of the school. But the Committee of Council was not reduced to one of the three alternatives, of either proposing a county rate, or else asking Parliament, *in the face of a recent exposure*, for a large increase of the grant;

or else, those two courses being impossible, economiz-
ing. It might surely have made itself quite certain,
whether an *exposure* had actually befallen its system,
and to what this *exposure* amounted. It might have
made some inquiry on this matter of its own officers,
whose credit was greatly concerned. It made none. If it
had satisfied itself, as we are persuaded it might have
satisfied itself, that the Royal Commissioners had not
clearly seen the real truth of this matter of the elementary instruction; that *well* and *ill*, in this matter, are
relative terms; that of the children in our inspected
schools much more than the Commissioners' one-
fourth read well, considering their condition and
opportunities—very much less than the Commissioners'
three-fifths could be brought, with their present condition and opportunities, to read well absolutely;—if it
had explained this, if it had declared, as it might have
declared with perfect truth, that it had itself emphatically insisted on the importance of the elementary
instruction; that it had struggled for its advancement,
that it was prepared to struggle for it still;—such an
explanation, we are convinced, would have been
willingly accepted. The Committee might have proved
its sincerity by very simple administrative changes. It
had already directed its inspectors to pay special attention to the elementary instruction, but it had retained
(and still retains) its crowded programme of subjects
for examination. By striking out the great majority of
these, by reducing the subjects entered on the official
programme from twenty-three to five—religious knowledge, reading, writing, arithmetic, and *general information*—and by directing the inspector to refuse to
examine in the last if he be dissatisfied with the results
of his examination in the four others; by permitting

him to recommend *partial* stoppage of grants when thus dissatisfied (at present he can recommend entire stoppage only)—the Committee of Council, at the same time that it would have somewhat diminished its consumption of stationery (no light merit), would, we feel certain, have done far more to promote elementary instruction than the Revised Code will ever effect.

But we must not forget that we write for the general reader, and that we have promised him to avoid official details as much as possible. We will not trouble him with the very simple expedients by which, as Sir James Shuttleworth shows, the minor administrative knots which fill Mr. Lingen with such dismay—the multiplication of Post-office orders and of petty separate payments in the same school—might have been untied without the sword of the Revised Code. Nor will we discuss even more important changes which it was time to bring about, but which, like the consolidation of small payments just mentioned, might have been brought about without a revolution. The details of the Privy Council Office system have grown up gradually; some of them must have been the result of accident; all of them are fit matter for revision. It can hardly have been by the deliberate judgement of men of sagacity that that meritorious work, *Morell's Analysis of Sentences*,[77] was made the intellectual food of girls of sixteen. It can hardly have been by the deliberate judgement of men of taste that another meritorious work, *Warren's Extracts from Blackstone's Commentaries*,[78] was selected, for the astonishment of Quintilians yet unborn, to be the authorized textbook for readers, the chosen field in which the student of elocution should exhibit his powers. It must have been by an accident that those two odious words, *male* and *female* (for *man* and *woman*, *boy* and *girl*), established themselves so firmly in the vocabulary of a department charged with the propagation of humane letters and refinement, from whence they are invading the common language of the whole country, carrying into the relations of social human life the terminology of the Zoological Gardens. The Revised Code contains, we see, regulations for changing certain matters in the training of pupil-teachers and students. It must have been by an accident that these were omitted. But we will not discuss these things here. We will not discuss the organization of inspection; inspection with its sixty inspectors, all performing the independent functions and receiving something like the salary of inspectors-general, but not chosen (they are far too numerous) with the care with which inspectors-general should be chosen; not possessing (they are far too numerous) that access to their chief by which inspectors-general enlighten him as to what is really going on outside the walls of the central office;—inspection which the Revised Code reorganizes not at all, but proposes to make, by introducing a plan of immense examinations, more vast, more expensive, and more unwieldy. We will only say in passing, that we are convinced the right course to follow is not to increase the number of Privy Council Office inspectors, but rather to reduce it; that the State—instead of attempting itself to carry out a vast system of minute local examinations by means of its own inspectors in chief, highly paid and sent from a distance—should avail itself for such purposes of a local and cheaper machinery, supervising the operations of this by their own inspectors greatly reduced in number. This is what is done in Holland with signal success, and we are sure it might be done here. Our denominational system affords, indeed, peculiar facilities for it. We feel certain that in the case of National schools (which form the vast majority of those aided by the Committee of Council), the ordinary inspection of these would be perfectly well performed by the diocesan inspectors—appointed as at present, but receiving a small allowance from the Committee of Council for their travelling expenses—acting under the supervision of the Committee of Council's inspector in chief, and removeable from the Committee of Council's service (but from that only) by the Lord President. The diocesan inspectors are in general men of precisely the same age, standing and experience as the majority of the young clerical inspectors. They could hardly be asked to act under the supervision of these; but under the supervision of an inspector in chief much their superior in standing and experience they would willingly act. These inspectors in chief would have large districts, would be few in number (ten or fifteen would probably suffice for all England), might therefore be selected with great care and discrimination, and would be, like the provincial inspectors in Holland, the only salaried inspectors of the State. As in Holland, they would yearly re-inspect a certain number of the schools inspected by their local inspectors, and would maintain among these uniformity of practice and standard. At the same time, they would form a body of men not too numerous to have concert among themselves, and to communicate with the central office. Similar means might be found to provide for the inspection of British, Wesleyan, or Roman Catholic schools, which lie chiefly in or about the large towns. The inspectors at present are at once very expensive, and a mob. Under the Revised Code they will be still more expensive, and still more a mob.

Finally, we will not even discuss the much vexed question of the teachers' augmentation grants,[79] by its handling of which the Revised Code has raised such a storm. We will not attack this handling. We will even say that the teachers have not, in our opinion, either a vested interest or a legal claim. They have only what is called, in common life, *a very hard case*. We think a payment in consideration of a teacher's place in an examination for honours a bad form of help for the State's help towards school-maintenance to take. We do not think it the State's business itself to hold examinations for honours, any more than we think it its business itself to examine all the little readers in the country. We should be sorry to see less mental life and activity among the young schoolmasters, but we should be glad if this could find its vent and look for its honours (as it is beginning to look for them) in the examinations of bodies such as the London University[80] and its affiliated institutions, rather than in the examinations of a Government Department. The examinations of the Committee of Council should address themselves to ascertain a teacher's *competence* only; there we agree with the framers of the Revised Code. But we think they might have managed to establish this principle for their future operations, without wholly disregarding the hopes, the legitimate confidence, engendered by their own past operations; without throwing twenty thousand persons into despair. So, again, with the aid to training colleges. We do not blame the framers of the Revised Code for wishing to set some limits to this. The State has aided the creation of too many of these institutions, often in the wrong places, and at needless expense. Limitation was necessary. But we could wish some better means had been originally devised for accomplishing this limitation, by processes which the training colleges might have accepted, and which would not have abruptly deranged all their operations; by processes which their inventors might not have been, after all, forced to abandon.

These are matters, however, in which the Council Office authorities might perfectly well have proposed any needful changes, although it behoved them to plan such changes prudently. Everyone admits that the old system, *in its details*, was, as Mr. Lowe called it, 'a tentative, provisional, and preliminary one.' But recognising that the mind of the country was not yet ripe for the final settlement of this question of popular education, not able to adopt the country rate of the Royal Commissioners, but explaining what had been the real success of the system they administered, explaining what there was erroneous in the complaints against it, proposing certain salutary administrative changes, the Council Office authorities might, we are convinced, with the cheerful acquiescence of the country, have asked Parliament, not 'for a large increase of their grant,' but for a continuation of their former grant, for the means of carrying on their old system for the present; thus saving intact for the future the vital principle of that system,—the principle, that the State owes to schools for the poor support 'in consideration of their discipline, efficiency, and general character,' and a supervision which addresses itself, above all, to these. *Their strength was to sit still.*[81]

Instead of this, they have accepted with alacrity the first summons of their adversaries, and are cheerfully preparing to abandon all their positions. If these are ever to be reoccupied they will all have to be fought for over again. Instead of reserving this question for the future, they settle it now; by proposing a change which abandons the essential part of their old system, severs all vital connection between the State and popular education, substitutes for the idea of a *debt* and a *duty* on the State's part towards this, the idea of a *free gift*, a gratuitous boon of *prizes;* for a supervision of the whole movement of popular education,—its method, its spirit, and its tendency,—a mechanical examination of certain scholars in three branches of instruction. For to this must State-inspection inevitably dwindle, when to these the grants of the State are confined. Where the State's treasure is bestowed, there will its heart be also.[82]

But Lord Granville and Mr. Lowe have just announced certain concessions.[83] Some of these are slight, others are more important. They none of them remove the worst faults of the Code, although two of them partially correct its greatest absurdities. The framers of the Code have actually discovered that they 'pushed their principle too far when they proposed to examine infants under six years of age!' They have positively found out that to discourage the retention in school of all children over eleven years of age is not a good way of promoting popular education! From such quickness of apprehension what might not be expected? But then throughout the whole speech of the real author of this Code—Mr. Lowe—shines clearly forth the spirit which still animates him, and which makes even his concessions valueless. That spirit is a spirit of hostility to the system which he administers, and to its fundamental principles. It is in vain that he declares—to conjure[84] the alarm which he has excited—that 'he has no wish to disturb any of the fundamental principles of the present system.' With his next breath he avows that 'his only plan is to sweep away the existing system.'

Reproached with inconsistency, he explains that he only means to sweep away the *annual grants* of the present system. That is, he means to sweep away just what is essential in the present system—its *maintenance-grants*, its recognition of the State's duty to aid schools for the poor 'in consideration of their discipline, efficiency, and general character.' And this he calls 'not disturbing any fundamental principle of the present system!' We suppose he must imagine that the 'fundamental principle of the present system' is its vice-president, and that so long as that functionary subsists, the system is whole. So, again, he consents to spare the training colleges a little longer, but he consents to this unwillingly and with menaces. So, too, forced to give up his examination of infants—forced to mar in this particular the beautiful simplicity of his scheme, forced to admit into it, in some small measure, the accursed thing, the maintenance-grant, the *subsidy*—he relieves his mind by lamenting over the decay of that voluntary spirit which once regarded all State-grants with such jealousy, by intimating that, 'were he at liberty to choose abstractedly what he thought best for the education of the country,' he would have no such grants at all. He has the air of apologizing to the Voluntaries for not being able to give them perfect satisfaction. We are convinced they will receive his apologies most indulgently. His momentary bowing in the house of Rimmon[85] will be forgiven him. It is so evident that his heart is in the right place! It is so manifest that his desires are in the heaven of Voluntaryism with Mr. Baines, even though his practice be condemned to grope a little longer in the earthly gloom of State-connexion!

But of his enmity to the present system, Mr. Lowe

gave a yet more striking proof than these apologies. It is understood that the inspectors are, as a body, favourable to that system, and averse to the Revised Code: their reports are quoted in contradiction of the assumptions on which the Code is based. Mr. Lowe determined to punish them. The habits of English public life, the high tone of English public men, in general prescribe to a Minister the most punctilious consideration for those who serve under him. He spares and screens these, though it be to his own hindrance. His generosity in this respect is one of Lord Palmerston's most popular qualities; rather than resist its impulse, he has incurred on more than one occasion serious embarrassment. From no such embarrassment will Mr. Lowe suffer. With the unscrupulousness of passion—growing desperate as the dangers of his 'little subject' thickened round him—he, in his late speech, flung to the winds every restraint of official delicacy. In his Code he had sacrificed the principles of his department; in his speech he sacrificed its persons. The best part of that performance was an elaborate attack upon his own inspectors. Of this Lord Granville is incapable. But Lord Granville is not the real leader in this struggle.

What will be the issue of the discussion now impending? We have good hopes. The disposition hitherto shown by the House of Commons has been excellent; the attachment of the country at large to a system from which vast practical benefit has been derived is strong. But we are not confident. The friends of the Revised Code are numerous, resolute, and powerful. There is Mr. Lowe, a political economist of such force, that had he been by when the Lord of the harvest[86] was besought 'to send labourers into his harvest,' he would certainly have remarked of that petition that it was 'a defiance of the laws of supply and demand,' and that the labourers should be left to come of themselves. There is the *Times*, which naturally upholds Mr. Lowe. There is the *Daily News*, unable on this subject to shake off what it has shaken off on so many others, a superstitious reverence for old watchwords of those extreme Dissenters, who for the last ten years have seemed bent on proving how little the future of the country is to owe to their intelligence. There are the friends of economy at any price, always ready to check the hundreds of the national expenditure, while they let the millions go. There are the selfish vulgar of the upper classes, saying in their hearts that this educational philanthropy is all rubbish, and that the less a poor man learns except his handicraft the better. There are the clever and fastidious, too far off from its working to see the substantial benefits which a system, at all national, of popular education confers on the lower classes, but offended by its superficial faults. All these will be gratified by the triumph of the Revised Code, and they are many. And there will be only one sufferer;—*the education of the people.*

EXTRACTS FROM ARNOLD'S REPORTS ON ELEMENTARY SCHOOLS, 1852–1882

Statement of the rôle of the Inspector of Schools[87]

There is an advantage in the same Inspector, where it is possible, continuing to see the same school year after year; he acquires in this way a knowledge of it which he can never gain from a single visit, and he becomes acquainted not with the instruction and discipline only of the school, but also with its local circumstances and difficulties.

These local circumstances and difficulties, it is of advantage, no doubt, that the Inspector should know: it is a most important question, and one the necessity of a clear resolution of which becomes daily more and more apparent to me, in what manner and to what extent this knowledge should affect his report on a school to your Lordships. I constantly hear it urged that consideration for local difficulties and peculiar circumstances should induce him to withhold the notice in his report of shortcomings and failures, because these may have been caused by circumstances for which neither managers nor teacher were to blame, and because the statement of them may unfavourably affect a struggling school. There is some plausibility in this plea for silence; but it is based, I feel sure, on a misconception of what the peculiar province and duty of an Inspector is. His first duty is that of a simple and faithful reporter to your Lordships; the knowledge that imperfections in a school have been occasioned wholly or in part by peculiar local difficulties, may very properly restrain him from recommending the refusal of grants to that school; but it ought not to restrain him from recording the imperfections. It is for your Lordships to decide how far such imperfections shall subsequently be made public; but that they should be plainly stated to you by the Inspector whom you employ there can be, I think, no doubt at all. It is said that the Inspector is sent into his district to encourage and promote education in it; that often, if he blames a school, he discourages what may be, from local difficulties, a struggling effort, and an effort whose inferiority is owing to no fault of its promoters. I answer, that it is true that the Inspector is sent into his district to encourage education in it: but in what manner to encourage education? By promoting the efficiency, through the offer of advice and of pecuniary and other helps, to the individual schools which he visits in it; not by seeking to maintain by undeserved praise, or to shelter by the suppression of blame, the system, the state of things under which it is in the power of this or that local hindrance to render a school inefficient, and under which many schools are found inefficient accordingly.

A certain system may exist, and your Lordships may offer assistance to schools established under it; but you have not, surely, on that account committed yourselves to a faith in its perfect excellence; you have not pledged yourselves to its ultimate success. The business of your Inspector is not to make out a case for that system, but to report on the condition of public education as it evolves itself under it, and to supply your Lordships and the nation at large with data for determining how far the system is successful. If, for fear of discouraging voluntary efforts, Inspectors are silent respecting the deficiencies of schools—respecting the feeble support given to this school, the imperfect accommodations in another, the faulty discipline or instruction in a third, and the failure of all alike to embrace the poorest class of children—if everything is represented as hopeful and prosperous, lest a manager should be disappointed or a subscriber estranged—then a delusion is prolonged in the public mind as to the real character of the present state of things, a delusion which it is the very object of a system of public inspection, exercised by agents of the Government on behalf of the country at large, to dispel and remove. Inspection exists for the sake of finding out and reporting the truth, and for this above all.

But it is most important that all Inspectors should proceed on the same principle in this respect—that one should not conceal defects as an advocate for the schools, while another exposes them as an agent for the Government. If this happens, besides that the general picture of the state of education will be unfaithful, there is also a positive hardship inflicted on the schools which are frankly reported on; they will appear at a disadvantage compared with other schools, not because these are really in a better state, but because the statement of their defects is softened down or altogether suppressed.

It is an ungrateful task to seem to deprecate, under any circumstances, consideration and indulgence. But consideration and indulgence, the virtues of the private man, may easily become the vices of the public servant; and I have ventured to submit the foregoing remarks to your Lordships because I think that in the inspection of schools there is a peculiar temptation to exercise these qualities unduly. A factory or a workhouse is, to most people, a less interesting and attaching object than a school; it has less power of making a friend of its visitor, and of leading him, often half insensibly, to become its advocate rather than its reporting Inspector. The character of school inspection, too, is, it appears to me, at present such as to render difficult the adoption of a uniform principle in reporting by all the Inspectors. The inspection of a school is now, upon a plan founded when a far smaller number of schools were under your Lordship's supervision than at present, carried out into such detail as to afford every facility to an Inspector, desirous to give a favourable report upon a school, for doing so, by enabling him to call attention to special points of detail in which the school may be strong, rather than to others where it may be weak, or to its general efficiency, which may be small. At present, for instance, an Inspector finding an advanced upper class in a school, a class working sums in fractions, decimals, and higher rules, and answering well in grammar and history, constructs, half insensibly whether so inclined or not, but with the greatest ease if so inclined, a most favourable report on a school, whatever may be the character of the other classes which help to compose it. But it is evident that the attention of your Lordships is especially concentrated on those other classes, and that an elementary school excites your interest principally as it deals with these; as it deals with the mass of children who, remaining but a short time at school, and having few or no advantages at home, can acquire little but rudimentary instruction; not as it deals with the much smaller number, whose parents can enable them to remain long at school, to pursue their studies at home, to carry on their education, in short, under favourable circumstances, and who therefore less need the care and assistance of your Lordships.

The difficulty of obtaining an exact report on a school is still further complicated, if the Inspector is to think himself bound to ascertain (in a single morning) what is called the moral tone of a school, and to make the condition in which he imagines himself to have found this tell considerably upon the character of his report.

Should a state of things ever arise which placed a very greatly increased number of schools under your Lordship's supervision; should your Inspectors ever have to work under a really national system of education; the range of details to which their attention in inspecting each particular school is now addressed would no doubt be necessarily narrowed. Variety of judgement would then be less probable, when that which had to be judged of was less various. They would then, perhaps, have to look only to certain broad and ascertainable things: on the one hand, the commodiousness of the school buildings, the convenience of the school fittings, the fulfilment of the necessary sanitary conditions; on the other the competence of the teacher, the efficiency of the discipline, the soundness of the *elementary* secular, and (in certain cases) of the *elementary* religious instruction. But they would not occupy themselves in inquiring with what success the three or four head boys (sons, probably, of tradesmen in good circumstances) out of a school of 100 or 150 children, could work an equation, or refer words to their Greek or Latin constituents.

Until this time arrives (if it ever should arrive) the true duty of an Inspector towards your Lordships, the truest kindness towards the managers and teachers of schools, seems to me to be this—that the Inspector, keeping his eye above all upon the most tangible and cognisable among those details into which he is directed to inquire, and omitting, as much as possible, the consideration of what is not positive and palpable, should construct a plain matter-of-fact report upon each school which he visits, and should place it, without suppression, before your Lordships. But, although I thus press for the most unvarnished and literal report on their schools, I can assure the teachers of them that it is from no harshness or want of sympathy towards them that I do so. No one feels more than I do how laborious is their work, how trying at times to the health and spirits, how full of difficulty even for the best; how much fuller for those, whom I too often see attempting the work of a schoolmaster—men of weak health and purely studious habits, who betake themselves to this profession, as affording the means to continue their favourite pursuits: not knowing, alas, that for all but men of the most singular and exceptional vigour and energy, there are no pursuits more irreconcilable than those of the student and of the schoolmaster. Still, the quantity of work actually done at present by teachers is immense: the sincerity and devotedness of much of it is even affecting. They themselves will be the greatest gainers by a system of reporting which clearly states what they do and what they fail to do; not one which drowns alike success and failure, the able and the inefficient, in a common flood of vague approbation.

(1854)

The effect of the Revised Code on the work of the Inspectorate

The great school event of the year has, of course, been the introduction, in the latter half of it, of the new system of examinations prescribed by the Revised

Code. I have not hitherto applied to your Lordships for any help in conducting these examinations in my district, but have, so far, accomplished them all myself, because I was anxious fully to observe their working. I have not to make any remarks upon their financial working, its effect upon schools, and its acceptability to managers. I confine myself entirely to their practical working as a system of school *examinations*, and to points in which they make the inspection of a school now a different matter from what it used to be formerly.

It might have been wished and intended, perhaps, that the old inspection should take place just as before, and that the examination should be merely a new thing super-added to it. Practically this is not so, and I think, without a very large increase in the body of Inspectors, and a strict discrimination of their separate kinds of function, it cannot be so; practically the old inspection tends, and I think will tend more and more, to disappear. I am speaking of the old inspection considered as an agency for testing and promoting the intellectual force of schools, not as an agency for testing and promoting their discipline and their good building, fitting, and so on. For their discipline and for their material suitability, the new system furnishes the same or nearly the same means of care as the old one. For their intellectual force it furnishes no longer the same means of care, but a different one; I do not say a means of care less valuable or not more valuable than that furnished by the old inspection, but a different one. It is important to point out this difference, in order that one undoubtedly useful sort of care which inspection used to provide for the intellectual progress of schools, but which it provides no longer, or in a much lesser degree than formerly, the managers may take measures to provide in some other way.

Inspection under the old system meant something like the following. The Inspector took a school class by class. He seldom heard each child in a class read, but he called out a certain number to read, picked at random as specimens of the rest; and when this was done he questioned the class with freedom, and in his own way, on the subjects of their instruction. As you got near the top of a good school these subjects became more numerous; they embraced English grammar, geography, and history, for each of which the Inspector's report contained a special entry, and the examination then often acquired much variety and interest. The whole life and power of a class, the fitness of its composition, its handling by the teacher, were well tested; the Inspector became well acquainted with them, and was enabled to make his remarks on them to the head teacher; and a powerful means of correcting, improving, and stimulating them was thus given. In the hands of an able Inspector...this means was an instrument of great force and value.

The new examination groups the children by its standards, not by their classes; and however much we may strive to make the standards correspond with the classes, we cannot make them correspond at all exactly. The examiner, therefore, does not take the children in their own classes. The life and power of each class as a whole, the fitness of its composition, its handling by the teacher, he therefore does not test. He hears every child in the group before him read, and so far his examination is more complete than the old inspection. But he does not question them; he does not, as an examiner under the rule of the six standards, go beyond .

the three matters, reading, writing, and arithmetic, and the amount of these three matters which the standards themselves prescribe; and, indeed, the entries for grammar, geography, and history, have now altogether disappeared from the forms of report furnished to the inspector. The nearer, therefore, he gets to the top of the school the more does his examination, in itself, become an inadequate means of testing the real attainments and intellectual life of the scholars before him. Boys who have mastered vulgar fractions and decimals, who know something of physical science and geometry, a good deal of English grammar, of geography, and history, he hears read a paragraph, he sees write a paragraph, and work a couple of easy sums in the compound rules or practice. As a stimulus to the intellectual life of the school—and the intellectual life of a school is the intellectual life of its higher classes— this is as inefficient as if Dr Temple (to recur to him again for illustration), when he goes to inspect his fifth form, were just to hear each boy construe a sentence of delectus, conjugate one Latin verb, and decline two Greek substantives.

I know that the aim and object of the new system of examination is not to develop the higher intellectual life of an elementary school, but to spread and fortify, in its middle and lower portions, the instruction in reading, writing, and arithmetic, supposed to be suffering. I am not contesting the importance of this subject, or the adequacy of the means offered by the new examination for attaining it. I am only pointing out the real value of a certain mode of operation on schools which the old inspection undoubtedly supplied, and which the new examination does not and by its nature cannot supply.

It will be said that we must conjoin the old inspection with the new examination; undoubtedly we must so far as we can. But I think no one who is much acquainted with schools and examinations will imagine that we can do this at all completely. The whole school felt, under the old system, that the prime aim and object of the Inspector's visit was, after insuring the fulfilment of certain sanitary and disciplinary conditions, to test and quicken the intellectual life of the school. The scholars' thoughts were directed to this object, the teacher's thoughts were directed to it, the Inspector's thoughts were directed to it. The scholars and teacher co-operated therefore with the Inspector in doing their best to reach it: they were anxious for his judgement on their highest progress, anxious to profit by this judgement after he was gone. At present the centre of interest for the school when the inspector visits it is changed. Scholars and teacher have their thoughts directed straight upon the new examination, which will bring, they know, such important benefit to the school if it goes well, and bring it such important loss if it goes ill. On the examination day they have not minds for anything else. If it were possible for the Inspector to make the old inspection, unaltered so far as he was concerned, precede the new examination, it would no longer be the same inspection, for he would no longer have the children's spirit in it, and without this he could no longer make the same test of their intellectual life; he would no longer have the master's whole interest and attention in it, and without these he would no longer criticize and counsel with profit, and so be able to stimulate the school's intellectual life for the future. I think, if the peculiar valuable effect of the old inspection is to be retained, this inspection ought, on these grounds, to be disjoined from the new examination.

But on other, and purely material grounds, it *must* be disjoined from it. The new examination is in itself a less exhausting business than the old inspection to the person conducting it; it does not make a call as that did upon his spirit and inventiveness; but it takes up much more time, it throws upon him a mass of minute detail, and severely tasks hand and eye to avoid mistakes. Few can know till they have tried what a business it is to enter in a close-ruled schedule, as an examination goes on, three marks for three different things against the names of 200 children whom one does not know one from the other, without putting the wrong child's mark in the wrong place. Few can know how much delay and fatigue is unavoidably caused before one can get one's 600 communications fairly accomplished, by difficulty of access to children's places, difficulty in seeing clearly in the obscurer parts of the schoolroom, difficulty of getting children to speak out—sometimes of getting them to speak at all—difficulty of resisting, without feeling oneself inhuman, the appealing looks of master or scholars for a more prolonged trial of a doubtful scholar. Then there are inquiries and returns to be made by the Inspector about log-book, portfolio, accounts, pupil-teachers' engagement and stipends, which had not to be made formerly. An inquiry has just been added respecting the means and position in life of school children's parents, to discover whether they are proper objects of State aid. All this makes the new examination a business of so much time and labour, as to deprive the Inspector of the needful freshness and spirit (to conduct the old inspection properly needed a good deal of spirit) for joining with it, on the same occasion, the old inspection. If I insist on this, it is that I may exhort managers themselves to supply, in case of need, a mode of stimulus to their schools, which was very useful to them. The clergy, who are the usual managers of National schools, could probably supply what is wanted without difficulty; and I think the managers of British and Wesleyan schools, with a little exertion and good-will, might find means to supply it to their schools also.

I have been struck by one result of the practical working of the new examinations which I am sure your Lordships never intended. I mean the peculiar severity with which they tell upon the younger classes in a school owing to the timidity natural to this age. When a boy of eleven or twelve years of age is so shy that he cannot open his mouth before a stranger, one may without harshness say that he ought to have been taught better and refuse him his grant; but when a child of seven is in this predicament one can hardly, without harshness, say the same thing, and to refuse him his grant for a timidity which is not, in his case, a school fault, seems to be going beyond the intention of your Lordships, who designed the refusal of your grants to be a punishment for school faults.

The attention which has been drawn by the Revised Code to the elementary subjects of reading, writing, and arithmetic has already had the happiest effect in improving the quality of school reading books. At last the compilers of these works seem beginning to understand that the right way of teaching a little boy to read is not by setting him to read such sentences as these (I quote from school works till lately much in vogue): 'the crocodile is viviparous', 'quicksilver, antimony, calamine, zinc, etc., are metals', 'the slope of a desk is oblique, the corners of the door are angles'; or the right way of teaching a big boy to read better, to set him to read: 'some time after one meal is digested we feel again the sensation of hunger, which is gratified by again taking food'; 'most towns are supplied with water and lighted by gas, their streets are paved and kept clean, and guarded by policemen'; 'summer ornaments for grates are made of wood shavings and of different coloured papers'. Reading books are now published which reject all such trash as the above, and contain nothing but what has really some fitness for reaching the end which reading books were meant to reach. Some of them even go a little too far in the effort to avoid dryness and pedantry and to be natural and interesting; they contain rather too many abbreviations, too many words meant to imitate the noises of animals, and too much of that part of human utterance which may be called the *interjectional*. The little children, for whom the books are designed, are apt to be rather puzzled by words of this kind, and, even if they were not, it is a fault in a short reading lesson to contain too much of them. But this fault, which certainly some of the best of the new reading books do not quite avoid, has at least the merit of being a fault on the right side.

(1863)

The effect of the Inspector under the Revised Code

Again, it is urged that an Inspector is not forbidden by the Revised Code to retain 'a liberal and intelligent inspection' along with the new examination, and that an inspector who has an assistant has ample time for such inspection. But the question is, not whether an Inspector can make such an inspection, but whether the school will care much for it when it is the new examination which brings the grant, and whether it will do as much good as it formerly did when it is no longer much cared for.

All test examinations, it is said again, may be said to narrow reading upon a certain given point, and to make it mechanical. If a man wants a certificate or diploma of you, you say you will give it him if he learns this and that, which you prescribe; and you may be said to cramp his studies by thus limiting them. Certainly, if a man wants a certificate, or a diploma, or honours, of you, you must fix just what he shall get them for, which is by no means of the same extent as a liberal education. But this is a reason against making an excessive use of such test examinations, of turning too much of a man's reading into reading for certificates, diplomas, or honours. That is why our University system of examinations, competitions, and honours, is so little favoured in Germany.* But, at any rate, to make a narrowing system of test examinations govern the whole inspection of our primary schools, when we have before us, not individuals wanting a diploma from us, but organisations wanting to be guided by us into the best ways of learning and teaching, seems like saddling ourselves with a confessed cause of imperfection unnecessarily.

Admitting the stimulus of the test examination to be salutary, we may therefore yet say that when it is overemployed it has two faults: it tends to make the instruction mechanical, and to set a bar to duly extending it. School grants earned in the way fixed by the Revised

* The least studious of German countries, Austria, is the one most abounding in university examinations like our own. '*Le pays à examens, l'Autriche, est précisément celui dans lequel on ne travaille pas*', says M. Laboulaye.

Code—by the scholar performing a certain *minimum* expressly laid down beforehand—must inevitably concentrate the teacher's attention on the means for producing this *minimum*, and not simply on the good instruction of his school. The danger to be guarded against is the mistake of treating these two—the producing this *minimum* successfully and the good instruction of a school—as if they were identical. The safeguard seems to be in reducing the overwhelming preponderance of this examination and its results, at the same time that we retain all its useful stimulus.

In my report two years ago I said: '*More free play for the Inspector, and, in consequence, more free play for the teacher.*' As long as the whole grant-earning examination turns on results precisely and literally specified by the Department beforehand, so long the inspection will be mechanical and unintelligent, and it will inevitably draw the teaching after it.   (1869)

The school as a humanizing and civilizing agency; with some observations on the effects of the Revised Code[88]

The school's physical environment as a humanizing force in a depressed area

...nowhere are good school-buildings, and, above all, a good playground, such a potent means of attraction to scholars as in London; for nowhere are the benefits of air, light, space, and free means of exercise, so scantily possessed by them in their homes. The spacious playgrounds attached to the Wesleyan practising schools in Westminster, in the midst of a densely crowded and poverty-stricken locality, form, in my opinion, one of the most delightful features of that institution; and form also one of its best agents in the work of humanizing and civilising the neighbourhood in which it is placed.

(1855)

Arnold's praise for the Wesleyan Methodists

Amongst the local efforts for the promotion of public education which I have witnessed in my district during the last five years, none, perhaps, is so remarkable as that which the Wesleyan Methodists have been making during that period in South Staffordshire. In no part of my district, except in London, are the schools under my inspection so thickly scattered; in none are they so well attended; in none have they multiplied so fast and improved so rapidly in efficiency.[89] Mr Tremenheere's reports on the state of the mining population have sufficiently made known the moral and social condition of the working-classes in South Staffordshire;[90] and, while that condition is such as it is there described, the elementary schools in that part of the country will not, as a body, be equal to the best elementary schools in other parts of the country. The home education of the children must make itself felt. But that these South Staffordshire schools have attained, as a whole, the thoroughly respectable and satisfactory condition in which I now find them, a condition of efficiency quite out of all proportion with the barbarism of the district in which they are found, does infinite credit to the zeal of their promoters and to the labour of their teachers, and cannot fail in the end to tell powerfully upon the civilisation of the neighbourhood. When first these schools came under my inspection in 1851, the rate of attainment which I found in them was far lower (with one or two striking exceptions) than that

which I found in any other part of my district; it was so
low that, in order to obtain pupil-teachers here at all, I
was in many cases forced to recommend the admission
of candidates whose deficiencies would elsewhere have
ensured their instant rejection. The rate of attainment
in these schools generally is now, as I have said, equal
to that of respectable schools in the best parts of my
district; I am enabled to demand the same proficiency
of candidates for apprenticeship here as elsewhere; the
actual apprentices perform, with credit, the same examination as others. And the new aspect of the school
buildings (often, with the neighbouring Wesleyan
chapel, the only considerable edifices, except the fur-
naces, in their locality) sufficiently indicates how recent
is the effort which has produced these results. (1856)

Humanizing instruction

The candour with which school inspectors in France
avowed to me their dissatisfaction with the school-
books in use there, led me to reflect on the great imperfection exhibited by our school-books also. I found
in the French schools good manuals for teaching special
subjects—a good manual for teaching arithmetic, a
good manual for teaching grammar, a good manual for
teaching geography; what was wanting there, as it is
wanting with us, was a good *reading-book*, or course of
reading-books. It is not enough remembered in how
many cases his reading-book forms the whole literature,
except his Bible, of the child attending a primary
school. If then, instead of literature, his reading-book,
as is too often the case, presents him with a jejune
encyclopaedia of positive information, the result is that
he has, except his Bible, no literature, no *humanizing*

instruction at all. If, again, his reading-book, as is also too often the case, presents him with bad literature instead of good—with the writing of second or third-rate authors, feeble, incorrect, and colourless—he has not, as the rich have, the corrective of an abundance of good literature to counteract the bad effect of trivial and ill-written school-books; the second or third-rate literature of his school-book remains for him his sole, or, at least, his principal literary standard. Dry scientific disquisitions, and literary compositions of an inferior order, are indeed the worst possible instruments for teaching children to read well. But besides the fault of not fulfilling this, their essential function, the ill-compiled reading-books I speak of have, I say, for the poor scholar, the graver fault of actually doing what they can to spoil his taste, when they are nearly his only means for forming it. I have seen school-books belonging to the cheapest, and therefore most popular series in use in our primary schools, in which far more than half of the poetical extracts were the composition either of the anonymous compilers themselves, or of American writers of the second and third order; and these books were to be some poor child's Anthology of a literature so varied and so powerful as the English! To this defectiveness of our reading-books I attribute much of that grave and discouraging deficiency in anything like literary taste and feeling, which even well-instructed pupil-teachers of four or five years' training, which even the ablest students in our training schools, still continue almost invariably to exhibit; a deficiency, to remedy which, the progressive development of our school system, and the very considerable increase of information among the people, appear to avail little or nothing. I believe that nothing would so much contribute to remedy it as the diffusion in our elementary schools of reading-books of which the contents were really well selected and interesting. Such lessons would be far better adapted than a treatise on the atmosphere, the steam-engine, or the pump, to attain the proper end of a reading-book, that of teaching scholars to read well; they would also afford the best chance of inspiring quick scholars with a real love for reading and literature in the only way in which such a love is ever really inspired, by animating and moving them; and if they succeeded in doing this, they would have this further advantage, that the literature for which they inspired a taste would be a good, a sound, and a truly refining literature; not a literature such as that of most of the few attractive pieces in our current reading-books, a literature over which no cultivated person would dream of wasting his time.   (1860)

What was happening under the Revised Code

The mode of teaching in the primary schools has certainly fallen off in intelligence, spirit, and inventiveness during the four or five years which have elapsed since my last report. It could not well be otherwise. In a country where every one is prone to rely too much on mechanical processes, and too little on intelligence, a change in the Education Department's regulations, which by making two-thirds of the Government grant depend upon a mechanical examination, inevitably gives a mechanical turn to the school teaching, a mechanical turn to the inspection, is and must be trying to the intellectual life of a school.[91] In the inspection, the mechanical examination of individual scholars in reading a short passage, writing a short passage, and working two or three sums, cannot but take the lion's share of room and importance, inasmuch as two-thirds of the Government grant depend upon it; yet I find, that of this examination, into which, in schools like British and Wesleyan schools where the religious instruction of the children is withdrawn from inspection, the whole inspection tends to resolve itself, more than 49 per cent of the children in average attendance in the schools inspected by me this last year had no share. More than 14 per cent of the children in average attendance were under six years of age, and therefore not examined for the grant; more than 27 per cent of them did not appear on the capitation schedule at all, not having attended school often enough; there are left, therefore, as subjects of examination, not more than about 58 per cent of the scholars. The inspection, therefore, is not now that stimulus to the whole school which it was when a proportion of each class, picked at random by the inspector, were freely examined by him.

In the school teaching the decline of intellectual life caused by a more mechanical method of instruction shows itself in increasing weakness in even those very matters which our changes were designed to revive and foster. In my district the proportion of children presented in the three higher standards and doing their work, therefore, on paper, and that presented in the three lower standards, and doing their work on slates, were as nearly as possible the same last year as the year before. Just 27 per cent last year were in paper-work, and 73 per cent in slate-work; the year before, 26·7 per cent were in paper-work, and in slate-work 73·3 per cent. The proportion, therefore, remained as nearly as possible the same; but I find that whereas of the children presented in paper-work only 14·9 per cent failed the year before last, 18 per cent failed last year. Among the children presented in slate-work the increase in the rate of failure is smaller, but an increase there is; 10·8 per cent failed the year before last, 11·2 per cent last year. The total rate of failure, which the year before last was 11·9 per cent, rose last year to 13 per cent.

Meanwhile, the matters of language, geography, and history, by which, in general, instruction first gets hold of a child's mind and becomes stimulating and interesting to him, have in the great majority of schools fallen into disuse and neglect. The Minute of last February, which makes them subjects of a grant-bringing examination has, by recalling attention to them, made manifest into what decay they had sunk. That Minute is, in my opinion, chiefly valuable as an indication to school managers and school teachers that the Education Department thinks these matters of importance. The grant is so trifling, and is saddled with such conditions, that many of the schools in my district, decline, as I have said, to avail themselves of it. But even if they availed themselves of it, I doubt whether a decline of intellectual life, itself due chiefly to the mechanical mode of examination the Revised Code has introduced, can be well cured by a palliative, which, while it extends the examination beyond the elementary matters, yet arranges it, for the higher matter as for the elementary ones, in such a way as to give it the character of an intricate and mechanical routine. More free play for the Inspector, and more free play, in consequence, for the teacher, is what is wanted...In the game of mechanical contrivances the teachers will in the end beat us; and as it is now found possible, by ingenious preparation, to get children through the

Revised Code examination in reading, writing, and ciphering, without their really knowing how to read, write, or cipher, so it will with practice, no doubt, be found possible to get the three-fourths of the one-fifth of the children over six through the examination in grammar, geography, and history, without their really knowing any one of these three matters.   (1867)

The great fault of the Revised Code

During the school year more than 25,000 children passed under my inspection; of these, about 13,000 were presented for examination grants.

The total rate of failure which in 1866–7 was 13 per cent, rose in 1867–8 to 14·56 per cent, but declined in 1868–9 to 11·3 per cent. Of last year's failures 20 per cent were in arithmetic, 7·7 per cent in writing, and 6 per cent in reading.

This gradation not ill represents the degrees of difficulty in teaching by rote the three matters of arithmetic, writing and reading. I have repeatedly said that it seems to me the great fault of the Revised Code, and of the famous plan of *payment by results*, that it fosters teaching by rote; I am of that opinion still. I think the great task for friends of education is, not to praise *payment by results*, which is just the sort of notion to catch of itself popular favour, but to devise remedies for the evils which are found to follow the applications of this popular notion. The school examinations in view of *payment by results* are, as I have said, a game of mechanical contrivance in which the teachers will and must more and more learn how to beat us. It is found possible, by ingenious preparation, to get children through the Revised Code examination in reading, writing, and ciphering, without their really knowing how to read, write, and cipher.

To take the commonest instance: a book is selected at the beginning of the year for the children of a certain standard; all the year the children read this book over and over again, and no other. When the Inspector comes they are presented to read in this book; they can read their sentence or two fluently enough, but they cannot read any other book fluently. Yet the letter of the law is satisfied, and the more we undertake to lay down to the very letter the requirements which shall be satisfied in order to earn grants, the more do managers and teachers conceive themselves to have the right to hold us to this letter. Suppose the inspector were to produce another book out of his pocket, and to refuse grants for all the children who could not read fluently from it. The managers and teacher would appeal to the Code, which says that the scholar shall be required to read 'a paragraph from a reading book used in the school', and would the Department sustain an Inspector in enforcing such an additional test as that which has been mentioned?

The circle of the children's reading has thus been narrowed and impoverished all the year for the sake of a *result* at the end of it, and the *result* is an illusion.

(1869)

Great stress has been laid on the declaration of the Duke of Newcastle's Commission, that 'the object is to find some constant and stringent motive to induce teachers to do that part of their duty which is at once most unpleasant and most important'. This unpleasant and important part of their duty, according to the same Commission, is, 'to see that all the children under their charge really learn to read, write, and cipher thoroughly well'...but is a child's elementary grounding in thorough working order, because he can read fluently a sentence in a short book which he has been reading and re-reading all the year? (1869)

What are wanted

The animation of mind, the multiplying of ideas, the promptness to connect, in the thoughts, one thing with another, and to illustrate one thing by another, are what are wanted; just what *letters*, as they are called, are supposed to communicate.[92] (1874)

Natural science and crude minds[93]

A stir of life is certainly more and more visible again in our schools. Scholars and teachers alike show it, and I have good hopes for the future. In what is properly to be called culture, in feeling, taste, and perception, the advance is least; and this is, perhaps inevitable. Even second year students still show in this respect, an astonishing crudeness. 'Doctor, can you fulfil the duties of your profession in curing a woman who is distracted?' or again, 'Can you not wait upon the lunatic?'—these are paraphrases of Shakespeare's *Canst thou not minister to a mind diseased*, from which I am even now fresh. 'The witches who are under the control of Hecate, and who love the darkness because their designs are best accomplished then, have assembled at their meeting place with no other protection than a wolf for their sentinel, and by whose roar they know when their enemy Tarquin is coming near them.' It seems almost incredible that a youth who has been two years in a training college, and for the last of the

221

two years has studied *Macbeth*, should, at his examination, produce such a travesty of the well-known passage in that play beginning *Now witchcraft celebrates*. Yet such travesties are far too common, and all signs of positive feeling and taste for what is poetically true and beautiful are far too rare. At last year's meeting of the British Association the President of the Section for Mechanical Science told his hearers that, 'in such communities as ours, the spread of natural science is of far more immediate urgency than any other secondary study. Whatever else he may know, viewed in the light of modern necessities, a man who is not fairly versed in exact science is only a half-educated man, and if he has substituted literature and history for natural science, has has chosen the less useful alternative.' And more and more pressure there will be, especially in the instruction of the children of the working classes, whose time for schooling is short, to substitute natural science for literature and history as the more useful alternative. And what a curious state of things it would be if every scholar who had passed through the course of our primary schools knew that, when a taper burns, the wax is converted into carbonic acid and water, and thought, at the same time, that a good paraphrase for *Canst thou not minister to a mind diseased*, was, *Can you not wait upon the lunatic!* The problem to be solved is a great deal more complicated than many of the friends of natural science suppose. They see clearly enough, for instance, how the working classes are, in their ignorance, constantly violating the laws of health, and suffering accordingly and they look to a spread of sound natural science as the remedy. What they do not see is that to know the laws of health ever so exactly, as a mere piece of positive knowledge, will carry a man in general no great way. To have the power of using, which is the thing wished, these data of natural science, a man must, in general, have first been in some measure *moralised*; and for moralising him it will be found not easy, I think, to dispense with those old agents, letters, poetry, religion. So let not our teachers be led to imagine, whatever they may hear and see of the call for natural science, that their literary cultivation is unimportant. The fruitful use of natural science itself depends, in a very great degree, on having effected in the whole man, by means of letters, a rise in what the political economists call *the standard of life*.   (1876)

Poetry and the formation of character

I find that of the specific subjects English literature, as it is too ambitiously called—in plain truth the learning by heart and reacting of a hundred lines or two of standard English poetry—continues to be by far the most popular. I rejoice to find it so; there is no fact coming under my observation in the working of our elementary schools which gives me so much satisfaction. The acquisition of good poetry is a discipline which works deeper than any other discipline in the range of work of our schools; more than any other, too, it works of itself, is independent of the school teacher, and cannot be spoiled by pedantry and injudiciousness on his part. Some people regard this my high estimate of the value of poetry in education with suspicion and displeasure. Perhaps they may accept the testimony of Wordworth with less suspicion than mine. Wordsworth says, 'To be incapable of a feeling of poetry, in my sense of the word, is to be without love of human nature and reverence for God'. And it is only through acquaintance with poetry, and with good poetry, that this 'feeling of poetry' can be given.

Good poetry does undoubtedly tend to form the soul and character;[94] it tends to beget a love of beauty and of truth in alliance together, it suggests, however indirectly, high and noble principles of action, and it inspires the emotion so helpful in making principles operative. Hence its extreme importance to all of us; but in our elementary schools its importance seems to me to be at present quite extraordinary.   (1880)

Priorities and frills

...an earnest and widely lamented friend of popular education said once, I remember, that he should like to have Greek and Sanscrit taught to the children in board schools, if it were possible. Aspirations safeguarded by an *if it were possible* cannot, it may be thought, do much harm; nevertheless such aspirations do tend to make us lose sight of the actual present conditions of our problem in popular education, and so far they do harm. Sir John Lubbock talks of the variety of subjects which we make our own children study, and I am not at all sure that we do not make them study too great a variety. But at any rate, there is this difference: take thirty of our own children between the ages of ten and thirteen, and you will not find one of them who does not know what *a steed* is or what *a ford* is. You have, therefore, a totally different material to work upon. And even to talk of lessons in Greek and Sanscrit for such scholars as those whom in our elementary schools we have to deal with, is dangerous trifling, because it tends to make us forget the pressing reality.

Not that the ideal which we should propose to our-selves for the school-course in these schools is not a high or a large one. It is the ideal admirably fixed long ago by Comenius, an early and wise school reformer, who is now too much forgotten. 'The aim is', says Comenius, 'to train generally all who are born men to all which is human.' Without pedantry and without platitudes, we should all seek to reach this aim in the most practical manner. (1880)

Creative activity and information

No doubt the quantity of mental exertion required for examinations is often excessive, but the strain is much the more severe, because the quality and character of mental exertion required are so often injudicious. The mind is less strained the more it reacts on what it deals with, and has a native play of its own, and is creative. It is more strained the more it has to receive a number of 'knowledges' passively, and to store them up to be reproduced in an examination. But to acquire a number of 'knowledges', store them, and reproduce them, was what in general those candidates for Indian employ-ment had had to do. By their success in doing this they were tested, and the examination turned on it. In old days examinations mainly turned upon Latin and Greek composition. Composition in the dead languages is now wholly out of favour, and I by no means say that it is a sufficient test for candidates for Indian employment. But I will say that the character and quality of mental exertion required for it is more healthy than the character and quality of exertion required for receiving and storing a number of 'knowledges'. And the candidate whom the former test brings to the front is likely to be a healthier man in body and mind, both then and afterwards, than the man whom the latter test brings to the front.

Of such high importance, in relieving the strain of mental effort, is the sense of pleasurable activity and of creation. Of course a great deal of the work in elementary schools must necessarily be of a mechanical kind. But whatever introduces any sort of creative activity to relieve the passive reception of knowledge is valuable. The kindergarten exercises are useful for this reason, the management of tools is useful, drawing is useful, singing is useful. The poetry exercise, if properly managed, is of very great use, and this is why I have always been in favour of it and am glad to see further development given to it by the New Code. People talk contemptuously of 'learning lines by heart'; but if a child is brought, as he easily can be brought, to *throw himself into* a piece of poetry, an exercise of creative activity has been set up in him quite different from the effort of learning a list of words to spell, or a list of flesh-making and heat-giving foods, or a list of capes and bays, or a list of reigns and battles, and capable of greatly relieving the strain from learning these and of affording a lively pleasure. It is true, language, and geography, and history, and the elements of natural science are all capable of being taught in a less mechanical and more interesting manner than that in which they are commonly taught now; they may be so taught as to call forth pleasurable activity in the pupil. But those disciplines are especially valuable which call this activity forth most surely and directly.

As to 'knowledges', a teacher should, in my opinion, aim at having every child who passes through an elementary school not only taught reading, writing, and

arithmetic, but furnished in addition with some knowledge of the English language and of grammar, and also
with some instruction in natural science, geography, and
history. A select class capable of being carried further
with profit should be formed for specific subjects. But
governing the teacher's whole design of instruction in
these knowledges should be the aim of calling forth, by
some means or other, in every pupil a sense of pleasurable activity and of creation; he should resist being
made a mere ladder with 'information'.

There is an admirable sermon of Butler's[95] preached
in 1745 on behalf of the charity schools of London and
Westminster, which every one concerned with popular
education ought to read. It is far too little known; the
Christian Knowledge Society would do well to reprint it,
as they have reprinted Bishop Wilson's manual. Every
point is taken in it which most needs to be taken: the
change in the world which makes 'knowledges' of
universal necessity now which were not so formerly, the
hardship of exclusion from them, the absurdity and
selfishness of those who are 'so extremely apprehensive
of the danger that poor persons will make a perverse use
of even the least advantage, whilst they do not appear
at all apprehensive of the like danger for themselves or
their own children, in respect of riches or power, how
much soever; though the danger of perverting these
advantages is surely as great, and the perversion itself
of much greater and worse consequence'. But there is,
perhaps, no sentence in the sermon which more deserves
to be pondered by us than this: 'Of education,' says
Butler, '*information itself is really the least part.*'

(1882)

School teachers, their education, rôles, and status

Teachers or drudges?

I hear many complaints that too high a standard of attainment is now required in elementary schools; that the exact point up to which it is desirable to instruct the children attending them has been considerably outpassed; that the children are more and more instructed in subjects injudiciously chosen, and in a manner to unfit them for their future station and business in life...

Much of the exaggeration respecting the overteaching in elementary schools arises, I think, in the following way. People read the examination papers, which are printed from year to year in your Lordships' Minutes, and exclaim at the rate of attainment demanded; as if the rate of attainment demanded by those examination papers was the rate of attainment demanded in elementary schools. They forget that these examination papers are for *teachers*, not for *scholars*.

Yes; but, they say, why demand so much learning from those who will have to impart so little? Why impose on those who will have to teach the rudiments only of knowledge to the children of the poor, an examination so wide in its range, so searching in its details?

The answer to this involves the whole question as to the training of the teachers of elementary schools. It is sufficient to say, that the plan which these objectors recommend, the plan of employing teachers whose attainments do not rise far above the level of the attainments of their scholars, has already been tried. It has been tried, and it has failed. Its fruits were to be

seen in the condition of elementary education throughout England, until a very recent period. It is now
sufficiently clear, that the teacher to whom you give
only a drudge's training, will do only a drudge's work,
and will do it in a drudge's spirit: that in order to ensure
good instruction even within narrow limits in a school,
you must provide it with a master far superior to his
scholars, with a master whose own attainments reach
beyond the limits within which those of his scholars
may be bounded. To form a good teacher for the
simplest elementary school, a period of regular training
is requisite: *this period must be filled with work:* can the
objectors themselves suggest a course of work for this
period, which shall materially differ from that now
pursued; or can they affirm that the attainments
demanded by the certificate-examination exceed the
limits of what may without overwork be acquired
within the period of his training, by a man of twenty
or twenty-one years of age, of fair intelligence, and of
fair industry?   (1855)

Learning to teach[96]

It is certain, that the present arrangement, imposed as
it has been on the Government by the necessity of circumstances, and rendering as it has rendered all the
benefit possible under those circumstances, fails to
assist certain schools which stand greatly in need of
assistance. Professing as it does to improve the quality
rather than to increase the quantity of elementary
schools, it is most sufficient and successful in large
towns and populous neighbourhoods. In these principally I had, until lately, witnessed its operation, and by
its success in these I had been profoundly impressed;

for here it is, above all, the *quality* of elementary education which needs improvement. On becoming more
acquainted with its operation in poorer and more thinly
peopled districts, I cannot but be impressed with the
conviction that its adequacy is here no longer the same;
for here it is the increase in the *quantity* of education, it
is the very establishment and maintenance of schools
which is in many cases the thing required.

The high rate of payment which the services of a
trained teacher now command forms the obstacle in
the case of schools of the poor class just mentioned, to
their acquisition of such a teacher, and, therefore, to
their participation in your Lordships' grants. To improve the position of the teacher in respect of his salary
as well as in other respects, has been a constant endeavour of your Lordships, and that this endeavour has
been crowned with success is a public benefit. The
formation of a class of *principal teachers* paid at a low
rate is by no means to be desired; and, therefore, while
I lament the difficulty in which their inability to pay a
high salary to a teacher places the managers of certain
poor schools, I should be sorry to see that difficulty
removed by any change which lowered the present
standard of *principal teachers'* salaries.

For the wants of these schools, therefore, it is not
easy, under the present system, to suggest a provision;
there is, however, in the higher class of schools under
my inspection, a want which is at this moment strongly
felt, and to which it lies, I think, in your Lordships'
power in some degree to afford relief. In this higher
class of schools there is a great and growing demand for
regularly trained *secondary* or *assistant teachers*, which is
at present most inadequately supplied. Such teachers
would be employed under the supervision of the prin-

cipal teacher whose salary would remain at the present rate; but the richest body of school-managers is generally unable, even were it desirous, to pay the assistant at the same rate as the principal. But the increase in the number of schools aided by your Lordships, and requiring trained teachers is at present so rapid, that it still fully keeps pace with, or even outstrips, the supply of such teachers; a student in a training school, therefore, after he had finished the shortest period of training which is permitted, finds no difficulty in at once obtaining his appointment to an elementary school at a principal teacher's salary. There is not at present left, after the existing elementary schools have been provided with principal teachers, any class of students unprovided for, and willing, therefore to accept a less remunerative, although, for them, more instructive and more improving employment.

For not merely is the teacher of a large and important school greatly benefited by the service of a highly trained student, infinitely superior in training, information, and authority, not alone to the class of pupil-teachers, but also to the class of assistants established by your Lordships' Minute of July, 1852, but the student, too, on his side, may be greatly benefited by such service. Under the successful and experienced teacher of a large and thriving school he may learn what the training school cannot teach him, what his own experience can only teach him slowly, and after many mistakes—the practical methods by which great schools are made and kept thriving. It is well worth his while for the sake of such knowledge, for the sake of learning, in a good practical school, how to manage children, how to deal with parents and managers—it is well worth his while, in consideration of such advantages, to content himself for a year or two with a somewhat lower salary.

The time will no doubt arrive when the present extension of the pupil-teacher system will bear its natural fruits, and when, after all the principal teacher-ships of elementary schools are occupied, there will yet remain year by year a considerable class of students not posted as principals, and willing, therefore, as in Holland and Prussia, to begin their career as assistants; but this period has not yet arrived. Its arrival will greatly benefit elementary schools, and will benefit in a scarcely less important degree the trained students also. Even under the present circumstances, I have been greatly struck with the keen and just sense which I have found existing among the students themselves of the advantage to be derived from serving for a certain period under an experienced master in a formed and successful school; more than one student has expressed to me his readiness to forego the higher rate of salary which he might obtain as a principal teacher, for the sake of obtaining this invaluable experience as an assistant. At present, however, it is only in a school of the very first order, and offering, therefore, to the student the most extraordinary advantages as a place of practical training, that I feel warranted in urging him to accept an engagement as assistant, to the temporary detriment of his condition as respects salary. Indeed the authorities of the training schools would at present be opposed to any extensive employment of their trained students as assistants; for not only are they naturally unwilling to allow them to forfeit the tangible benefit of the best-paid situations offered, but they cannot leave the schools in connection with them without principal teachers, which they would do if they now diverted to other employment any considerable portion of their yearly supply of students.

It is desirable, however, and I am sure your Lordships will feel it to be desirable, to encourage as much as possible among the managers of schools their growing wish for this highly trained and efficient class of assistants; this only aid which can considerably lighten the labours of a chief teacher, or enable him to feel really at ease with respect to the management of those parts of his school which are not for the moment under his own personal tuition and superintendence.   (1857)

Gross blunders of taste and expression

On one other topic, in connection with the subject of pupil-teachers, I am anxious to touch in conclusion. In the general opinion of the advantages which have resulted from the employment of them, I most fully concur; and of the acquirements and general behaviour of the greater number of those of them whom I have examined I wish to speak favourably. But I have been much struck in examining them towards the close of their apprenticeship, when they are generally at least eighteen years old, with the utter disproportion between the great amount of positive information and the low degree of mental culture and intelligence which they exhibit. Young men, whose knowledge of grammar, of the minutest details of geographical and historical facts, and above all of mathematics, is surprising, often cannot paraphrase a plain passage of prose or poetry without totally misapprehending it, or write half a page of composition on any subject without falling into gross blunders of taste and expression. I cannot but think that, with a body of young men so highly instructed, too little attention has hitherto been paid to this side of education; the side through which it chiefly forms the character; the side which has perhaps been too exclusively attended to in schools for the higher classes, and to the development of which it is the boast of what is called classical education to be mainly directed. I attach little importance to the study of languages, ancient or modern, by pupil-teachers, for they can seldom have the time to study them to much purpose without neglecting other branches of instruction which it is necessary that they should follow; but I am sure that the study of portions of the best English authors, and composition, might with advantage be made a part of their regular course of instruction to a much greater degree than it is at present. Such a training would tend to elevate and humanise a number of young men, who at present, notwithstanding the vast amount of raw information which they have amassed, are wholly uncultivated; and it would have the great social advantage of tending to bring them into intellectual sympathy with the educated of the upper classes. (1852)

Hopeless want of tact and apprehensiveness

No more useful change has in my opinion ever been introduced into the programme of the pupil-teachers' studies than that which has lately added to it the learning by heart of passages from some standard author. How difficult it seems to do anything for their taste and culture I have often said. I have said how much easier it seems to get entrance to their minds and to awaken them by means of music or of physical science than by means of literature; still if it can be done by literature at all, it has the best chance of being done by the way now

234

proposed. The culture both of the pupil-teacher and of the elementary schoolmaster with us seems to me to resist the efforts made to improve it and to remain unprogressive, more than that of the corresponding class on the Continent. Ignorance is nothing; such a blunder as this of an English student, 'Pope lived a little prior to the Christian era', a French or Swiss student might also commit; but the hopeless want of tact and apprehensiveness shown by such a sentence as this, 'I should consider Newton as a great author; firstly, *on account of the style and value of his works;* secondly, on account of his most valuable and wonderful discoveries, *coupled with the pains he took to diffuse his self-acquired knowledge among the people*', no French or Swiss student, who had read the books and heard the lectures which the English student who wrote that sentence had heard and read, would, in my opinion, ever equal. It is true that if you take the bulk of the scholars, even in schools for the richer classes, the rate of culture is very low; but then it is to be remembered that our pupil-teachers and students are a select body, not the bulk of a class, and have gone through a careful training and schooling. (1863)

How the Revised Code affected the teacher

The performance of the reduced number of candidates is weaker and more inaccurate than was the performance of the larger number six years ago, and for the last year or two has been becoming weaker and weaker. No Inspector can be surprised at this who compares the present acquirements of the vast majority of the pupil-teachers of his district in the yearly examinations which they have to pass before him with those which he remembers ten years ago. Nor, again, can this difference in their acquirements surprise him when he compares the slackness, indifference, and loose hold upon their profession which is to be remarked in the pupil-teachers now, and contrasts it with what he remembers ten years ago. The service of the pupil-teacher was then given under an indenture which he was accustomed to regard as absolutely binding him for five years; now it is given under an agreement which expressly declares itself to be always terminable by notice or payment. He then had seven and a half hours of instruction every week from the principal teacher, out of school hours and when all the attention of the principal teacher could be given to him; now he has only five hours of instruction, and these may be given in the night school, when the principal teacher's attention is divided. The work of teaching in school is less interesting and more purely mechanical than it used to be. But, above all, the pupil-teacher has continually before him, he continually sees and hears, a master who ten years ago was rewarded for teaching him, was proud of his own profession, was hopeful, and tried to communicate this pride and hope to his apprentice. Ten years ago the schoolmaster was under the impulse given by the celebrated letter of instructions to the Secretary to the Committee of Council in 1848, which, in establishing the certificate examination, said:—'For the first time in this country schoolmasters will be assembled by the invitation of the Government, as candidates, for the formal recognition of their capacity to instruct the humbler classes of Her Majesty's subjects, and, as a consequence of such recognition, to receive immediately from the State an annual stipend proportioned to their merits and exertions. It is important that the assembled candidates should be impressed with a conviction of the anxiety of Government, by means of a higher description of moral and religious education, to improve the condition of the poor, and of their determination, as an indispensable means to this end, to elevate the position of the elementary teacher, by qualifying him to occupy a higher station, and by rewarding his more efficient services by superior endowments. They ought to receive from the Inspectors the impression that they are called upon to co-operate with them and with the Committee of Council on Education for the attainment of great national objects.'

To the trainer thus rewarded, thus animated, thus encouraged to value his profession, thus proclaimed a fellow-worker with the national Government, has succeeded a trainer no longer paid or rewarded, a trainer told that he has greatly over-rated his importance and that of his function, that it is most inexpedient to make a public servant of him and that the Government is determined henceforth to know no one in connection with his school but the managers. It is wonderful that such a trainer should be slack in seeking pupil-teachers whom he has to instruct without reward; that he should communicate to what pupil-teachers he has his own sense of the change in the schoolmaster's position, his own slackness, his own discouragement; and that under these influences the pupil-teacher's heart should no longer be in his work, that his mind should be always ready to turn to the hope of bettering himself in some more thriving line, and his acquirements meanwhile weak and scanty?

At a moment when popular education is at last becoming a question of immediate public interest, and when the numbers, spirit, and qualifications of our teaching staff will have a great call made upon them, it is important to take precise note of their actual condition and prospects. Undoubtedly the present educational movement finds us ill-prepared for it, in so far as our teaching staff is less vigorous in spirit, is more slackly recruited, and with weaker recruits, than it was a few years ago. Complaints and recriminations as to the measures which have led to this falling-off are now vain; let it be conceded that these measures may have had grounds which made them, in spite of this falling-off, politic and sound. But it is still most desirable to see if this falling-off cannot be stopped and what are the means which afford the best hope of stopping it.

The best thing for a teacher to do

The best thing for a teacher to do is surely to put before himself in the utmost simplicity the problem he has to solve. He has to instruct children between the ages of four and thirteen, children, too, who have for the most part a singularly narrow range of words and thoughts. He has, so far as secular instruction goes, to give to those children the power of reading, of writing and (according to the good old phrase) of casting accounts. He has to give them some knowledge of the world in which they find themselves, and of what happens and has happened in it; some knowledge, that is, of the great facts and laws of nature, some knowledge of geography and of history, above all of the history of their own country. He has to do as much towards opening their mind, and opening their soul and imagination, as is possible to be done with a number of children of their age and in their state of preparation and home surroundings.

There is the problem for him. He will find that in seeking to solve it he can quite well work on the old lines without busying himself with new and (so-called) scientific theories of education. It is not true that he must of necessity begin geography, for instance, with the geography of a child's own parish if he is to interest the child in geography. He will find he can interest him in it quite well by beginning with the old-fashioned four quarters of the globe, and coming round to the child's own parish by way of Africa and Zululand. But the great thing is to give the power of reading. It may be doubted whether this is not given more seldom than the power of writing and of casting accounts, although more children fail in the examination in these than in the examination in reading. The power of reading, as has been already said, is not in itself formative. Nevertheless, a power of reading, well trained and well guided, is perhaps the best among the gifts which it is the business of our elementary schools to bestow; it is in their power to bestow it, yet it is bestowed in much fewer cases than we imagine. Time is much better spent on enlarging and securing, by copious, well-chosen, and systematic readings, our school children's power to read, than in giving to them, at their age, the rudiments of this or that new science over and above the simple instruction in *Natur-kunde*[97] on which I have already insisted. The reading lessons should be used not only to secure the bare power of reading—a most valuable power, yet capable, no doubt, like other good things, of being employed amiss later on in the pupil's life as well as of being employed for his good. Nor should they be used only to increase a child's stock of what is called information. They should be treated as in connection with the good and sterling poetry learned for recitation, and should be made to contribute to the opening of the soul and imagination, for which the central *purchase* should be found in that poetry. The more the teacher extends his own culture the better he will be able to do this, and here is an additional reason for extending his own culture. (1878)

EXTRACTS FROM ARNOLD'S
SPEECH ON HIS RETIREMENT

Arnold sees himself as he really was

I do not mean to say that I think I have been altogether
a bad inspector. (Cheers.) I think I have had two
qualifications for the post. One is that of having a serious
sense of the nature and function of criticism. I from the
first sought to see the schools as they really were. Thus
it was soon felt that I was fair (hear, hear), and that the
teachers had not to apprehend from me crochets,
pedantries, humours, favouritism, and prejudices.
(Cheers.) That was one qualification. Another was that
I got the habit, very early in my time, of trying to put
myself in the place of the teachers whom I was inspecting. I will tell you how that came about. Though I am
a schoolmaster's son I confess that school teaching or
school inspecting is not the line of life I should naturally have chosen. I adopted it in order to marry a lady
who is here to-night, and who feels the kindness as
warmly and gratefully as I do. (Cheers.) My wife and I
had a wandering life of it at first. There were but three
inspectors for all England. My district went right across
from Pembroke Dock to Great Yarmouth. We had no
home; one of our children was born in a lodging at
Derby, with a workhouse, if I recollect right, behind and
a penitentiary in front. (Laughter.) But the irksomeness
of my new duties was what I felt most, and during the
first year or so this was sometimes almost insupportable.
But I met daily in the schools with men and women
discharging duties akin to mine, duties as irksome as
mine, duties less well paid than mine, and I asked

myself, Are they on roses? Would not they by nature prefer, many of them, to go where they liked and do what they liked, instead of being shut up in school? I saw them making the best of it; I saw the cheerfulness and efficiency with which they did their work, and I asked myself again, How do they do it? Gradually it grew into a habit with me to put myself into their places, to try and enter into their feelings, to represent to myself their life, and I assure you I got many lessons from them. This placed me in sympathy with them. Seeing people once a year is not much, but when you have come into sympathy with them they do not fade from your mind, and I find myself able to recall, and almost daily recalling, names and faces and circumstances of teachers whom I have not seen for years. That is because I have been in sympathy with them. I will not accept all the praise you have given me, but I will accept this—I have been fair and I have been sympathetic. (Cheers.)

His concluding reflection

My reflection is one to comfort and cheer myself, and I hope others, at this our parting. We are entering upon new times, where many influences, once potent to guide and restrain, are failing. Some people think the prospect of the reign of democracy, as they call it, very gloomy. This is unwise, but no one can regard it quite without anxiety. It is nearly 150 years since the wisest of English clergymen told the Lord Mayor and Sheriffs of London in a hospital sermon that the poor are very much what the rich make them. (Hear, hear.) That is profoundly true, though perhaps it rather startles us to hear it. On the other hand, it is almost a commonplace that children are very much what their teachers make them. I will not ask what our masses are likely to be if the rich have the making of them. I prefer to ask what they are likely to be so far as the teachers have the making of them. And on the whole—and here is the consoling reflection with which I shall end—though the teachers have, of course, their faults as individuals, though they have also their faults as a class, yet, on the whole, their action is, I do think and believe, powerful for good. (Hear, hear.) And not in England only, but in other countries as well, countries where the teachers have been much spoken against, I have found it so. I find plenty of deleterious and detestable influences at work, but they are influences of journalism in one place, in another influences of politicians, in some places both the one and the other; they are not the influences of teachers. The influence of the elementary teacher, so far as my observation extends, is for good; it helps morality and virtue. I do not give the teacher too much praise for this; the child in his hands so appeals to his conscience, his responsibility is so direct and palpable. But the fact is none the less consoling, and the fact is, I believe, as I have stated it. Burke speaks of the ancient and inbred integrity and piety of the English people; where should this influence of the teachers for good be so strong sustained as here? Thus, in conclusion, we are carried beyond and above the question of my personal gratitude, although that, too, is very deep and real. I love to think of the elementary teachers, to whom I owe so much and am so grateful, as more and more proving themselves to deserve, and more and more coming to possess, in the days which are now at hand for us, the esteem and gratitude of the entire country. (Cheers.)

NOTES

DEMOCRACY

1. p. 41, From 'Thoughts on the Cause of the Present Discontent'.

2. p. 46, Super quotes Spinoza, *Ethics*, Part III, Propositions 6–7.

3. p. 52, For reaction to this Bill, see reports of debates in House of Lords in *The Times*, 23 February 1856, p. 9; and 26 February 1856, p. 5.

4. p. 58, The *Constitutionnel*, founded in 1815, was Bonapartist in sympathy, and prepared the public for the *coup* which made Louis Napoleon Emperor.

5. p. 58, The *Morning Star* was founded as a penny newspaper in 1856 by the Manchester school of radicals. For Arnold's views on the paper, see *Letters*, I, 204.

6. p. 59, S. Butler, *Hudibras*, I, i, 215–16.

7. p. 63, The Conventicle Act, etc. were laws passed by the Restoration Parliament of 1661–5 with the intention of suppressing the Nonconformists.

8. p. 65, Arnold uses the phrase 'Classical and Commercial Academy' to refer to the type of private school patronised by middle-class parents. They were profit-making establishments and, as the only extensively available form of middle-class education, were the object of Arnold's persistent attack. See *Friendship's Garland*, Super, V, 70–1.

9. p. 75, Matt. v. 48.

10. p. 75, Phil. iii. 13.

A FRENCH ETON

11. p. 76, Probably Matthew James Higgins (1810–68), a renowned controversialist who, using the pseudonym of 'Paterfamilias', wrote three articles in the *Cornhill Magazine* (May 1860, December 1860, March 1861) which were very critical of the principal public schools, especially Eton.

12. p. 76, The Clarendon Commission which was set up in 1861, and reported in 1864.

13. p. 81, François Pierre Guillaume Guizot (1787–1874), French statesman and historian who, as Minister of Education (1832–9), prepared and put into action the first law on primary education.

14. p. 84, *Télémaque* is a didactic novel written by Fénelon between 1693 and 1694. For many years it was an almost indispensable part of a French child's education.

15. p. 90, Charles-Forbes-René, comte de Montalembert (1810–70), a Catholic writer and speaker, sought to secure a more liberal system of education in France. Early in his life he wrote in a letter what was to become his motto: 'Would it not be a splendid thing to show that religion is the mother of liberty?'

16. p. 95, Henri du Vergier, comte de La Rochejaquelein (1772–94), was a cadet at the military academy at Sorèze when the French Revolution broke out; he subsequently led the Vendean insurrection (1793) against the revolutionary forces, an activity which cost him his life.

17. p. 100, For a page of such advertisements, see *The Times*, 16 April 1863, p. 16. Of these advertisements the *Saturday Review* wrote: 'It is a curious speculation who the persons can be, of what condition in life and cast of character, by whom the advertisements and prospectuses which we have here attempted to classify are accepted as oracles' (2 February 1861, 118–19).

18. p. 101, Arnold here refers to the annual grant, first made in 1833 and administered by the Committee of Council on Education, which was to assist in the provision of elementary education. By 1839 all schools in receipt of aid had to submit to inspection.

19. p. 102, Many of our present public schools were founded subsequent to Dr Thomas Arnold's success at Rugby, where, as G. M. Young says, he 'reconciled the middle classes to the public schools'. Cheltenham was founded 1841, Marlborough 1843, Bradfield 1850.

20. p. 103, George Granville Bradley (1821–1903), a scholar and later a master at Rugby. He was appointed Headmaster of Marlborough in 1858 at a time when the school was heavily in debt. It was for this reason that he raised the fees, and objected, as Super points out, to Arnold's statement.

21. p. 104, Sir John Coleridge (1790–1876), a judge and nephew of the poet, and a life-long friend of Dr Thomas Arnold. Almost simultaneously with the appearance in the *Cornhill* of the first article by 'Paterfamilias' (May 1860), Coleridge delivered a lecture at Tiverton on public school education. His lecture was similarly critical, and was published as *Public School Education: a Lecture Delivered at the Athenaeum, Tiverton* (London, 1860).

22. p. 106, Nathaniel Woodard (1811–91), a clergyman who, like Arnold, was deeply impressed with the lack of good schools for the middle classes, especially those which would offer definite Church of England teaching. His response was to found a society which was to provide such schools, and by 1864 Hurstpierpoint and Lancing Colleges were already operating.

23. p. 109, Early in 1862 it was alleged that the Woodard schools enforced Romish practices. When Woodard submitted to examination by the Bishop of Chichester he was completely exonerated in 1863.

24. p. 109, Thomas Dyke Acland (1809–98), politician and educational reformer. Dr Frederick Temple (1821–1902), at one time headmaster of Rugby, and later Archbishop of Canterbury. Both men were involved in the movement in the late fifties to set up a system of examinations for students in the middle-class schools in the West country. These were taken over by the Universities and became known as the Oxford and Cambridge Local Examinations. Acland published *Some Account of the Origin and Objects of the new Oxford examinations* (1858).

25. p. 111, The Society of Arts was chartered in 1847 under the presidency of the Prince Consort. In 1856 it began its long career of awarding certificates of proficiency in certain subjects based on examinations. Originally its examinations were open to members of certain Mechanics' Institutes, but, as the Royal Society of Arts, its examinations are now open to all.

26. p. 113, Stephen Thomas Hawtrey (1808–86), a master at Eton and incumbent of Holy Trinity, Windsor. In 1851 he founded St Mark's School for the education of the choirboys of his parish. See his *St Mark's by Seaside in 1861* (1861).

27. p. 118, For Sir John Coleridge's letters, see *Guardian*, 18 and 25 November 1863.

28. p. 120, Arnold here refers to the mismanagement of Bedford School which resulted from the misappropriation of the school's endowed funds to purposes other than the school's welfare, and to the unsatisfactory relations between the governing body and the teaching staff.

29. p. 124, See Burke, 'Reflections on the Revolution in France', *Select Works*, ed. E. J. Payne (3 vols. Oxford, 1874–8), II, 69 and 114.

30. p. 126, See F. Temple, 'The Revised Code', *The Times*, 25 March 1862, p. 5. Arnold, rather reluctantly, did contemplate answering the letter, but felt that the compromise subsequently reached absolved him of the need to do so (*Letters*, I, 169).

31. p. 126, See 'Reflections on the Revolution in France', *Select Works*, ed. Payne, II, 70.

32. p. 127, Nimrod, 'a mighty hunter before the Lord'; Numa, a model, for the Romans, of wisdom and piety.

33. p. 129, Charles Adderley, M.P. for North Staffordshire. For his contribution to the debate on the Revised Code see Hansard's *Parliamentary Debates*, 3rd ser., CLXVI, cols. 177–8. Reported in *The Times*, 28 March 1862, p. 7. Arnold quotes Adderley in 'The Function of Criticism at the Present Time', Super, III, 272.

34. p. 130, In February 1863 Lord Derby opposed one of the many bills providing for the establishment of railways in Metropolitan London. See Hansard's *Parliamentary Debates*, 23 February 1863, 3rd ser., CLXIX, cols. 623–7.

35. p. 130, Sir John Pakington (1799–1880), a conservative politician whose ideas on educational reform were far in advance of those held amongst men of his own party and of the liberals.

36. p. 130, The Government Annuities Bill aimed at allowing those of small income to buy annuities and life insurance from the Government, which, unlike many of the unsound Friendly and Insurance societies, would offer stability and safety.

37. p. 134, J. A. Roebuck (1801–79), a prominent radical politician, was a favourite object of Arnold's attack. See *Culture and Anarchy*, Super, V, 96, and 'The Function of Criticism', Super, III, 272. Arnold is here quoting from Roebuck's speech in the House of Commons, 7 March 1864, on the Government Annuities Bill, which he opposed. See Hansard's *Parliamentary Debates*, 3rd ser., CLXXIII, cols. 1593–5. Reported in *The Times*, 8 March 1864.

38. p. 134, n., At Sheffield Roebuck was speaking at the annual conference of the Yorkshire Union of Mechanics' Institutes held on 18 May 1864. See *The Times*, 20 May 1864, pp. 10–11.

39. p. 136, See 'Reflections on the Revolution in France', *Select Works*, ed. Payne, II, 69.

40. p. 137, Sir Edward Baines (1800–90), M.P. for Leeds. A determined opponent of State intervention in public affairs; he opposed, for instance, the Government Annuities already mentioned. He was particularly opposed to Government intervention in education, and together with Edward Miall led the Noncomformist movement known as 'voluntaryism in education', whose ambition was to free education entirely from Government interference.

41. p. 141, Sir Archibald Alison (1792–1867), historian and staunch tory. His *History of Europe*, to which Arnold is referring, was written 'to show the corruption of human nature and the divine superintendence of human affairs; or as Disraeili said of Mr Wordy in *Coningsby* to prove that Providence was on the side of the tories' (*Dictionary of National Biography*).

42. p. 144, Matt. xix. 16–22.

43. p. 144, For similar ideas about the aristocracy, see 'The Function of Criticism', Super, III, 262–3.

44. p. 146, Isa. xl. 31.

45. p. 147, The Church-Rate was levied on all parishioners, including Nonconformists, for the upkeep of the parish church. It was felt to be an injustice, and the Nonconformists long struggled to rid themselves of it; they were successful when the Act relieving them of paying the rate was finally passed in July 1868.

46. p. 147, For the 'voice of thunder', see Rev. xiv. 2.

47. p. 148, John Bright (1811–89), radical politician and famous and stirring orator who was vigorously campaigning for the Reform Bill during the sixties. Arnold often took issue with him; see, for instance, *Culture and Anarchy*, Super, v, 240.

48. p. 148, Richard Cobden (1804–65), the famous M.P. (1841–65) who played such a large part in the repeal of the Corn Law, by the fervour with which he supported the Anti-Corn Law League. 'In the company of Mr Bright, whose name and his own became a pair of household words, he year after year traversed the island from end to end, arguing, replying, exhorting, organising, and raising funds . . . ' (*DNB*). He stood, of course, for free trade and non-intervention.

49. p. 148, Henry Ward Beecher (1813–87), the most popular Congregational minister in New York. A strong anti-slavery man, he visited England in 1863, where he lectured to huge audiences.

50. p. 150, Goldwin Smith (1823–1910), a controversialist and academic, was, among many other things, a fellow-member with Arnold of the Newcastle Commission. He was a firm supporter of Cobden, Bright, and the leaders of the Manchester School.

51. p. 153, Hugh Fortescue, third Earl Fortescue (1818–1905), politician and M.P. till his father's death. A social reformer of much earnestness, he wrote a number of pamphlets upon such social topics as local government, health in towns, and middle-class education; they include *Public Schools for the Middle Classes* (1864).

52. p. 153, Edward Miall (1809–81), politician and Congregational minister, who was first editor of the *Nonconformist* newspaper. He was often mentioned by Arnold in his social criticism. See, for instance, *Culture and Anarchy*, Super, v, 128.

THE TWICE-REVISED CODE

53. p. 157, The Archbishop of Canterbury's speech was reported in *The Times*, 4 October 1861, p. 10.

54. p. 157, Sir James Kay-Shuttleworth (1804–77), first secretary of the Committee of Council, and credited by the *DNB* with the foundation of the English system of popular education. Arnold refers to his pamphlet, *Letter to Earl Granville, K.G., on the Revised Code . . .* (1861).

55. p. 157, n., Arnold refers to Charles John Vaughan, *The Revised Code . . . Dispassionately Considered* (1861).

56. p. 158, The Code was due for debate on 25 March 1862.

57. p. 158, Archdeacon Sinclair was secretary of the National Society for Promoting the Education of the Poor.

58. p. 159, Lord Lansdowne, to whom Arnold was private secretary 1847–51, was Lord President of the Privy Council, 1830–41 and 1846–52, and presided over the Committee of Council on Education.

59. p. 160, Edward Miall: see note 52 above.

60. p. 160, Edward Baines: see note 40 above.

61. p. 160, Here Arnold is quoting from a speech by Gathorne Hardy, reported in *The Times* of 5 October 1861, p. 8.

62. p. 161, See the *Report of the Commissioners Appointed to Inquire into the State of Popular Education in England*, 1861 (i.e. the report of the Newcastle Commission).

63. p. 163, In the House of Commons, 13 February 1862. See *The Times*, 14 February 1862, p. 5.

64. p. 168, The Rev. F. Watkins was the Inspector of Church of England schools in Yorkshire.

65. p. 171, The Rev. J. P. Norris was a pupil at Rugby under Dr Arnold and subsequently Inspector of Church of England schools in Cheshire, Shropshire, and Staffordshire.

66. p. 173, See James Fraser, *The Revised Code . . . The Principles, Tendencies, and Details*. 1861.

67. p. 175, Luke xxii. 53.

68. p. 176, 'The Poor and their Public Schools: the New Minute', *Blackwood's Magazine*, XCI (January 1862), 77–102. The periodicals and magazines of the period make frequent reference to the issue. See, for instance, H. G. Robinson, 'State Education, its Past and Future: the Revised Education Code', *Macmillan's*, V (November 1861), 72–80; and 'The Education Minute and its Critics', *Saturday Review*, 12 October 1861, pp. 379–80.

69. p. 176, See S. T. Coleridge, *On the Constitution of the Church and State*, ch. 6. Cf. Basil Willey, *Nineteenth Century Studies*, pp. 44–50, where he suggests that Coleridge's ch. 7 anticipates *Culture and Anarchy*.

70. p. 176, Charles François Marie, comte de Rémusat (1797–1875), French liberal, journalist, and politician. His works include *England in the XVIII Century, Bacon*, and *John Wesley*.

71. p. 178, Lord Stanley spoke at a meeting of the Leeds Mechanics' Institute and Literary Society; see *The Times*, 23 October 1861, p. 8.

Edward Henry Stanley, fifteenth Earl of Derby (1826–93), politician, pamphleteer, and active supporter of the Mechanics' Institutes and Free Libraries; he almost became King of Greece in 1863.

72. p. 179, See *The Times*, 14 February 1862.

73. p. 182, See 'Note on Minute of the Committee of Council on Education of the 29th July', *Edinburgh Review*, CXIV.

74. p. 183, R. R. W. Lingen (1819–1905) succeeded Kay-Shuttleworth as secretary of the Committee of Council on Education. For his views, see the *Report of the Newcastle Commission*, VI, 76. No doubt Lingen was among those of whom Arnold wrote to his wife on 28 March 1862: 'I have no doubt the more it (his *Fraser's* article) makes an impression the more incensed against me will the chiefs of the office become.' *Letters*, I, 168.

75. p. 187, Arnold's plea that schools have to do with more than mere instruction recurs throughout his *Reports* (see above, p. 225–7) and corresponds closely with the views of Bulwer-Lytton in *England and the English* (2 vols. 1833), book III, ch. 3 and appendix (B).

76. p. 187, 'Cartouch-boxes'—cartridge boxes.

77. p. 189, J. D. Morell, *The Analysis of Sentences Explained and Systematized* (1852). Cf. Arnold's *Reports*, ed. Marvin, pp. 86–7.

78. p. 189, S. Warren (ed.), *Select Extracts from Blackstone's Commentaries, Carefully adapted to the Use of Schools and Young Persons* (1837).

79. p. 192, Teachers' augmentation grants were supplements, paid by the Government, to increase the salaries of teachers who had taken certificate-examinations.

80. p. 192, For Arnold's enthusiasm for these examinations of the University of London, see his *Report* for 1874 ed. Marvin, pp. 164–5.

81. p. 193, Isa. xxx. 7.

82. p. 194, 'There will its heart . . . '—Matt. vi. 21.

83. p. 194, For Lowe's speech to House of Commons on 13 February 1862, see *The Times* of 14 February 1862, pp. 5–7.

84. p. 194, 'To conjure'—to convey away, as by magic.

85. p. 195, 'The House of Rimmon . . . '—2 Kings v. 18.

86. p. 196, 'Lord of the harvest . . . '—Luke x. 2.

EXTRACTS FROM ARNOLD'S REPORTS ON ELEMENTARY SCHOOLS, 1852–1882

87. p. 198, 'Matthew Arnold's position as an officer of the Education Department was exceptional and, in some respects, unique. When he was first appointed, there was a concordat between the Council Office and the various religious bodies, in virtue of which none but clergymen were charged with the duty of inspecting Church of England schools . . . His own duty, therefore, as a lay Inspector, was to visit schools connected with the British and Foreign School Society, Wesleyan, and other Protestant schools not connected with the Church of England. As these schools were far less numerous than others, the district assigned to him at first was very large, comprising nearly one-third of England. After the Education Act of 1870, the system of denominational inspection was necessarily, and very properly, abandoned; districts became smaller, and the official Inspector was required to visit all the schools which received Government aid in the area assigned to him. From this time his official work became less laborious, and was practically limited to one of the easiest divisions of the metropolis,—the borough of Westminster,—a district so well provided with voluntary denominational schools that for a long time there was in it only one school provided by the London School Board.' (J. Fitch, *Thomas Arnold and Matthew Arnold and their Influence on English Education* (1897), pp. 176–7.)

For all his protestations of ineptitude and boredom, it is clear that Arnold took his duties as Inspector seriously. As Jowett, the Master of Balliol, put it: 'The world has been pleased to say many complimentary things of him since his death, but they have scarcely done him justice because they did not understand his serious side —hard work, independence, and the most loving and careful fulfilment of all the duties of life.' (*The Life of Benjamin Jowett*, II, 338. Quoted in Fitch, p. 260.)

G. H. Bantock observes: 'One is not surprised to read accounts of the hastiness and superficiality of his inspections.' Is this not a trifle naïve? Are we not all *occasionally* hasty and superficial? Would we agree to posterity's judgement being based—as a generalisation —on such occasions?

88. p. 212, About half-way through his service as an Inspector, Arnold wrote: 'I find, after all, the education of the middle and upper classes a less important and interesting affair than popular education, as a matter of public institution I mean. So many other influences tell upon those classes that the influence of a public system of education has not the same relative importance in their case as in that of the common people, on whom it is almost the only great civilising agency directly at work.' (*Letters*, I, 302. Letter to Lady de Rothschild, 22 September 1865.)

89. p. 213, For a disinterested outsider's view, compare the views of the American Consul in Birmingham: 'There are many ... reformatory and educational institutions in Birmingham and its suburbs, established on the voluntary principle for which the town is distinguished. Indeed, one who looks forward in the expectation or hope to see a uniform or unsectarian system of education adopted, must notice, with a little concern, the rapid rise and extension of *denominational* schools. The number of churches and chapels that have opened day schools as an integral part of their establishments, seems to be increasing to an extent which may interpose an obstacle to a national system. In many cases, the school house is a part or continuation of the church or chapel building, and frequently numbers several hundred children. It is a matter of common occurrence to hear of the opening of a chapel and school room, as if they were part and parcel of the same denominational establishment.' (Elihu Burritt, *Walks in the Black Country* (1869), pp. 81–2.)

90. p. 213, G. H. Bantock, misinterpreting the tone of Arnold's observation on the working class—'And so they are thrown back upon themselves, upon their beer, their gin, and their *fun*'— mounts a solemnly heavy broadside attack on Arnold for despising the 'fun' of the people, and continues: 'but Arnold's rejection of it gives us an indication of why he *never* [our italics] saw the problems of the elementary school children in relation to their background'. This is a very odd assertion in the light of the abundant evidence to the contrary, both in the school reports and elsewhere: see, for example, his letter, 'The Principle of Examination', in *Essays, Letters and Reviews of Matthew Arnold*, ed. Neiman, pp. 36–9, especially paragraph 9. Bantock says that he feels 'a certain, difficult to define, but nonetheless insistent, disappointment' with Arnold's school reports . . . 'there is something lacking'. The vagueness of the formulation at this crucial point is itself disappointing, not to say surprising in the writing of one who demands stringency.

91. p. 216, Arnold constantly returned to this question of examinations, their place in education, and their effects on teachers and pupils. His wittiest sally is probably his letter in the *Daily News*, 25 March 1862, signed pseudonymously 'A Lover of Light', reprinted in Neiman, pp. 36–9.

Cf. also his article 'Schools', in T. H. Ward's *The Reign of Queen Victoria* (1887), and the following extract from his Report to the School Inquiry Commission of 1865: 'The French have plenty of examinations; but they put them almost entirely at the right age for examinations, between the years of fifteen and twenty-five, when the candidate is neither too old nor too young to be examined with advantage. To put upon little boys of nine or ten the pressure of a competitive examination for an object of the greatest value to their parents, is to offer a premium for the violation of nature's elementary laws, and to sacrifice, as in the poor geese fatted for Strasbourg pies, the due development of all the organs of life to the premature hypertrophy of one. It is well known that the cramming of the little human victims for their ordeal of competition tends more and more to become an industry with a certain class of small schoolmasters, who know the secrets of the process, and who are led by self-interest to select in the first instance their own children for it. The foundations are no gainers, and nervous exhaustion at fifteen is the price which many a clever boy pays for over-stimulation at ten; and the nervous exhaustion of a number of our clever boys tends to create a broad reign of intellectual deadness in the mass of youths from fifteen to twenty, whom the clever boys, had they been rightly developed and not unnaturally forced, ought to have leavened. You can hardly put too great a pressure on a healthy youth to make him work between fifteen and twenty-five; healthy or unhealthy, you can hardly put on him too light a pressure of this kind before twelve.' (*Schools and Universities on the Continent*, Super, IV, 92–3.)

Cf. Dickens, *Dombey and Son*, ch. XII; John Brown's essay, 'Education through the Senses', in *Horae Subsecivae*; and essays II and VI in *Essays on a Liberal Education*, ed. F. W. Farrar (1867).

92. p. 221, In 1872 Arnold wrote *Bible Reading for Schools*, subsequently reissued for the lay reader and published, in revised form, in 1875 as *The Great Prophecy of Israel's Restoration*. It was a presentation, in an intelligently edited form, of Isaiah xl–lxvi, and in the preface to the school edition he wrote: 'Why is this attempt made? It is made because of my conviction of the immense importance in education of what is called *letters*; of the side which engages our feelings and imagination. Science, the side which engages our faculty of exact knowledge, may have been too much neglected; more particularly this may have been so as regards our knowledge of nature. This is probably true of our secondary schools and Universities. [Cf. essay VI in *Essays on a Liberal Education*, ed. Farrar.] But on our schools for the people (by this good German name let us call them, to mark the overwhelmingly preponderant share which falls to them in the work of national education) the power of letters has hardly been brought to bear at all; certainly it has not been brought to bear in excess, as compared with the power of the natural sciences. And now perhaps, it is less likely than ever to be brought to bear . . . '

His justification for his choice of this particular part of the Old Testament is fascinating: 'To make a great work pass into the popular mind is not easy, but our series of chapters have one quality which facilitates this passage for them—their boundless exhilaration. Much good poetry is profoundly melancholy; but the life of the people is such that in literature they require joy. If ever that "good time coming" for which they long, was presented with energy and magnificence, it is in these chapters.' In a letter to Sir Joshua Fitch, he slightly changed his emphasis: 'It is the educational side of the question that I particularly care for. It does not much matter whether or no one thing more or less is produced which in literature is happy and brilliant, there is so much of this in literature already; but whether the people get hold of a single thing in high literature, this point of education is of immense matter.' (Fitch, *Thomas and Matthew Arnold*, p. 198.)

93. p. 221, This passage can be read as part of a continuing debate: in the 1860s and 1870s between such men as Arnold, T. H. Huxley, and Farrar; in our own day between C. P. Snow and F. R. Leavis. Perhaps by now we should be learning to think in terms of both/and, rather than either/or. It is a lesson writ large in both Arnold's and Huxley's contributions to the debate. Cf.: ' . . . the more that men's minds are cleared, the more that the results of science are frankly accepted, the more that poetry and eloquence come to be received and studied as what in truth they really are,— the criticism of life by gifted men, alive and active, with extraordinary power at an unusual number of points;—so much the more will the value of humane letters, and of art also, which is an utterance having a like kind of power with theirs, be felt and acknowledged, and their place in education be secured.' (M. Arnold, 'Literature and Science', *Discourses in America* (1896), pp. 124–5.)

94. p. 224, It is clear that at this point, especially, Arnold is influentially perpetuating the ideas of his father. Such trust was shared by some of his contemporaries; see, for instance, G. H. Lewes, 'The Principles of Success in Literature', *Fortnightly Review*, I (1865), 85: 'Literature is at once the cause and the effect of social progress. It deepens our natural sensibilities, and strengthens by exercise our intellectual capacities . . . There is no need in our day to be dithyrambic on the glory of Literature. Books have become our dearest companions, yielding exquisite delights and inspiring lofty aims.'

We find it difficult, perhaps, to share their confidence; certainly, however positive we may feel, we would tend to formulate our position with rather more subtlety and diffidence. But cf. Vincent Buckley, *Poetry and Morality*, and William Walsh, *The Use of Imagination*.

95. p. 227, The sermon of Butler's is one that Arnold refers to again in his Speech on his Retirement. It is sermon II of 'Six Sermons Preached upon Public Occasions', *The Works of Joseph Butler*, II, 305.

96. p. 229, 'I must go back to my charming occupation of hearing students give lessons. Here is my programme for this afternoon: Avalanches—The Steam-Engine—The Thames—India Rubber—Bricks—The Battle of Poictiers—Subtraction—The Reindeer—The Gunpowder Plot—The Jordan. Alluring, is it not?

Twenty minutes each, and the days of one's life are only threescore years and ten.' (*Letters*, I, 242. Letter to Lady de Rothschild, 14 October 1864.)

97. p. 239, *Natur-kunde*: nature study; or in T. H. Huxley's terminology, Physiography—an elementary knowledge of the facts and laws of nature.

CHRONOLOGICAL TABLE

1822   Born December 24.

1842   June 12: death of Thomas Arnold.

1847   Becomes private secretary to Lord Lansdowne, President of the Council.

1851   Becomes a member of Her Majesty's Inspectorate.

1852   Submits his first General Report on Elementary Schools.

1856   Education Department established.

1857   Elected to the Chair of Poetry at Oxford.

1858   June 30: the Duke of Newcastle's Commission appointed 'to consider and report what Measures, if any, are required for the Extension of sound and cheap elementary Instruction to all classes of the People'.

1859   April–August: visits schools in France, Switzerland and Holland, as Foreign Assistant Commissioner on the Newcastle Commission. Robert Lowe becomes vice-president of the Committee of Council on Education.

1861   March 18: Newcastle Commission publishes its report. July 29: Minute on Revised Code laid before the Commons. Publishes *The Popular Education of France*.

1862   February 13: debate on the Revised Code in the Commons. Re-elected to the Chair of Poetry.

1864   Publishes *A French Eton*.

1865   April–October: visits schools in France, Germany, Switzerland and Italy for the Taunton Commission, set up to investigate the secondary education of the middle class.

1868   Publishes report to the Schools Inquiry Commission as *Schools and Universities on the Continent*.

1869   Publishes *Culture and Anarchy* in book form.

1870   Forster's Education Act.

1871   Publishes *Friendship's Garland* in book form.

1886   Retires from the Inspectorate.

1888   Dies April 15.

SELECT BIBLIOGRAPHY

ARNOLD, MATTHEW. *The Works of Matthew Arnold.* Edition de luxe. 15 vols. 1903–4.

Culture and Anarchy. Ed. J. Dover Wilson. Cambridge, 1932.

Essays, Letters, and Reviews by Matthew Arnold. Ed. Fraser Neiman. Cambridge, Mass., 1960.

Letters of Matthew Arnold. Ed. G. W. E. Russell. 2 vols. 1895.

The Complete Prose Works of Matthew Arnold. Ed. R. H. Super. Vols. I–V published to date. Ann Arbor, 1960–.

BANTOCK, G. H. 'Matthew Arnold, H.M.I.', *Freedom and Authority in Education.* 1965.

CHAMBERS, E. K. *Matthew Arnold, a Study.* 1947.

CONNELL, W. F. *The Educational Thought and Influence of Matthew Arnold.* 1950.

FITCH, J. *Thomas Arnold and Matthew Arnold and their Influence on English Education.* 1897.

MCCARTHY, P. J. *Matthew Arnold and the Three Classes.* 1964.

Humanism in the Continuation School. Board of Education Pamphlet no. 43. H.M.S.O., 1921.

ADAMSON, J. W. *English Education, 1789–1902.* 1930.

BRIGGS, ASA. *Victorian People.* 1954.

FARRAR, F. W. (ed.). *Essays on a Liberal Education.* 1867.

HOLLOWAY, J. *The Victorian Sage.* 1962.

HOUGHTON, W. E. *The Victorian Frame of Mind, 1830–1870.* 1957.

HUXLEY, T. H. *Science and Education: Essays.* 1893.

JUMP, J. D. *Matthew Arnold.* 1955.

STANLEY, A. P. *Life and Correspondence of Thomas Arnold, D.D.* 1844.

TAWNEY, R. H. *Equality.* 1931. Rev. ed. with intro. by R. M. Titmuss. 1964.

YOUNG, G. M. *Victorian England: Portrait of an Age.* 1937.

INDEX

Acland, T. D., 109
Adderley, C. B., 129
Agricultural Journal, 143
aristocracy, 43–6, 51–7, 116, 127–30, 138–9, 142–5, 150–2

Baines, Edward, 137–8, 153, 160, 195
Beecher, H. W., 148
Bradley, G. G., 103
Bright, John, 148
Burke, Edmund, 41–2, 71, 124, 126, 136, 243

Chesterfield, Lord, 55
Clarendon Commission, 76, 79–80, 98–9, 102, 119, 139, 142–3
Cobden, Richard, 148
Coleridge, Sir John T., 104, 111, 118
Coleridge, Samuel T., 176
Comenius, 225
Committee of Council on Education, 157, 160, 182, 187–8, 191–2, 236–7
Constitutionnel, 58
Crossley, Francis, 159
Cumin, Patrick, 174–5

Daily News, 197
Derby, Lord, 130

Edinburgh Review, 182
elementary schools
    curriculum, 214–16, 221–7
    environment, 212–13
    and the Revised Code, 157–97, 203–12, 216–21, 235–8
    their teachers, 228–40

Fortescue, Lord, 153
Fraser, James, 170, 173
France
    curriculum at Lyceum, 84–6
    fees at Lyceum, 86–8
    lyceums, 64–5, 120–2
    lyceum at Toulouse, 81–7, 101, 103
    private school at Sorèze, 88–97, 101, 103

Granville, Lord George, 176, 178–80, 194, 196
Guardian, 118, 172, 186
Guizot, François, 81, 84, 90

Hawtrey, Stephen, 113–14

Inspector, of Schools, his rôle 198–203

Lacordaire, J. B. H., 88–97, 103, 152
Lansdowne, Lord, 159, 184
Larochejaquelein, Henri de, 95
Lingen, R. R. W., 183–4, 189
Lowe, Robert, 158, 163, 166, 177, 179, 181, 187, 193–7
Lubbock, Sir John, 224

Methodist schools, 213–14
Miall, Edward, 153, 160, 185
Mirabeau, Honoré, 42, 45, 77
middle class
    culture, 67–9, 144–7
    examinations, 109–11
    importance of, 69–71
    secondary schools, 65–7, 97–116, 152–6
    and the State, 62–4, 131–42

middle class (*cont.*)
  transformation of, 145–7,
    152–3
Morning Star, 58

National Society, 158
Newcastle Commission, 159–
    62, 164–5, 167–73, 177,
    187–8, 220–1
Norris, J. P., 171

Pakington, Sir John, 130
public schools, 65, 76–9, 85–6,
    98–100, 102–3, 113–14

Rémusat, Charles, 176
Revised Code, 157–97
  declared aim of, 160–4
  examinations under, 203–12
  financial results of, 158–60
  grants under, 164–7, 173–4,
    176–82, 192–7, 211–12
  and higher instruction, 174 6
  and Inspectors, 161, 164–
    70, 172–3, 179–82, 186–91,
    194–6, 203–12
  payment by results, 162–4,
    179–82, 193–5, 219–20
  real meaning of, 166–7, 182
  and teachers, 235–8
Roebuck, J. A., 134, 137

Shakespeare, W., 221–2
Shuttleworth, Sir James Kay-,
    157–9, 168, 183–4, 186,
    189
Sinclair, John, 158, 163
Smith, Goldwin, 150
Spectator, 186
Stanley, Lord, 178, 180
State, the,
  in England, 41–2, 57–61, 71–
    4, 125–42, 183–7
  and elementary education,
    101, 157–97, 198–240
  in France, 50–1, 57–9, 64–5
  and secondary education, 64–
    6, 106–9, 116–20, 122–5

Temple, Frederick, 109, 126–7
Thierry, Amédée, 132
Times, The, 77, 100–1, 126, 129,
    143, 153, 197
Tocqueville, Alexis de, 49

Vaughan, C. J., 157, 163, 170,
    179

Watkins, Frederick, 168
Wood, R., 55
Woodard, Nathaniel, 106–9,
    119, 125, 154
Wordsworth, W., 223